Declare His Glory

among the Nations

edited by
David M. Howard

InterVarsity Press
Downers Grove
Illinois 60515

InterVarsity Press is the book publishing
division of Inter-Varsity Christian
Fellowship, a student movement active on
campus at hundreds of universities, colleges
and schools of nursing. For information
about local and regional activities,
write IVCF, 233 Langdon St.,
Madison, WI 53703.

All Scripture quotations, unless otherwise
indicated, are from the Revised Standard
Version Bible, copyrighted 1946, 1952,
© 1971, 1973.

ISBN 0-87784-784-3
Library of Congress Catalog
Card Number: 77-74847

Printed in the United States of America

Contents

Preface

It was bitterly cold in central Illinois as the stroke of midnight ushered out the year 1976 and welcomed the year 1977. Seventeen thousand students bowed in hushed silence in the huge Assembly Hall of the University of Illinois. Urbana 76 was about to end as they remembered together the death and the coming again of our Lord Jesus Christ in the celebration of the Lord's Supper. Shortly after midnight the final benediction was pronounced, the final Alleluias were sung and the final embraces and farewells were expressed.

As these students, along with missionaries, faculty, pastors, IVCF staff and others filed out and prepared to return to campuses and homes all over North America and even to other parts of the world, each one could honestly say with the Apostle John, "We have beheld his glory." For the glory of Jesus Christ, only begotten of the Father, had been the theme of the past five days. Every major address was related to the great exhortation found in Psalm 96:3: "Declare his glory among the nations."

Nearly three years of intensive prayer and planning had gone into those five days. The theme had been chosen for three reasons. First, it focused on the glory of God and of his Son, Jesus Christ, as the heart of the gospel message. Second, it reflected the worldwide scope of the church's task with its phrase "among the nations." Third, it spoke of the personal and corporate responsibility of the church to declare that glory to all nations.

Participating in the program which developed this great theme were missionaries from India, Ecuador, Zaire, Costa Rica and Colombia; evangelists from Uganda, Argentina and the United States; pastors from India, Canada, London and Mississippi; students from North America; student workers from Singapore, the Philippines, Canada and the United States; a theologian from the United States; a music director from Canada; and a variety of widely read authors among the aforementioned people. The cosmopolitan nature of the worldwide body of Christ was evident among those who participated in the program. Voices from the Third World spoke clearly and biblically about our mutual task. Veteran missionaries and young people, world renowned evangelical leaders and some lesser known but faithful servants of God gave valuable insights into God's work today.

In addition to the major addresses (all of which are found in this book) over one hundred workshops were offered throughout the week where students could interact with competent leaders on a wide variety of topics related to world evangelism. Personal discussion with speakers was a highlight of every afternoon as students crowded into classrooms where each speaker was available to answer questions. The Intercristo matching service provided computer print-outs showing job opportunities around the world which students could discuss with representatives from 125 mission agencies who were present at booths in the Armory.

Students were encouraged to begin the day alone with the Lord in a quiet time using material provided by the convention to help lay a biblical foundation for each day. After breakfast small groups of ten gathered in the dormitories for inductive study of the passage already used in the quiet time for that morning. The same groups met each evening to end the day in prayer, thanksgiving and sharing of what God was doing in their lives.

Urbana 76 purposely and unashamedly emphasized world missions following the precedent of the ten previous Inter-Varsity Christian Fellowship student missionary conventions. We were told at Urbana 76 that there are still 2.7 billion people in the world who have never had an adequate opportunity to hear the message of salvation through Jesus Christ. Of these approximately thirty million, or one percent, are found in North America. Thus nearly ninety-nine percent of the unreached peoples of the earth are to be found outside the continent where Urbana 76 was held. Therefore, the emphasis on cross-cultural evangelism was a key to understanding how we are to fulfill the Great Commission which Jesus Christ left with his church.

The response of the students to the commands from God's Word and the challenge of a world still to be reached with that Word was heartwarming. When an offering was received to help in reaching students around the world for Jesus Christ, they responded with $247,000 in cash and approximately $43,000 in pledges. When World Evangelism Decision Cards were distributed to help students make a firm commitment to God for whatever he might ask of them, 8,529 students signed these cards indicating their willingness to go wherever God might choose to send them. Hundreds more were signed in months following the convention as students continued to pray and consider the call which had come to them during those days.

Only eternity will show the true and lasting results of Urbana 76. But in the meantime the message of the convention lives on in these pages. It is our prayer that all who read this book may also be challenged to declare his glory among the nations.

David M. Howard
Director, Urbana 76

Introduction

one
Foundation Stones for Declaring God's Glory

John W. Alexander

It is a pleasure extending my welcome to you for this Missionary Convention sponsored by Inter-Varsity Christian Fellowship, and I do so on behalf of the Inter-Varsity Board of Trustees, on behalf of our staff, our Local Committee members and all of our student members across the nation.

There is a second—and rather personal—basis on which I welcome you. Urbana is my home town. And when I thumb through this Convention Handbook and come to the map, I can see in the upper right-hand corner the 1000 block on Stoughton Street, the location of my boyhood home, and Lincoln Grade School where I spent my early years.

Also, as an alumnus of the University of Illinois, I welcome you. Little did I realize in September of 1936 when I enrolled here as a freshman that the day would come when I would return to this, my alma mater, with thousands of fellow Christians to sing God's praises, to hear his Word expounded, to focus attention on reaching a needy world for the sake of Christ Jesus. It is a thrill for me to be here with you.

The theme of the Convention is "Declare His Glory among the Nations." The purpose is to help us all do a better job of declaring his glory. And if that purpose is to be fulfilled, we need to build the Convention on solid truth and solid response to that truth.

There is an analogy here with constructing a building. The principle holds that beneath substantial buildings there must be substantial foundations. May I propose this evening that we lay in place two major foundation stones upon which to construct our part of this Missionary Convention?

The first stone can be labeled convictions, the second, confessions.

In laying the first foundation, let us direct attention to a portion of God's Word found in the New Testament—in the letter to the Church at Ephesus (Eph. 1:3-10). I have selected this portion because the paragraph deals with purpose—God's purpose. Notice what it says concerning God's purpose for the dimension of time, for the dimension of space, his purpose for people and his purpose for the Lord Jesus Christ.

Blessed be the God and Father of our Lord Jesus Christ, who has blessed us in Christ with every spiritual blessing in the heavenly places, even as he chose us in him before the foundation of the world, that we should be holy and blameless before him. He destined us in love to be his sons through Jesus Christ, according to the purpose of his will, to the praise of his glorious grace which he freely bestowed on us in the Beloved. In him we have redemption through his blood, the forgiveness of our trespasses, according to the riches of his grace which he lavished upon us. For he has made known to us in all wisdom and insight the mystery of his will, according to his purpose which he set forth in Christ, as a plan for the fulness of time, to unite all things in him, things in heaven and things on earth.

God is a long-range planner. He has a long-range purpose in mind. His purpose is an expression of his will. It is his will to bring all human history to a great climax in Jesus Christ. His purpose includes all of time—which includes all of the year 1976—which includes these days in late December. It is a stirring thought to realize that the five days of this Convention do not repose in a time vacuum. They are part of God's plan. His purpose includes all people. None of his creatures is outside the scope of his will. His plan includes not just this crowd of 17,000 people; it includes you as an individual and me as a person. If we have been following the Lord Jesus Christ in glad obedience, we are here at Urbana not primarily because we chose to come to Illinois but because the sovereign Lord of the universe willed that we be here.

What then are some of the truths which we believe are serving as the foundation stones upon which this Convention is to be constructed?

First is the conviction that God is the great active agent in all that we do—in this Convention in particular.

Second is the conviction that God's overriding purpose in his work is the pre-eminence of Jesus Christ: "That in all things he might be pre-eminent."

Third, God's Holy Spirit is at work in the lives of people today, drawing them to Christ.

Fourth, God speaks through Scripture revealing something of his character, his deeds and his ways, communicating to men, revealing enough information on which to respond. Our attitude toward the Bible is very important. The choice of what attitude to adopt is one of the most difficult and important decisions in life.

In my own case, I have wrestled with this problem for years and have chosen to believe that the Bible is the infallible revelation of the infallible God—which means that it is entirely trustworthy and reliable. How about errancy? Admittedly there are parts of the Bible which are problems. These I recognize. When I've done my best to find solutions, but without success, I stand silent before them, not knowing how to explain them. But I refuse to pronounce a verdict of "error" for two reasons: First, I then would have to commence the process of sifting out biblical error from biblical truth. This is something even the Lord Jesus refused to suggest when he was on earth. Second, to what more reliable source would I turn for the criteria by which to distinguish biblical truth from biblical error? My belief in biblical inerrancy readily admits all the problems; but I refuse to set myself up as judge of Scripture and commence deciding which statements are biblical errors.

Fifth, as God gives people new life in Christ, he makes them one with all who believe. This group is called the church. We recognize that there are many definitions of *church.* But I want to underline the fact that we in IVCF believe wholeheartedly that the church is the body of Christ composed of all who have committed themselves to Jesus Christ. The church is God's own institution through which he has chosen to work in the world.

Sixth, God is building his church in all parts of the world and in all segments of society. This includes colleges, universities, schools of nursing and technical schools. God has not bypassed the college world in spite of pessimism on the part of some Christians that his Spirit does not operate there.

We also believe that God's Spirit is working through students and faculty at those schools. This is what we mean by the "indigenous witness." To be sure, an important ministry can be had by outsiders visiting the campus. But the main witness must be done by students and faculty who are inside that college, inside that university, inside that school.

Further, we believe that God has chosen you to be such a witness: you who are students, you who are faculty. We believe that you are at your particular school—this particular year—because the sovereign Lord of all space and of all time has chosen you to be there.

Moreover, we believe that your vision of the witness to Christ extends beyond your campus to include other parts of society in your home land and to include other lands of the world—not only here and now but also in the years ahead.

Finally, we believe that you desire help in being a witness—not only for the present, but also for the future. Thus, the fundamental purpose of this Convention is to provide you with such assistance. Inter-Varsity does not pretend to be the only agency raised up by God to help students. There are several other movements which glorify God on campus. But we believe the Lord has given Inter-Varsity a portion of that ministry. And this convention is one of the efforts to give college students some help in discerning God's will as members of Christ's worldwide body today, and as maturing participants in his body throughout all the tomorrows.

The second foundation I propose we lay beneath this Convention can be labeled *confession.* I believe it would be in order for the 17,000 of us in this the opening session of Urbana 76 to unite in a prayer of humble confession. In response to the foregoing statements of convictions concerning God and his purpose in Christ, let our opening response be that of repentant sinners who, in the presence of his wondrous holiness, are moved to confess our sin.

Now I realize this is difficult. We hear the words from Scripture in 1 John 1:9: "If we confess our sins, he is faithful and just, to forgive us our sins and to cleanse us from all unrighteousness." We nod our heads in agreement. But when it comes to the uncomfortable business of privately facing our own sin and our many sins, we turn away. It is more comfortable to apply this truth to the sins of other people. We generally do not squirm when applying it corporately, but when the spotlight of a holy God's convicting power floods in upon us we prefer to display our proud peacock feathers and leave the confession to the other fellow.

We agree that the United States should confess its sins (and indeed it should), but we find great difficulty in confessing our own. We agree that the church should confess its sins (and well it might), but let's leave the spotlight on the church—comfortably keeping it off us. If only certain mission boards would confess their sins—but don't ask me to confess mine. If only certain people would confess their terrible sin of race prejudice—but be careful not to embarrass me by asking me to confess the race prejudice in my heart.

And so it goes. On and on. Let me ask you this question: How can God's will be carried out in this Convention if you and I, as individuals, decide to go through these next five days as proud, self-righteous Pharisees, leaving it up to the other person to confess his sins while we refuse to confess ours.

For several months I have had a strong conviction that this opening message of Urbana 76 should close on the note of repentance and confession. Accordingly, I invite you now to join me in coming humbly before our heavenly Father—to truly confess our sin. I know of no better way than to read a prayer of confession which has been offered by our forefathers for at least 400 years in scattered places around the world. I will read the prayer slowly so that each of us can focus mind and heart on the words. I invite you to respond silently, making confession in the privacy of your own heart.

Almighty and most merciful Father;
We have erred and strayed from thy ways like lost sheep.
We have followed too much the devices and desires of
*   our own hearts.*
We have offended against thy holy laws.
We have left undone those things which we ought to
*   have done.*
We have done those things which we ought not to
*   have done.*
There is no health in us.
But thou, O Lord, have mercy upon us miserable
*   offenders.*
Spare thou those, O God, who confess their faults,
Restore thou those who are penitent, according to thy
*   promises declared unto mankind in Christ Jesus our Lord.*
And grant, O most merciful Father, for his sake, that we
*   may hereafter live a godly, righteous, and sober life,*
*   to the glory of thy holy Name.   Amen.*

two
Beyond
Urbana

Edward Beach

Earlier this year I was taking a shower. It was one of those invigorating, blood-chilling, only-happens-at-camp type of showers. That's partly why I'll never forget the conversation that I overheard on the other side of the dormitory wall. One Christian said to another, "I could never be a missionary! I have no idea at all what God has in mind for me after college—but for sure it's not missionary work."

Six years ago tonight I had reached a similar conclusion. As a student who had just arrived for Urbana 70, I sat in this Assembly Hall thinking, "I could never be a missionary! For one thing, missionaries speak all kinds of exotic languages that are impossible to learn. I failed high school French, so I know that God can't possibly want me to be a missionary. I'm going to be an architect. That's what I'm studying and that's what excites me, so that's what I'll be."

Well, my life has turned out quite unexpectedly, and I want to tell you about it. I want to share with you how God has changed my plans and blessed me in ways that I had never conceived of.

My future seemed to be in architecture and I was eagerly looking forward to it. So I went to Urbana full of the confidence that everything was set. It was fun to go to a mission conference "knowing" that I was not one of the elect bound for Bungabungaland. But God wanted to change that attitude, and Urbana 70 was the place where he did it. It was there that he planted a seed of desire in me to do *whatever he* wanted, *wherever he* wanted me to do it.

At the end of the conference, I said, "God, I want you to exercise your sovereign lordship over my life. I want you to make my future to suit your desires, whatever they are, rather than mine. I do not know whether you want me in overseas work or right here at home. But I will pray and follow wherever you lead."

But my willingness did not indicate my readiness. In contrast to my own immaturity and lack of vision, I saw the quality of life that characterized the speakers at Urbana 70 and a number of the people in our Inter-Varsity group. I wanted to see that same kind of quality in my life as a student.

Personally, I've never found it all that *easy* to be both a Christian and a student at the same time. There always seemed to be enough activities vying for my attention to fill a 48-hour day. So often I wished that I could give up being a student just long enough to do the 854 zillion items on my list of things to do. But I saw clearly that God wanted me to integrate my Christianity and my student role, not to divide them. He wanted me to bear witness to my fellow students *not* as a non-student but as one who shares in their joys and dreams, troubles and trials. And plainly the Lord regarded a 24-hour day as being plenty long enough. Gradually, out of the kaleidoscope of exams and Bible study, prayer meetings and sleepless nights in the design studio, evangelism projects and computer programs came a growing understanding of my priorities as a Christian student.

The fellowship and training of our IVCF group was always an invaluable help to me. The friendship of those brothers and sisters who so patiently loved me is still an encouragement and model to me. They showed me in living-walking-talking terms what it means to be a servant like the Lord Jesus. For instance, their desire to pray for people, both alone and together, was infectious. I'd never talked to God so much in all my life! Nor had I ever known that prayer was so refreshing! I remember sitting in the deserted shadows of this Assembly Hall on some bitter cold winter nights, sometimes praising God, sometimes pouring out my troubles to him. I found that the stress and strain of being a student gave me a lot to pray about.

It was through IVCF that I learned the in-depth Bible study methods that helped me to dig deeply into God's Word and to apply scriptural truths to my life as a student. I doubt that I would ever have established a daily time of prayer and Bible study if it had not been for the encouragement and instruction that I received. That "daily quiet time" with the Lord meant more for my growth as a Christian student than anything else. And it is still that way.

I'll never forget some of the struggles that I encountered trying to maintain that time alone with the Lord. I always found it hard to concentrate with the typical distractions of speakers rumbling away at peak power, water balloons and hallway arguments. One day I decided to see what calmness the local cemetery might add to my devotions. As I was praying there with thankfulness that God should provide such a place, I looked up and—behold! —coming towards me was a fleet-footed pair of aspiring Olympic runners hurdling tombstones while a sketching class was busily capturing the frenzied serenity of my graveyard. When the gardener came by tractoring his gang-mower, I said, "Amen," and left.

Finally a whole year had passed since Urbana 70 and still I was unsure where the Lord wanted me to serve him. I began to spend hours writing out long prayers. I asked him again and again what I was supposed to do with my life. I talked with missionaries whenever I could, read missionary biographies and investigated different types of cross-cultural ministries. The more I prayed and investigated, the more and more desirous I became of getting into some kind of overseas work. Out of my muddled confusion came a confidence that God was indeed leading me and that I needed to stay ready and be open to whatever direction he might point me in. But student life was the role and mission field that God had given me. So I continued to involve myself in the work at hand. Whether in the design studio or snack bar, I tried my best to share with people in both verbal and non-verbal terms what the gospel meant. I never felt that I had any unusual evangelistic ability but the more I talked with people about Jesus, the more I sensed an overwhelming priority that the gospel needed to be heard and understood and acted on.

The last exam of my junior year was finally over. The broiling heat of an Urbana summer had begun to set in and I looked forward to trading it for the cool forests of Canada and a job at Ontario Pioneer Camp. One day a Wycliffe couple stopped in at the camp to show a film about the Aguacatec people of Guatemala they had been working with. That excited me because I was already very interested in Wycliffe. The film told how this couple had gone to live with the Aguacatecos and had translated the Scriptures for them. As a result, first one man became a Christian, then his family and then practically the whole village. As native evangelists brought the translated Scriptures to surrounding towns, many more people became Christians and a maturing indigenous church was raised up.

When I saw that, I knew beyond all doubt that that was what God wanted me to do. The need was clear: 2000 languages existed where God's Word was not available. Moreover, I had become a Christian through reading the Bible on my own. I knew personally the power and importance of God's Word. My months of prayers were answered as the Holy Spirit seemed to say within me, "I want you to translate my Word for those who do not have it." God has many ministries for his people, but finally I knew which one he had for me.

It was after this happened that God guided in other decisions. Most important was that Elenore and I became engaged just before our senior year. That was an exciting year, and part of the excitement was sharing with people the new plans that God had given us. I remember telling one of my design instructors. She thought that the whole thing was a ridiculous idea and that I should forget such nonsense and stick with architecture. Unfortunately for her side, her argument made me more determined than ever to get into translation work.

Elenore's anthropology professor couldn't find enough ways to encourage her in her studies—until the day she told him that she was going to do a Bible translation for a minority language group. Instantly he began to tell her how huge and horrid and lethal the mosquitoes were in the kinds of regions that we would be working in. We were thankful, to say the least, for the more positive encouragement of fellow Christians.

Soon we had graduated, were married and were working 40-hour weeks. It was during that first year of marriage that we applied to join Wycliffe and to take the first semester of training that they required for translators.

We were flying high when we arrived for the summer-long course in linguistics. We sensed that we were right in the center of God's will.

Then the bomb hit. The work was hard. I don't mean just hard. To me, it seemed impossible. "How can I do this for the rest of my life?" I thought. That's what I said the first week. Then the second week came. "What do you think I am, God? Can't you see that this is impossible? Yes, I know about Philippians 4:13, but did you ever study linguistics? There's a hundred things I can do better than this! And at least a thousand things that I would rather do! I'm simply no good at this, God. I can't do it!"

But I did do it. And somehow, the Lord kept me going through all nine weeks. I learned to analyze the grammar and phonology of languages that I had never even heard of before. Learning to say those "exotic, impossible-to-learn" sounds turned out to be quite possible and even fun.

I began to learn some other things that summer too. Like about how the Lord provides strength and ability when my strength is nil and my ability worthless. I realized that maybe the reason God wanted me there was not because I had all the qualifications of a great missionary—as I had hoped I had—but rather because he wanted me to come to know more of himself and to be made just a little bit more like his Son.

We became more convinced than ever that we were where

God wanted us. And when Wycliffe accepted us as members, it was a confirmation that they too knew where God wanted us. Our two home churches were both very excited about how the Lord was leading, so that was yet another confirmation of his will. We sensed that our next step should be to go to Wycliffe's Jungle Training Camp in southern Mexico.

The word jungle conjures up all sorts of nightmares in people's minds. They think of giant boa constrictors dropping out of trees or of being lost in a steaming tropical rain forest. But Jungle Camp is none of that. It is training in the skills of cross-cultural living and has been the most valuable experience that God has given me along that line.

What do I mean by a "valuable" cross-cultural experience? I mean things like learning successfully to handle the stress of a new system of relationships, learning genuinely to enjoy another culture and learning to be a gracious guest in a land that is not your own. Everybody and everything around you becomes your teacher.

Some of my teachers were pint-sized—like the little boy who came just to stare at me and wouldn't go away because I was the closest thing to a Martian that he had ever seen. Situations taught me a lot too—like battling with the "Aztec two-step" when the only out-house in the village was still under construction. You see, Jungle Camp is training in real life problem-solving.

We had the opportunity to experience all kinds of stresses like coping with a change of roles. The greenhorn missionary leaves home as a leader, an innovator and supposedly a spiritual giant. But in Jungle Camp all that the Tzeltal Indians noticed was that I couldn't swing a machete without getting blisters, that I had an awful time speaking their language (they had no trouble at all with it) and that I owned enough pairs of shoes to shod all of the important men in town. The only way that I was a giant to them was by my physical stature.

Village living is the most romantic part of Jungle Camp. We were assigned by pairs to live in a Tzeltal village for six weeks. That means living in a one-room hut with all the ancient conveniences of a dirt floor, mud walls, a thatch roof and running water, of course, down the path about 200 meters. Our forty days and forty nights there were both traumatic and a barrel of laughs.

To get water each day I had to walk through the cluster of other dwellings to the stream. Often I tried to slink past, hoping to spare myself another awkward conversation. But one day someone stepped out from the shadows and said, "Don Eduardo, bin yac apas?" I knew the question. I had to answer it a hundred times a day. He wanted to know what I was doing. But now I didn't know how to answer.

Finally I just gave up and said, "Ma' jna." ("I don't know what I'm doing.") Then my friend would look at me very puzzled, contemplate the water buckets I was carrying and my direction of travel and say, "Max ana, don Eduardo." ("You don't know what you're doing.")

That really bothered me. Of course he was just trying to be friendly but why did he always call me "don"? Don Eduardo. I had no idea what "don" meant and I had never heard them address each other that way. To my ears, it sounded like "dumb." Don Eduardo. Dumb Edward.

"Dumb Ed, what are you doing?"

"I don't know."

"Dumb Ed, you don't know."

Later, I humbly learned that "don" is a Spanish term of respect. I also finally realized that I was the only man in the village making those daily trips to the stream. That was an embarrassing way to be reminded that their culture is drawn on a different map than mine.

How would you communicate something of the gospel to people who only speak a language that you are just beginning to learn? Put yourself in our shoes as I translate an attempt that Elenore and I made after only a few weeks of Tzeltal study.

Gringo: "Do you know where you are going after you die?"

Tzeltali: "No. Do you know where you'll go after you die?"

Gringo: "Yes."

Tzeltali: "Where?"

Gringo: "To heaven. To be with Jesus."

Tzeltali: "Can I go too?"

Gringo: "Yes!"

Tzeltali: "Tell me how."

Silence.

What a fantastic opportunity! But I don't know enough Tzeltal to answer! Here I am, supposedly a real live missionary standing right in the field white unto harvest and I can't do what 536 people back home are praying that I'll do.

When the silence seemed unbearable, my wife grabbed a Tzeltal translation of the New Testament and asked one of the more educated fellows to read John 3:16 to everybody present. So he read it. And then he read verse 17, and then 18 and then 19. Syllable by syllable he read them, all the way through to the end of the chapter. And after each syllable there was a thoughtful pause while the next one was studied out. The powerful sword of the Spirit glanced off the coat of illiteracy. We were reminded again that part of our disciple-making ministry would obligatorily include teaching people to read.

A friend of ours has said that the missionary's first months away from the homeland is the world's best kept secret. You can't send home thrilling accounts about conquering the powers of darkness or of thousands being saved. It's hard to tell people that you're still trying to figure out how to talk. It's tough to explain all of your Charlie Brown experiences, all of the blunders that make you feel like a dummy. Under the stress of cross-cultural living, my humanness sticks out all over the place. I've seen how some of the fruits of the Spirit were not as ripe in me as I'd thought. I've been forced to ask myself, "Who am I for this task? Why does God want me? Why did he change my plans?"

I believe that he has changed my plans because he wants me to know more of the glory, more of the infinite expanse of love, wisdom and power that is uniquely his. And he wants others to know it who do not. He wants me to worship him in a way that I would not have otherwise, as well as to bring other worshipers into his kingdom. He wants to make me, and you and others more and more like Jesus.

Beyond Urbana. I wonder what's beyond Urbana 76 for us. In August, Elenore and I made our first visit to the area of Guatemala where we hope to work. It's a beautiful place. The rugged mountains soar up from valleys at three-thousand foot altitude to peaks of ten and eleven thousand feet. The people are beautiful too and we loved them at first sight. But there is a great darkness in that place because God's Word has never been available in their language. We are so anxious to bring them that message which will dispel their darkness. We long for the Lord to build part of his kingdom there. We want to see men and women who are truly disciples, growing strong in faith and in their knowledge of God and his Word. We desire for the glory of the Lord to be declared and praised in that place.

I've told you how God has led and blessed me since being a student at Urbana 70. I knew nothing then of what he had in store for me. But I asked him to lead me. Since then, he has directed me on a totally unexpected path and I've experienced his abundant goodness at every turn. I wonder what he has for you beyond Urbana. Although none of us knows for certain what lies ahead, I do know one thing for certain. I want nothing else but to follow him.

part I

The Biblical Basis of Declaring God's Glory

three
The Living God Is a Missionary God
John R. W. Stott

Millions of people in today's world are extremely hostile to the Christian missionary enterprise. They regard it as politically disruptive (because it loosens the cement which binds the national culture) and religiously narrow-minded (because it makes exclusive claims for Jesus), while those who are involved in it are thought to suffer from a kind of arrogant imperialism. And the attempt to convert people to Christ is rejected as an unpardonable interference in their private lives. "My religion is my own affair," they say. "Mind your own business, and leave me alone to mind mine."

It is essential, therefore, for Christians to understand the grounds on which the Christian mission rests. Only then shall we be able to persevere in the missionary task, with courage and humility, in spite of the world's misunderstanding and opposition. More precisely, biblical Christians need biblical incentives. For we believe the Bible to be the revelation of God and of his will. So we ask: Has he revealed in Scripture that "mission" is his will for his people? Only then shall we be satisfied. For then it becomes a matter of obeying God, whatever man may think or say.

So the overall title of this series of four expositions is *The Biblical Basis of Missions*. Their purpose is to convince us that world mission (the endeavor under God to bring the whole world to the feet of Jesus) is neither an unwarranted intrusion into other people's privacy, nor a regrettable Christian deviation, nor the hobby of a few eccentric enthusiasts, but a central feature of the historical purpose of God according to Scripture and, moreover, a responsibility which he lays (in some measure at least) upon all his people. It is no exaggeration to say that the Bible is a missionary book, because the God of the Bible is a missionary God.

What we are going to do is look at the four major sections into which the Bible is divided (the Old Testament, the Gospels, the Acts and the Letters) and see that in each section the unfolding purpose of God (Father, Son and Holy Spirit) for his church is a missionary purpose. Thus, according to the Old Testament, the living God is a missionary God; according to the Gospels the Lord Christ is a missionary Christ; according to the Acts the Holy Spirit is a missionary Spirit; and according to the Letters the Christian church is a missionary church. We cannot escape this. The evidence is overwhelming. If we listen and submit to God's word it will change our perspective and is likely to change our lives as well.

The Call of Abraham

Our story begins about 4,000 years ago with a man called Abraham, or more accurately, Abram as he was called at that time. Here is the account of God's call to Abraham.

> *Terah took Abram his son and Lot the son of Haran, his grandson, and Sarai his daughter-in-law, his son Abram's wife, and they went forth together from Ur of the Chaldeans to go into the land of Canaan; but when they came to Haran, they settled there. The days of Terah were two hundred and five years; and Terah died in Haran. Now the LORD said to Abram,*

*"Go from your country and kindred and your father's house
to the land that I will show you. And I will make of you a great
nation, and I will bless you, and make your name great, so
that you will be a blessing. I will bless those who bless you,
and him who curses you I will curse; and by you all the families of the earth shall bless themselves." So Abram went, as
the LORD had told him; and Lot went with him. Abram was
seventy-five years old when he departed from Haran. (Gen.
11:31—12:4, RSV).*

God made a promise (a composite promise, as we shall see) to
Abraham. And an understanding of that promise is indispensable to an understanding of the Bible and of the Christian mission. These are perhaps the most unifying verses in the Bible;
the whole of God's purpose is encapsulated here.

By way of introduction we shall need to consider the setting
of God's promise, the context in which it came to be given. Then
we shall divide the rest of our study into two. First, *the promise*
(exactly what it was that God said he would do) and second—at
greater length—its *fulfillment* (how God has kept and will keep
his promise). We start, however, with the setting.

Genesis 12 begins: "And now the Lord said to Abram." It
sounds an abrupt opening of a new chapter. We are prompted to
ask: "Who is this 'Lord' who spoke to Abraham?" and "who is
this 'Abraham' to whom he spoke?" They are not introduced
into the text out of the blue. A great deal lies behind these words.

This illustrates, by the way, the great danger of the "microscopic" study of Scripture. Mind you, it is important that we get
out our microscopes, as it were, and examine small passages in
minute detail. At the same time, we must be careful not to make
the all-too-common mistake of isolating the text from its context, both its immediate context and its wider context in the
Bible as a whole. To do so is sure to lead to misunderstanding.
Instead, there is a sense in which every part of the Bible, however short, should be seen as a microcosm of the whole. We must
understand each in the light of all, and not in ignorance of it,
still less in defiance of it. Since we believe the whole Bible to be
the word of God, we also believe in its unity (though of course a
unity which contains a rich variety) and our expositions must

demonstrate this unity and not violate it.

This principle is never more true than of the first three verses of Genesis 12. They are a key which opens up the whole of Scripture. The previous eleven chapters lead up to them; the rest of the Bible follows and fulfills them.

What, then, is the background to this text? It is this. "The Lord" who chose and called Abraham is the same Lord who in the beginning created the heavens and the earth, and who climaxed his creative work by making man a unique creature in his own likeness. In other words, we should never allow ourselves to forget that the Bible begins with the universe, not with the planet earth; then with the earth, not with Palestine; then with Adam the father of the human race, not with Abraham the father of the chosen race. Since, then, God is the Creator of the universe, the earth and of all mankind we must never demote him to the status of a tribal deity or petty godling like Chemosh the god of the Moabites, or Milcom (or Molech) the god of the Ammonites, or Baal the male deity, or Ashtoreth the female deity, of the Canaanites. Nor must we suppose that God chose Abraham and his descendants because he had lost interest in other peoples or given them up. Election is not a synonym for élitism. On the contrary, as we shall soon see, God chose one man and his family in order through them to bless *all* the families of the earth. Nor (if we remember the context) should this surprise us, for the God of Abraham is the God of creation, "the God . . . of all the kingdoms of the earth," "the God of the spirits of all flesh" (2 Kings 19:15; cf. Gen. 18:25; Num. 16:22).

We are bound, therefore, to be deeply offended when Christianity is relegated to one chapter in a book on the world's religions as if it were one option among many, or when people speak of "the Christian God" as if there were others! No, there is only one living and true God, who has revealed himself fully and finally in his only Son Jesus Christ. Monotheism lies at the basis of mission. As Paul wrote to Timothy, "There is one God, and there is one mediator between God and men, the man Christ Jesus" (1 Tim. 2:5).

The Genesis record moves on from the creation of all things by the one God and of man in his likeness, to man's rebellion against his own creator and to God's judgment upon his rebel creature—a judgment which is relieved, however, by his first gospel promise that one day the woman's seed would "bruise," indeed "crush," the serpent's head (3:15).

The following eight chapters (Genesis 4—11) describe the devastating results of the Fall in terms of man's progressive alienation from God and from his brother man. First, Adam and Eve are driven from the garden and so denied access to the tree of life. Next, Cain murders his brother Abel. Later God saw that "the wickedness of man was great in the earth, and that every imagination of the thoughts of his heart was only evil continually" (6:5), and God destroyed those wicked sinners by the flood. Only Noah and his family were spared. Afterward God established his covenant both with human beings and with the subhuman creation, promising never again to judge the world with a comparable deluge, but to preserve the regularity of day and night, summer and winter. Nevertheless, the sin and degradation of man remained. Righteous Noah fell victim to drunkenness and one of his sons to immorality. And though the nations grew and "spread abroad" under the blessing of God's providence (10:32), they were later "scattered abroad" under his judgment after the proud rebellion of the Tower of Babel (11:9).

This was the setting in which God's call and promise came to Abraham. All around was moral deterioration, darkness and dispersal. Society was steadily disintegrating. Yet God the Creator did not abandon the human beings he had made in his own likeness (Gen. 9:6). Out of the prevailing godlessness he called one man and his family, and promised to bless not only them but through them the whole world. The scattering would not proceed unchecked; a grand process of ingathering would now begin.

The Promise
What then was the promise which God made to Abraham? It was a composite promise consisting of several parts.

First, it was the promise of *a posterity*. He was to go from his kindred and his father's house, and in exchange for the loss of his family God would make of him "a great nation." Later in order to indicate this God changed his name from "Abram" ("exalted father") to "Abraham" ("father of a multitude") because, he said to him, "I have made you the father of a multitude of nations" (17:5).

Second, it was the promise of *a land*. God's call seems to have come to him in two stages, first in Ur of the Chaldees while his father was still alive (11:31; 15:7) and then in Haran after his father had died (11:32; 12:1). At all events he was to leave his own land, and in return God would show him another country.

Third, it was the promise of *a blessing*. Five times the words *bless* and *blessing* occur: "I will bless you . . . so that you will be a blessing. I will bless those who bless you . . . and by you all the families of the earth shall bless themselves (or be blessed)." Thus the blessing God promised Abraham would spill over upon all mankind.

A posterity, a land and a blessing. Each of these promises is elaborated in the chapters that follow Abraham's call.

First, *the land*. After Abraham had generously allowed his nephew Lot to choose where he wanted to settle (he selected the fertile Jordan valley), God said to Abraham: "Lift up your eyes, and look from the place where you are, northward and southward and eastward and westward; for all the land which you see I will give to you and to your descendants for ever" (13:14-15).

Second, *the posterity*. A bit later God gave Abraham another visual aid, telling him to look now not to the earth but to the sky. On a clear, dark night he took him outside his tent and said to him, "Look toward heaven and number the stars." What a ludicrous command! Perhaps Abraham started, "1, 2, 3, 5, 10, 20, 30 . . . ," but he must soon have given up. It was an impossible task. Then God said to him: "So shall your descendants be."

Previously God had promised that his descendants would be as countless as the dust of the earth (13:16); now he said they would be as countless as the stars of the sky (15:5). Later still he combined the similes and confirmed his promise with an oath: "By myself I have sworn, . . . I will indeed bless you, and will multiply your descendants as the stars of heaven and as the sand which is on the seashore" (22:16-17). Indeed, it is remark-

able that the famous astronomer Sir James Jeans conjectured in
his book *The Mysterious Universe* that the two are approximately equivalent, that there are probably as many stars in space as
grains of sand on all the beaches of the world. *That* was to be
the size of Abraham's posterity! And we read: "He believed the
Lord." Although he was probably by now in his eighties, and
although he and Sarah were still childless, he yet believed God's
promise and God "reckoned it to him as righteousness." That is,
because he trusted God, God accepted him as righteous in his
sight.

Third, *the blessing.* "I will bless you." Already God has accepted Abraham as righteous or (to borrow the New Testament
expression) has "justified him by faith." No greater blessing is
conceivable than this acceptance with God which the Bible calls
"justification." It is the foundation blessing of the covenant of
grace, which a few years later God went on to elaborate to Abraham: "I will establish my covenant between me and you and
your descendants after you . . . for an everlasting covenant, to be
God to you and to your descendants after you . . . and I will be
their God" (17:7-8). And he gave them circumcision as the outward and visible sign of his gracious covenant or pledge to be
their God. It is the first time in Scripture that we hear the covenant formula which is repeated many times later: "I will be their
God and they shall be my people."

A land, a posterity, a blessing. "But what has all that to do
with mission?" you may be asking with impatience. My answer
is "Everything! Be patient a little longer and you will see." Let
us turn now from the promise to the fulfillment.

The Fulfillment

The whole question of the fulfillment of Old Testament prophecy is a difficult one in which there is often misunderstanding
and not a little disagreement. Of particular importance is the
principle, with which I think all of us will agree, that the New
Testament writers themselves understood Old Testament
prophecy to have not a *single* but usually a *triple* fulfillment—
past, present and future.

The first belongs to the past. It was an immediate or historical fulfillment in the life of the nation of Israel.

The second belongs to the present. It is an intermediate or gospel fulfillment in Christ and his church.

The third belongs to the future. It will be an ultimate or eschatological fulfillment in the new heaven and the new earth.

A good example is the repeated prophecy that the Temple, after its destruction by Babylonian soldiers in 586 B.C., would be rebuilt. First, it was rebuilt at the end of the same century when God's people were restored to the land. Second, God's temple is Christ and his church, for today God dwells in Christ among his people, as Jesus and his apostles repeatedly affirm (for example, Jn. 2:19; 1 Cor. 3:16; 6:19; Eph. 2:21, 22). Third, the regenerated universe will be God's temple, for his presence will fill it, and the saying will then have come true that "the dwelling of God is with men" (Rev. 21:3, cf. v. 22).

God's promise to Abraham received an immediate, historical fulfillment in his physical descendants, the people of Israel.

God's promise to Abraham of a numerous, indeed of an innumerable, posterity was confirmed to his son Isaac (26:4, "as the stars of heaven") and his grandson Jacob (32:12, "as the sand of the sea"). Gradually the promise began to come literally true. As the writer to the Hebrews put it centuries later: "Therefore from one man, and him as good as dead, were born descendants as many as the stars of heaven and as the innumerable grains of sand by the seashore" (11:12). Perhaps we could pick out some of the stages in this development.

The first concerns their years of slavery in Egypt, of which it is written, "the descendants of Israel were fruitful and increased greatly; they multiplied and grew exceedingly strong; so that the land was filled with them" (Ex. 1:7; cf. Acts 7:17). Or as Moses was to put it later, "Your fathers went down to Egypt seventy persons; and now the LORD your God has made you as the stars of heaven for multitude" (Deut. 10:22; cf. 1:10; 26:5; 28:62; Neh. 9:23).

The next stage I will mention came several hundred years later when King Solomon called Israel "a great people that cannot be numbered or counted for multitude" (1 Kings 3:8), "as many as the dust of the earth" (2 Chron. 1:9) and "as many as the stars of the heaven" (1 Chron. 27:23).

A third stage was some 350 years after Solomon; Jeremiah warned Israel of impending judgement and captivity, and then added this divine promise of restoration: "As the host of heaven cannot be numbered and the sands of the sea cannot be measured, so I will multiply the descendants of David my servant" (33:22).

So much for Abraham's posterity; what about the land? Again we note with worship and gratitude God's faithfulness to his promise. For it was in remembrance of his promise to Abraham, Isaac and Jacob that he first rescued his people from their Egyptian slavery and gave them the territory which came on that account to be called "the promised land" (Ex. 2:24; 3:6; 32:13), and then restored them to it some 700 years later after their captivity in Babylon. Nevertheless, neither Abraham nor his physical descendants fully inherited the land. As Hebrews 11 puts it, they "died in faith, not having received what was promised." Instead, as "strangers and exiles on the earth" they "looked forward to the city which has foundations, whose builder and maker is God" (see Heb. 11:8-16 and 39-40).

God kept his promises about the posterity and the land, at least in part. Now what about the blessing? Well, at Sinai God confirmed and clarified his covenant with Abraham, and pledged himself to be Israel's God (for example, Ex. 19:3-6). When Balaam was hired by Balak King of Moab to curse Israel, he not only remarked that "the dust of Jacob" was countless but added, "How can I curse whom God has not cursed? . . . Behold, I received a command to bless: he has blessed, and I cannot revoke it" (Num. 23:8-10, 20). And throughout the rest of the Old Testament God went on blessing the obedient, while the disobedient fell under his judgement.

Perhaps the most dramatic example comes at the beginning of Hosea's prophecy, in which Hosea is told to give his three children names which describe God's awful and progressive judgement on Israel. His firstborn (a boy) he called "Jezreel," meaning "God will scatter." Next came a daughter "Lo-ruhamah," meaning "not pitied," for God said he would no longer pity or forgive his people. Lastly he had another son "Lo-ammi," meaning "not my people," for God said they were not now his people: What terrible names for the chosen people of God! They sound like a devastating contradiction of God's eternal promise to Abraham.

But God does not stop there. For beyond the coming judgement there would be a restoration, which is described in words which once more echo the promise to Abraham: "Yet the number of the people of Israel shall be like the sand of the sea, which can be neither measured nor numbered" (Hos. 1:10). And then the judgements implicit in the names of Hosea's children would be reversed. There would be a gathering instead of a scattering ("Jezreel" is ambiguous and can imply either), "not pitied" would be pitied, and "not my people" would become "sons of the living God" (1:10—2:1).

The wonderful thing is that the apostles Paul and Peter both quote these verses from Hosea. They see their fulfillment not just in a further multiplication of Israel but in the inclusion of the Gentiles in the community of Jesus: "Once you were no people but now you are God's people; once you had not received mercy but now you have received mercy" (1 Pet. 2:9-10; cf. Rom. 9:25-26).

This New Testament perspective is essential as we read the Old Testament prophecies. For what we miss in the Old Testament is any clear explanation of just how God's promised blessing would overflow from Abraham and his descendants to "all families of the earth." Of course the nations are quite prominent in the Old Testament record. Sometimes they are used as instruments of God's judgement on Israel, and sometimes they are themselves judged because of their hostility to Israel. They are also depicted as watching God's dealings with his people, and coming in some sense to know that he is the Lord as they see him both judging and redeeming them. Yet, although Israel is described as "a light to lighten the nations," and has a mission to "bring forth justice to the nations" (Is. 42:1-4, 6; 49:6), we do not actually see this happening. It is only in the Lord Jesus himself that these prophecies are fulfilled, for only in his day are the nations actually included in the redeemed community. To this we now turn.

God's promise to Abraham receives an intermediate or gospel fulfillment in Christ and his church.

It's surely significant that almost the first word of the whole New Testament is the word *Abraham*. For Matthew's Gospel begins: "The book of the genealogy of Jesus Christ, son of David, son of Abraham. Abraham was the father of Isaac. . . ." So it is right back to Abraham that Matthew traces the beginning not just of the genealogy but of the gospel of Jesus Christ. He knows that what he is recording is the fulfillment of God's ancient promises to Abraham some 2,000 years previously. (See also Lk. 1:45-55, 67-75.)

Yet from the start Matthew recognizes that it isn't just *physical* descent from Abraham which qualifies people to inherit the promises, but a kind of *spiritual* descent, namely repentance and faith in the coming Messiah. This was John the Baptist's message to crowds who flocked to hear him: "Do not presume to say to yourselves 'We have Abraham as our father'; for I tell you God is able from these stones to raise up children to Abraham" (Mt. 3:9; Lk. 3:8; cf. Jn. 8:33-40). The implications of his words will have shocked his hearers, since "it was the current belief that no descendant of Abraham could be lost" (J. Jeremias, *Jesus' Promise to the Nations*, SCM Press, 1958, p. 48).

And God *has* raised up children to Abraham, if not from stones, then from an equally unlikely source, namely the Gentiles! So Matthew, although the most Jewish of all four gospel writers, later records Jesus as having said, "I tell you, many will come from the east and west and sit at table with Abraham, Isaac, and Jacob in the kingdom of heaven, while the sons of the kingdom will be thrown into outer darkness" (8:11-12; cf. Lk. 13:28-29).

It is hard for us to grasp how shocking, how completely topsy-turvy, these words will have sounded to the Jewish hearers of John the Baptist and Jesus. They were the descendants of Abraham; so they had a title to the promises which God made to Abraham. Who then were these outsiders who were to share in the promises, even apparently usurp them, while they themselves would be disqualified? They were indignant. They had quite forgotten that part of God's covenant with Abraham promised an overspill of blessing to *all* the nations of the earth. Now the Jews had to learn that it was in relation to Jesus the Messiah, who was himself seed of Abraham, that all the nations would be blessed.

The apostle Peter seems at least to have begun to grasp this in his second sermon, just after Pentecost. In it he addressed a Jewish crowd with the words: "You are the sons . . . of the covenant which God gave to your fathers, saying to Abraham, 'And in your posterity shall all the families of the earth be blessed.' God, having raised up his servant [Jesus], sent him to you first to bless you in turning every one of you from your wickedness" (Acts 3:25-26). It is a very notable statement both because he interprets the blessing in the moral terms of repentance and righteousness and because, if Jesus was sent "first" to the Jews he was presumably sent next to the Gentiles, whose "families of the earth" had been "far off" (cf. Acts 2:39) but were now to share in the blessing.

It was given to the apostle Paul, however, to bring this wonderful theme to its full development. For he was called and appointed to be the apostle of the Gentiles, and to him was revealed God's eternal but hitherto secret purpose to make Jews and the Gentiles "fellow heirs, members of the same body, and partakers of the promise in Christ Jesus through the gospel" (Eph. 3:6).

Negatively, Paul declares with great boldness, "Not all who are descended from Israel belong to Israel, and not all are children of Abraham because they are his descendants" (Rom. 9:6-7).

Who then are the true descendants of Abraham, the true beneficiaries of God's promises to him? Paul does not leave us in any doubt. They are Christian believers of whatever race. In Romans 4 he points out that Abraham not only received justification by faith but also received this blessing *before he had been circumcised*. Therefore Abraham is the father of all those who, whether circumcised or uncircumcised (that is, Jews or Gentiles), "follow the example of [his] faith" (Rom. 4:9-12). If we "share the faith of Abraham," then "he is the father of us all, as it is written, 'I have made you the father of many nations' " (vv. 16-17). Thus neither physical descent from Abraham, nor

physical circumcision as a Jew, makes a person a true child of
Abraham, but rather faith. Abraham's real descendants are believers in Jesus Christ, whether racially they happen to be Jews
or Gentiles.

What then is the "land" which Abraham's descendants inherit? The Letter to the Hebrews refers to a "rest" which God's
people enter now by faith (Heb. 3—4). And in a most remarkable
expression Paul refers to "the promise to Abraham and his
descendants, that they should inherit the world" (Rom. 4:13). One
can only assume he means the same thing as when to the Corinthians he writes that in Christ "all things are yours, whether
Paul or Apollos or Cephas or the world or life or death or the
present or the future, all are yours" (1 Cor. 3:21-23). Christians
by God's wonderful grace are joint heirs with Christ of the universe.

Somewhat similar teaching, both about the nature of the
promised blessing and about its beneficiaries, is given by Paul
in Galatians 3. He first repeats how Abraham was justified by
faith, and then continues: "So you see that it is men of faith who
are the sons of Abraham" and who therefore "are blessed with
Abraham who had faith" (vv. 6-9). What then is the blessing
with which all the nations were to be blessed (v. 8)? In a word,
it is the blessing of salvation. We were under the curse of the
law, but Christ has redeemed us from it by becoming a curse in
our place, in order "that in Christ Jesus the blessing of Abraham
might come upon the Gentiles, that we might receive the promise of the Spirit through faith" (vv. 10-14). Christ bore our curse
that we might inherit Abraham's blessing, the blessing of justification (v. 8) and of the indwelling Holy Spirit (v. 14). Paul sums
it up in the last verse of the chapter (v. 29): "If you are Christ's,
then you are Abraham's offspring, heirs according to promise."
The way to become a child of Abraham and qualify for the promise is to belong to Christ by faith, for he is the seed of Abraham
(v. 16), and then we become "heirs" (notice the language of in-
heritance as in verse 18) according to his promise of the fullness
of his salvation both here and hereafter.

Thus the apostle Paul on his great missionary journeys, as he
shared with the Gentiles the good news of salvation in Christ,

was convinced that he was preaching the very same gospel as had been preached 2000 years previously to Abraham in the words "in you shall all the nations be blessed" (Gal. 3:8). For "the nations" were the Gentiles, the "blessing" was justification and the gift of the Spirit, and "in you" or "your offspring" referred in the end to Christ (v. 16).

Not, of course, that God has ever repudiated his ancient people. On the contrary, the same Paul, the special apostle to the Gentiles, looks forward to the time when (in his vivid imagery) the broken-off branches of God's olive tree will be grafted in again and there will be a widespread turning of Jewish people to the Lord (Rom. 11:11-36).

But we have not quite finished yet. There is a third stage of fulfillment still to come.

God's promise to Abraham will receive an ultimate or eschatological fulfillment in the final destiny of all the redeemed.

In the Book of Revelation there is one more reference to God's promise to Abraham (7:9 ff). John sees in a vision "a great multitude which no man could number." It is an international throng, drawn "from every nation, from all tribes and people and tongues." And they are "standing before the throne," the symbol of God's kingly reign. That is, his Kingdom has finally come, and they are enjoying all the blessings of his gracious rule. He shelters them with his presence. Their wilderness days of hunger, thirst and scorching heat are over. They have entered the promised land at last, described now not as "a land flowing with milk and honey" but as a land irrigated from "springs of living water" which never dry up. But how did they come to inherit these blessings? Partly because they have "come out of the great tribulation" (evidently a reference to the Christian life with all its trials and sufferings), but mostly because "they have washed their robes and made them white in the blood of the Lamb," that is, they have been cleansed from sin and clothed with righteousness through the merits of the death of Jesus Christ alone. *"Therefore* are they before the throne of God."

Speaking personally, I find it extremely moving to glimpse this final fulfillment in a future eternity of that ancient promise of God to Abraham. All the essential elements of the promise may be detected. For here are the spiritual descendants of Abraham, a "great multitude which no man could number," as countless as the sand on the seashore and as the stars in the night sky. Here too are "all the families of the earth" being blessed, for the numberless multitude is composed of people from every nation. Here also is the promised land, namely all the rich blessings which flow from God's gracious rule. And here above all is Jesus Christ, the seed of Abraham, who shed his blood for our redemption and who bestows his blessings on all those who call on him to be saved.

Conclusion

Let me try to summarize what we learn about God from his promise to Abraham and its fulfillment.

First, he is the God of history. History is not a random flow of events. For God is working out in time a plan which he conceived in a past eternity and will consummate in a future eternity. In this historical process Jesus Christ as the seed of Abraham is the key figure. Let's rejoice that if we are Christ's disciples we are Abraham's descendants. We belong to his spiritual lineage. If we have received the blessings of justification by faith, acceptance with God, and of the indwelling Spirit, then we are beneficiaries today of a promise made to Abraham 4000 years ago.

Second, he is the God of the covenant. That is, God is gracious enough to make promises, and he always keeps the promises he makes. He is a God of steadfast love and faithfulness. Mind you, he does not always fulfill his promises immediately. Abraham and Sarah "died in faith, not having received what was promised, but having seen it and greeted it from afar" (Heb. 11:13). That is, although Isaac was born to them in fulfillment of the promise, their seed was not yet numerous, nor was the land given to them, nor were the nations blessed. All God's promises come true, but they are inherited "through faith and patience" (Heb. 6:12). We have to be content to wait for God's time.

Third, he is the God of blessing. "I will bless you," he said to Abraham (Gen. 12:2). "God ... sent him [Jesus] to you first, to bless you," echoed Peter (Acts 3:26). God's attitude to his people is positive, constructive, enriching. Judgement is his "strange work" (Is. 28:21). His principal and characteristic work is to bless people with salvation.

Fourth, he is the God of mercy. I have always derived much comfort from the statement of Rev. 7:9 that the company of the redeemed in heaven will be "a great multitude which no man could number." I do not profess to know how this can be, since Christians have always seemed to be a rather small minority. But Scripture states it for our comfort. Although no biblical Christian can be a universalist (believing that all mankind will ultimately be saved), since Scripture teaches the awful reality and eternity of hell, yet a biblical Christian can—even must— assert that the redeemed will somehow be an international throng so immense as to be countless. For God's promise is going to be fulfilled, and Abraham's seed is going to be as innumerable as the dust of the earth, the stars of the sky and the sand on the seashore.

Fifth, he is the God of mission. The nations are not gathered in automatically. If God has promised to bless "all the families of the earth," he has promised to do so "through Abraham's seed" (Gen. 12:3; 22:18). Now we are Abraham's seed by faith, and the earth's families will be blessed only if we go to them with the gospel. That is God's plain purpose.

I pray that these words, "all the families of the earth," may be written on our hearts. It is this expression more than any other which reveals the living God of the Bible to be a missionary God. It is this expression too which condemns all our petty parochialism and narrow nationalism, our racial pride (whether white or black), our condescending paternalism and arrogant imperialism. How dare we adopt a hostile or scornful or even indifferent attitude to any person of another color or culture if our God is the God of "all the families of the earth"? We need to become global Christians with a global vision, for we have a global God.

So may God help us never to forget his 4000-year-old promise to Abraham: "By you and your descendants *all* the nations of the earth shall be blessed."

four
The Lord Christ
Is a Missionary
Christ

John R. W. Stott

We have seen that "the Living God is a missionary God," and we have studied the foundational Old Testament promise and its fulfillment, that through Abraham's seed all the world's nations would be blessed. Now we move into the Gospels and affirm that "the Lord Christ is a missionary Christ."

At first sight you might come to a completely different conclusion. For the "Jewishness" of the story the Gospels tell is very obvious. By human parentage Jesus was a Jew, descended from King David and through him from Abraham. He was "born under the law" (Gal. 4:4), and was circumcised and presented to the Lord according to the law. His uncle Zechariah was a priest who took his turn to serve in the temple. Jesus himself lived in Palestine and never left it. His mind was steeped in the Old Testament. He observed the Jewish festivals. The twelve apostles he chose were all Jews too. He even restricted his ministry and theirs to the Jewish people, whom he called "the lost sheep of the house of Israel" (Mt. 10:5-6; 15:24).

But this limitation was only a temporary arrangement. It belonged to the period of his public ministry in which he presented himself to God's chosen people as their Messiah, that is, their Savior-King.

The Jewish background and sayings of Jesus have to be complemented with other material which presents him rather as the Savior of the world. Thus, if Matthew traced his genealogy back to Abraham, the head of the chosen race, Luke took it back further to Adam, the head of the human race (Lk. 3:38). For Jesus was truly and fully man. Next, it is amazing that those who paid homage to the child Jesus included not only Jewish shepherds but also Gentile magi. Probably they were Zoroastrian astrologer-priests from Persia; certainly they were forerunners of millions of other nationals who have bowed down to worship the Lord Jesus. Then when Simeon took the baby Jesus in his arms, he called him in words from Isaiah "a light to lighten the nations," just as Luke applied to him another text from Isaiah, namely that through him "all flesh shall see the salvation of God" (Lk. 2:32; 3:6).

The universal scope of the gospel of Christ is clearly set forth in his teaching. He likened the expansion of God's kingdom to the growth of a tiny mustard seed into a sizeable bush in which birds build their nests. He said that he the Good Shepherd would include within his "one flock" even the "other sheep"—Gentiles, in fact—who were outside the Jewish fold (Jn. 10:16). He indicated that just as a grain of wheat multiplies through its death, so by his death, his being "lifted up from the earth," "all men" (that is, people of all races like the Greeks who had just asked to see him) would be drawn to him (Jn. 12:20-33). He also promised that before the end of the world the good news of the kingdom would be preached "throughout the whole world, as a testimony to all nations" (Mt. 24:14).

This last saying of Jesus, which was part of his so-called "apocalyptic discourse" given on the Mount of Olives, also anticipated the Great Commission which he issued after the resurrection. To this we now turn. Many people seem to associate the Great Commission exclusively with the final verses of Matthew's Gospel. But during the forty days which elapsed between his resurrection and ascension Jesus evidently taught much about the worldwide mission of the church. Hence five different versions of his commission are recorded in our Bibles, one in each Gospel and the fifth in the Acts, although the longer ending of Mark's Gospel is almost universally acknowledged as being a later addition and not authentic.

The Great Commission: Four Indispensables

I have chosen for our study that version of the Great Commission found in John's Gospel, though we shall glance at the others. It is historically the first, having been given on Easter Day itself. It is also, I think, the most pregnant and the most neglected.

> On the evening of that day, the first day of the week, the doors being shut where the disciples were, for fear of the Jews, Jesus came and stood among them and said to them, "Peace be with you." When he had said this, he showed them his hands and his side. Then the disciples were glad when they saw the Lord. Jesus said to them again, "Peace be with you. As the Father has sent me, even so I send you." And when he had said this, he breathed on them, and said to them, "Receive the Holy Spirit. If you forgive the sins of any, they are forgiven; if you retain the sins of any, they are retained." (Jn. 20:19-23)

The essence of Christ's message is to be found in the three words of verse 21, "I send you." This is the commission; his other words are all commentary and explanation. So we must look carefully at these three English monosyllables. The "I" represents the emphatic Greek word ego. It expresses the authority of the Sender, an authority he was later specifically to claim when he said, "All authority in heaven and on earth has been given to me" (Mt. 28:18). This was—and still is—an almost incredible claim. God the Father has now committed to his Messiah Jesus the universal authority or dominion so often predicted of him in the Old Testament. So Jesus has authority over us, to send us where and when he chooses; authority over the nations to whom he sends us, and the right to receive their homage; authority too over demonic forces which may try to frustrate our mission. The words constitute a personal challenge to all Christian people who acknowledge the authority of Jesus. They are also a great encouragement, assuring us as they do that the authority to dispose and deploy the forces of God, to develop the worldwide Christian mission and to determine its consequences belongs to Christ the Lord and not to us.

"I send you." If the "I" is the Lord Christ who possesses universal authority, the "you" is all his servants. Although he addressed his commission in the first instance to the apostles, it cannot be restricted to them. We know from Luke's account of this occasion that others were present who were not apostles (Lk. 24:33). So the commission passes on beyond the apostles to embrace the whole church which deserves to be called "apostolic" only in so far as it is loyal to the apostles' mission and message.

"I send you." If "I" means Christ the universal Lord and "you" means all of us, then the verb "send" is his commission to us. What is it? In that Jerusalem upper room Jesus spoke four short sharp sentences which imprinted themselves indelibly on the memories of his hearers, and which define the nature of our mission.

The first (v. 19, repeated in v. 21) is "Peace be with you."

The second (v. 21) is "As the Father has sent me, even so I send you."

The third (v. 22) is "Receive the Holy Spirit."

And the fourth (v. 23) "If you forgive the sins of any, they are forgiven; if you retain the sins of any, they are retained."

These four sentences together indicate that a new day has dawned as a result of the death and resurrection of Jesus. They describe the particular shape which Jesus intends his mission to take. Indeed, each is an essential aspect of it. Without these four indispensables the "I-send-you" commission makes nonsense.

An Experience: Peace

The gospel committed to us to proclaim is, in the words of Peter, "good news of peace by Jesus Christ" (Acts 10:36). As the prophet cried out centuries before Christ: "How beautiful upon the mountains are the feet of him who brings good tidings, who publishes peace" (Is. 52:7). But how can we preach peace to others until we have received peace ourselves?

So Jesus said "peace be with you." It is the first official word that he spoke to the twelve after his resurrection. It is also the second, for he emphasized it by repetition. Of course it was the customary Hebrew greeting—shalom!—and still is in the State of Israel today. Yet we may be sure that, when Jesus used it, it was no empty convention. He wished them peace; he gave them peace. Without peace they could not go forth in his name. What sort of peace was it? There are three kinds of peace through Jesus Christ.

Peace of mind. The crucifixion of Jesus had shattered their hopes. In spite of his warnings, his death had plunged them into doubt whether after all he was the Christ in whom they had come to believe. But his word of peace reassures them. It is the same Jesus, the same voice with the same message, the same body with the same scars, though all transfigured by the resurrection. The certainty that he had risen dispelled their doubt and gave them peace, just as it can today.

Peace of conscience. Their peace had been disturbed not only by his death, but by their own complicity in his death. They had denied him, deserted him, left him in the lurch. They were overcome with a sense of guilt. But now Jesus speaks peace to their troubled conscience, and shows them his hands and his side as evidence that he has died for them and risen again. Had he not said in that same upper room that he would shed his blood for the forgiveness of sins? At least now they begin to understand that God has vindicated the achievement of the cross by raising Christ from the dead.

Jesus Christ still speaks peace to troubled minds and consciences. His death and resurrection are the foundation stones on which our Christian peace is built. He died for our sins; he was raised from death. So how can we doubt either his divine person or the efficacy of his atoning death? The resurrection powerfully declares him to be both Son of God and Savior of sinners. No wonder "the disciples were glad when they saw the Lord" (v. 20). Joy and peace flooded their hearts.

Still today Jesus adds to his word of peace a visible sign. For the bread and wine of Communion are like the hands and side of the Lord. At his table he seems to say to us, "Behold my hands and my side. Do you doubt that your sins are forgiven? See! I died for you and rose again." We too shall be glad when we see the Lord. Unutterable is the joy of Christians who know Jesus Christ as their once crucified and now risen Savior.

Without this double assurance about Christ, bringing peace to mind and conscience, we cannot go out on our mission. But once by word and sign Christ has given us his peace, nothing will be able to silence us.

Peace in the church. This is a third aspect of peace we must not overlook. The peace Christ gives is not just individual, but corporate; not just internal (in our hearts) but external (in our fellowship). For peace in the Bible is reconciliation, and this includes reconciliation with one another. Paul specially writes of "peace" in this sense of reconciliation in the Christian community—racial or social—in Ephesians 2. When there is quarreling and rivalry in the fellowship, racial prejudice or tribal pride, envy or bitterness, then our gospel lacks all credibility. How can we preach peace to others in such a way that they will believe us if we do not live in peace ourselves?

A Model: Jesus Christ

Christ's gift of peace is immediately followed by his summons to mission: "Peace be with you. As the Father has sent me, even so I send you" (v. 21). So the "peace" of Jesus gives us no excuse to remain in hiding, sheltered from conflict behind closed doors, withdrawn into ecclesiastical tranquility. On the contrary. With Christ's peace in our mind, conscience and fellowship we are all the better prepared to go out into the hostile world of which previously we were afraid.

And as we go, our mission is to be modeled on Christ's. Jesus does not merely issue a command ("The Father sent me; I send you"): He supplies a pattern ("*As* the Father sent me, *so* I send you"). There is thus to be a close parallel between the mission of the Son and the mission of the church. That being so, we must carefully consider the nature of *his* mission, in order thereby to discover the nature of *ours*. I choose three words to describe it.

Christ's mission was central. It occupied a central place in his mind and therefore in his life. The evidence is plain. Deep in the self-consciousness of Jesus was the knowledge that he had been "sent into the world" on a mission. At the outset of his public ministry, reading and preaching in the Nazareth synagogue, he applied to himself the words from Isaiah, "He has sent me to proclaim release to the captives" (Lk. 4:18); and soon after, when the crowds clamored to keep him in their district, he responded, "I must preach the good news of the kingdom of God to the other cities also; for I was sent for this purpose" (Lk. 4:43). Especially in John's Gospel he designated the Father "he who sent me" and himself "he whom the Father has sent" (for example, 3:34; 5:36-38; 6:29, 57; 7:29; 8:42; 10:36; 11:42; 17:3, 8, 18, 21, 23, 25). This sense of having been sent was a fundamental awareness of Jesus. It gave significance, urgency and compulsion to everything he did. "We must work the works of him who sent me while it is day," he said; "night comes, when no one can work" (Jn. 9:4). Thus his mission dominated his mind and actions. Indeed, the phenomenon of Jesus is inexplicable otherwise. Wherever we look in his earthly career—his birth and boyhood, his words and works, his sufferings and death—we are faced with the fact that he had been "sent," and that he knew it.

Now he says, "As the Father has sent me, so I send you." Therefore, if mission was central in the mind of Jesus, it must be central in our minds too. If Jesus is inexplicable apart from his mission, his church is equally inexplicable apart from its mission. If God was to Jesus "he who sent me," then Jesus must be to us "he who sent us." For this is part of the very nature of the church. The church is the community of Jesus who have first been chosen out of the world and then sent back into the world. "Mission is as fundamental to us as it was to Christ. An introverted church, turned in on itself, preoccupied with its own survival, has virtually forfeited the right to be a church, for it is denying a major part of its own being. As a planet which ceases to be in orbit is no longer a planet, so a church which ceases to be in mission is no longer a church. In order to qualify for the name "church" we must be a community deeply and constantly aware of our "sentness," and actively loyal to this part of our Christian identity.

Christ's mission was compassionate. The mission of Jesus was a mission of compassion. The words *mission* and *compassion* should always be bracketed, indeed almost hyphenated, so closely do they belong to one another. Again and again we read in the Gospels that Jesus "was moved with compassion"—now by the leaderless or hungry crowds, now by the sick, now by a single leprosy sufferer, now by a widow who had lost her only child. What aroused his compassion was always human need, in whatever form he encountered it. And out of compassion for people in need he acted. He preached the gospel, he taught the people, he fed the hungry, he cleansed the leper, he healed the sick, he raised the dead. All this was part of his mission. He had not come to be served, he said, but to serve (Mk. 10:45). Of course the climax of his self-giving service was his atoning death, by which he secured our salvation. Nevertheless, his mission of compassion was not limited to this, because human need is not limited to this. He was sent to serve, and his service was adapted with compassionate sensitivity to human need.

Now he says, "As the Father has sent me, so I send you." The Christian mission like Christ's is a mission of compassionate service. True, man's most fundamental need is salvation through the death and resurrection of Jesus. Nothing is more liberating, nothing more humanizing, than an experience of forgiveness, reconciliation to God and new birth. But this is not man's only need. And authentic Christian compassion forbids us to turn a blind eye to any human need. If Jesus did not restrict his mission to the preaching of the gospel, or even to dying for our sins and rising again in order that there might be a gospel to preach, then we have no right to limit our mission to evangelism alone.

It seems to me, therefore, that the recent controversy between the rival claims of evangelism and social action was a sterile controversy from the start. Some Christians have concentrated exclusively on evangelism, others on social and political involvement. But we have no liberty to pick and choose between the needs of our fellows, the needs of his body or of his soul or of his community. Christian evangelistic and social activity are both compassionate responses to human need. Both were included in Jesus' mission. So both must be included in ours.

Christ's mission was costly. To be sent into a hostile world, to feel compassion for sufferers, to give himself in service without reserve—all this was very costly for Jesus. It involved for him an identification with the people he had been sent to serve which included his birth, his life and his death.

First, his birth. Jesus could not have served human need by remaining aloof in the safe isolation of his heaven; he had to enter our world. And his entry was not a superficial visit like the arrival of an immigrant who refuses to become acculturated to the land of his adoption, or like a spaceship touchdown in which the astronaut protects himself from exposure in a spacesuit. No. He laid aside his immunity to pain, weakness, poverty, sorrow, suffering and temptation. He became flesh and lived among us. He made himself vulnerable when he made himself a human being like us.

Next, his life. There was no aloofness about Jesus. He never kept his distance, even from sinners. He did not share the Pharisees' false fear of contamination. He fraternized with dropouts and was criticized for it. "This man receives sinners and eats with them," people scoffed. "Friend of swindlers and sinners, that's what he is," they sneered. They hoped to ruin his reputation by this whispering campaign, but they succeeded only in enhancing it. The nickname they thought dishonorable was one of supreme honor. If Jesus were not the friend of sinners, he could be no friend of mine—or yours. So he touched untouchable lepers and allowed prostitutes to touch him. He shrank from nobody. He offered friendship, understanding, acceptance, love.

Third, his death. The ultimate of the self-identification of Jesus was the cross. He was despised and rejected by men. More than that, he gave himself for us. Already he had made himself one with us in our humanity and our sorrows; now he also identified himself with our sins, our guilt and our death. He who was "made flesh" for us was actually "made sin" and "made a curse" for us as well (Jn. 1:14; 2 Cor. 5:21; Gal. 3:13).

So then, Jesus took our nature, lived our life, tasted our sorrows, felt our pain, experienced our temptations, bore our sins, died our death. From his birth to his death, from the manger to the cross, Jesus made himself one with us. He could not have become more completely like us than he did, without ceasing to be himself. It was total identification, though without any loss of identity. And it was extremely costly.

Now he says, "As the Father has sent me, so I send you." The Lausanne Covenant states, "We affirm that Christ sends his redeemed people into the world as the Father sent him, and that this calls for a similar deep and costly penetration of the world. We need to break out of our ecclesiastical ghettos and permeate non-Christian society" (paragraph 6). Jesus calls us to apply to our mission in the world the same principle which characterized his. It is the principle of identification without loss of identity, the principle not of insulation but of incarnation. If I had to express it in a single word, I would choose *friendship* as opposed to *aloofness*. Jesus was the friend of sinners; we must be too. Without doubt there is a ministry to strangers, like distributing tracts to passers-by or signing checks for the relief of human need. Such actions can be right, good, Christian, responsible. Yet they are service-at-a-distance. They are the kind of service Jesus could have given if he had remained in heaven. But he *earthed* his service; and so must we. The most Christian context in which to offer service and share the gospel is genuine, caring friendship. No other kind necessitates anything like an incarnation, that is, an entering into another person's world.

Let me apply this principle in particular to our evangelism. The cross-cultural missionary knows all about it. He goes to another country, in which another language is spoken and another culture prevails. He has to learn that language and absorb that culture. It will take him years of toil, tears and sweat. Of the two tasks he has, he will find it easier to learn the language than understand the culture. I often wonder whether we are taking this charge seriously enough. Many are translating the Bible into the *languages* of the world. Thank God for their devotion. But who is translating the gospel into the *cultures* of the world? That is the pressing need.

Most of us are familiar with the distinctions between "E 1,"

"E 2" and "E 3" evangelism which Dr. Ralph Winter of the Fuller School of World Mission popularized at the 1974 Lausanne Congress. "E 1" is evangelizing people of the same language and culture, "E 2" people of a similar language and culture, while the "E 3" evangelist is the cross-cultural missionary. While gratefully accepting this clarification, I would like now to emphasize that there is a cross-cultural element in *all* evangelism, even in an E 1 context. That is, there is always a gap of ignorance or misunderstanding to be bridged. Sometimes the gap may be almost as wide as in an E 3 context, as when we are seeking to share the gospel with a student whose education has steeped his mind in scientific secularism. At other times the gap is narrow. Still it is a real gap, and an incarnation is needed to bridge it. To whatever degree the other person is alienated from God and from the gospel, to that degree there is need for an incarnation, a costly penetration into his mind and heart.

Does not this call and commission of Jesus condemn much of our modern superficiality? We do not follow in the footsteps of Jesus if we develop a ghetto mentality, if we withdraw from the world into our evangelical monasteries (though we do not call them that, and they have no walls) or even if we remain in our churches with a haughty come-and-get-it attitude to outsiders. Again too much so-called "personal evangelism" is very impersonal. We keep the other person at arm's length and build no human relationship with him. He (or she) remains a "contact," sometimes even a "client," but not a "friend." It is very depersonalized personal evangelism. Again, we must not put our confidence in slick evangelistic formulas, whose stereotype allows no sensitive responses to the Holy Spirit or to the existential situation. These are not the way of Jesus.

What we are called to is not "arm's length evangelism," but "incarnation evangelism." This will mean that we have to listen before we speak, for "if one gives answer before he hears, it is his folly and shame" (Prov. 18:13). We have to struggle to enter the other person's thought world, however alien it may be to our own. We must try to understand his misunderstandings and to grasp his hangups, problems, doubts and fears, in fact all those things which to him are obstacles to faith. We have to respect his

integrity as a person, and his convictions, however contrary
they may seem to us to be. In a word, we must feel the pain of
his alienation and weep the tears of his lostness, just as Jesus
wept over the blind folly of Jerusalem's impenitence.

When we see in Christ's mission a model for ours and thus
discern that genuine Christian mission is central, compassionate and costly, we may well be tempted to hang back. Incarna-
tional evangelism is not only costly; it is perilous. For it is a
call to identification with the non-Christian world *without any
loss of our Christian identity*. We are to think our way into the
thoughts of others without losing our Christian convictions, and
to love those whose lives are soiled without losing Christ's
standards of purity. He himself succeeded in this. He was both
"friend of sinners" and "separated from sinners" simultaneous-
ly (Lk. 7:34; Heb. 7:26). He calls us to the same ideal. But we are
very weak in both mind and character, and we need to take sensible precautions. Young Christians should wait until they have
first gained a measure of stability and maturity. And older Christians, remembering the warning, "Let anyone who thinks that
he stands take heed lest he fall" (1 Cor. 10:12), should keep waiting on the Lord to renew their strength, should seek the fire-
cover of other Christians' prayers and in some situations should
seek (like the apostles) to penetrate a hostile environment only
"two by two." Our need for divine power to strengthen and pro-
tect us brings us to Jesus' third sentence.

A Power: the Holy Spirit
The third way in which Jesus described our Christian mission is
in these words (v. 22): "He breathed on them and said to them,
'Receive the Holy Spirit.' " The apostles were not to go out on
their mission alone, or in their own puny strength. Nor must we.
We need power as well as peace, an equipment for mission as
well as a model. And this power, this equipment, is to be
found in the Holy Spirit. If we are to penetrate the non-Christian
world for Christ without being contaminated ourselves, we need
the power of the Holy Spirit to sanctify us. If we are to share the
gospel with others in such a way that they will listen, understand and respond, the power of the Spirit must be upon us.

So Jesus breathed on them and said, "Receive the Holy Spirit." I do not think we are intended to understand his words and his action as meaning that he actually bestowed the Spirit upon them there and then. We must compare Scripture with Scripture (the safest of all principles of biblical interpretation) and interpret this passage in its historical and biblical context. We know that the gift of the Spirit was poured out by the ascended Christ on the Day of Pentecost and that only then were they endued with power. We also know that during the forty days between his resurrection and ascension Jesus more than once promised them the power of the Holy Spirit and told them to wait before beginning their mission until the Spirit came and empowered them (Lk. 24:49; Acts 1:4-8). It is surely impossible to believe, therefore, that Jesus contradicted himself by bestowing upon them the very gift of the Holy Spirit which he was telling them they must wait to receive.

No. It is much better to understand these words as referring to the same promise, although given in another and more dramatic form. By saying to them, "Receive the Holy Spirit," he was pledging this gift to them and insisting that he himself the risen Lord would be the giver. And his breathing on them was an acted parable in anticipation of the Day of Pentecost. Just as he confirmed his promise of peace by a sign ("He showed them his hands and his side," v. 20), so he confirmed his promise of the Spirit by a sign ("He breathed on them," v. 22). They will never have forgotten that sacred moment when they felt upon them the breath of the risen Christ. Nor would they ever in future separate the second and third persons of the Trinity, as some of us moderns disastrously do, for Jesus' word and the breath of Jesus had plainly taught them that the Spirit was the gift of the Son, the Holy Breath of Jesus himself. Indeed I do not think there is any fundamental difference between this promise of the Spirit's power and Jesus' other promise which concludes the Gospel of Matthew: "Lo, I am with you always, to the close of the age." For it is in the person of the Holy Spirit that the presence and power of Jesus Christ are given to us today.

We need constantly to learn that Christian evangelism is more than a human enterprise. We cannot win souls to Christ merely by advertising or by preaching or by witnessing or by arguing. I do not say that these methods of evangelism are unnecessary, for the Holy Spirit can and does use them all. What I am saying is that they are *insufficient* without the work of the Holy Spirit in and through them. Only the Holy Spirit convicts of sin, testifies to Christ and imparts light and life in the new birth. So true, deep and lasting conversions are impossible without the Spirit. Our mission is God's mission: The Son supplies the model and the Holy Spirit the power.

A Message: Forgiveness
Supposing we have the peace of Christ and the power of the Spirit, and supposing we do go into the world on our mission as Christ went into the world on his, what shall we say? There can be no mission without a message. So Christ's fourth sentence commits to us the good news of the forgiveness of sins, though with the solemn addition of the bad news of the retention of sins.

"If you forgive the sins of any, they are forgiven; if you retain the sins of any, they are retained" (v. 23). This is admittedly a difficult verse; it has been variously interpreted. Mainly on the foundation of this text the Church of Rome has built its official teaching that the Catholic hierarchy has judicial power to absolve penitents. And for many centuries (though less today) they have applied it in practice to the hearing of confessions and the granting of absolution. Protestants, however, have always maintained that this verse cannot justly be interpreted in this "catholic" sense, for two reasons. The two major principles in interpreting a text are the principle of *history* (how did the original hearers understand it?) and the principle of *harmony* (how does it fit with its context and with other teaching being given at the same time?).

Applying the first principle, the fatal objection to the Catholic interpretation is that the apostles did not understand Christ's words in this way. There is no recorded instance in the Acts or the Letters in which they either required sinners to confess their sins to them (or to God in their presence privately) or gave judicial absolution to penitents. So what did the apostles do? Answer: They preached the gospel, its warnings as well as its promises. With clarity, courage and authority they declared the terms on which God forgives sins and without which he retains them. "Repent and be baptized," cried Peter on the Day of Pentecost, "for the forgiveness of your sins." "Repent . . . and turn again," he preached a few days later, "that your sins may be blotted out." Paul's message was the same: "Let it be known to you . . . that through this man [Jesus] forgiveness of sins is proclaimed to you" (Acts 2:38; 3:19; 13:38). And he went on to warn them of God's judgement if they refused the gospel invitation.

The second principle (that of harmony) confirms the rightness of this interpretation. Does it fit with what Jesus is known to have been teaching at that time? Yes, it does. Listen to Luke's version of the Great Commission (24:47): "that repentance and forgiveness of sins should be preached in his name [that is, in the name of Christ who had died and risen, v. 46] to all nations." The most probable explanation of the disputed verse in John 20, therefore, is that Jesus was giving the same commission to preach the gospel. The apostles were to proclaim the way of salvation, yes, and the way of damnation too. They were to explain as clearly as they could how sinners could be forgiven, and at the same time to warn them with equal plainness of the great danger inherent in rejecting the gospel offer. If you repent and believe, they were to say, your sins will be forgiven; if you refuse, they will not be forgiven. And this authoritative gospel Jesus expressed in the dramatic words, "if you forgive the sins of any, they are forgiven; if you retain the sins of any, they are retained."

Not that this constitutes the total message committed to us to proclaim. For those who respond to the gospel and are baptized are to be nurtured and grounded in their new-found faith. "Teach them," Jesus said, "to observe all that I have commanded you" (Mt. 28:20). We have no liberty to omit anything from our instruction of converts; we are to teach them "the whole counsel of God" (Acts 20:27).

Conclusion
Here then is the commission of Jesus, which itself was the logical

culmination of everything that had gone before. The four sentences he spoke in the upper room all issue from the fact of his death and resurrection, and are all indispensable to our Christian mission. It is the crucified and risen Savior alone who gives peace to a troubled mind, conscience and church, who sends us out into the world as he was sent into the world, who promises us the power of his Spirit as we go, and who puts on our lips the message of a full and free forgiveness to penitent believers and of a fearful judgement awaiting those who harden their hearts against him. From first to last our mission is a gift from Christ. The experience of peace, the model of identification, the power of the Spirit and the message of forgiveness all come from Jesus Christ.

In many respects we here today resemble those first people who received Christ's commission. For we too are Christians, and we too have met behind closed doors. True, we are not in hiding, but in conference. True also, what has motivated us to come together is not fear of hostile people outside but a compassionate concern for them. Nevertheless, we are a Christian assembly cut off from the non-Christian world—which is entirely legitimate so long as it is only temporary. It would be dangerous for us to stay together too long. For here the risen Christ comes to us, stands among us, speaks to us and shows us his hands and his side. Here too he breathes on us, promising us power for our task, and sends us back into the world from which we have come. As we hear his simple commission, "I send you," we could not respond better than in Isaiah's famous words, "Lord, here I am; send me."

five
The Holy Spirit Is a Missionary Spirit

John R. W. Stott

So far we have seen from the Old Testament that the living God is a missionary God and from the Gospels that the Lord Christ is a missionary Christ. Today we come to a third section of Scripture, the Book of Acts, and from it we shall learn that "tho Holy Spirit is a missionary Spirit," as the Lausanne Covenant puts it (paragraph 14).

Luke the physician wrote a two-volume history of the origins of Christianity, and dedicated both to a high-ranking Roman official called Theophilus. Volume I (his Gospel) is the story of Jesus Christ from his birth to his death, resurrection and ascension. Volume II (the Acts) is the story of the Church of Jesus Christ from its birth in Jerusalem the capital of Jewry to its conquest some thirty years later of Rome the capital of the world. It is an exciting tale of the early missionary expansion of the Church by the power of the Holy Spirit.

According to Acts 1:1, Luke recorded in his Gospel what

"Jesus *began* to do and teach" personally while he was on earth. This implies that in the Acts Luke was intending to record what Jesus *continued* to do and teach after his ascension, which was (v. 2) "after he had given commandment through the Holy Spirit to the apostles whom he had chosen." This commandment must surely refer primarily to the Great Commission, in which Jesus instructed the apostles to take the gospel to the nations in the power of the Spirit. Luke's second volume is correctly termed "the Acts of the Apostles," since it focuses on the exploits first of Peter and John (chap. 1—8), then of Peter alone (chap. 10—12) and finally of Luke's hero Paul (9 and 13 to the end). The book's full title, however, would be "the Acts of Jesus Christ by the Holy Spirit through the Apostles," for in verse 2 Christ, the Spirit and the apostles are all related to one another.

Before we leave the first two verses we should note how extremely significant they are. It would not be an exaggeration to claim that these verses set Christianity apart from all the religions of the world. For the world's religions regard their founder as having completed his work during his lifetime, whereas Luke says Jesus only "began" his. Of course he finished his *atoning* work on the cross. Yet that end was also a new beginning, in that after his resurrection, ascension and gift of the Spirit he continued to work through his apostles and now works through the post-apostolic church. Indeed (v. 2) he was "taken up" only after he had made provision for this future ministry. So this indicates what kind of a Christ we believe in. He is both the historic Christ who lived and the contemporary Christ who lives. He is the Christ who "began" to do and to teach on earth, and who has been active through his Spirit ever since.

The salient event of the early chapters of the Acts is, of course, the day of Pentecost. On this day the ascended and exalted Christ performed the final work of his saving career: He sent the Holy Spirit from heaven in order to work out in the church what he had achieved by his death and resurrection and to drive the church out into all the world to proclaim the good news. We are going to concentrate on the first two chapters of the Acts as follows:

Chapter 1 belongs to the period immediately *before* the day of

Pentecost, in which Jesus was telling the apostles to wait for the promised Spirit to come. So I entitle this "the promise of the Spirit."

Chapter 2:1-41 describes what happened on the day of Pentecost itself. So I shall call this section "the coming of the Spirit."

Chapter 2:42-47 portrays the church *after* the day of Pentecost and tells us what a Spirit-filled church looks like. Here, then, is "the community of the Spirit."

Before the Day of Pentecost: The Promise of the Spirit

Forty days elapsed between the resurrection and the ascension. During this period Jesus "presented himself alive ... by many proofs" (v. 3) and taught his apostles. He spoke to them (v. 3b) about "the kingdom of God," that is, God's gracious rule in the lives of his people, the topic which had been the burden of his teaching during his lifetime. He also told them (v. 4) not to leave Jerusalem until the Spirit had come, who had been promised. He was "the promise of the Father," for God the Father through the Old Testament prophets had promised an outpouring of the Spirit in the messianic age. He was the promise of the Son, since five times in the upper room he said that after he had gone the Spirit would come. This must be the meaning of the words at the end of verse 4: "which, he said, 'you heard from me.' " And he was promised by John the Baptist, who called the Messiah's expected gift or outpouring of the Spirit a "baptism," and had contrasted this "baptism of the Spirit" with his own water-baptism (v. 5).

Luke thus indicated that the main topics of our Lord's instruction during the forty days were the Kingdom of God and the Spirit of God. The Old Testament prophets constantly related the two. For they knew that the new age, when God would establish the Kingdom of the Messiah, would be the dispensation of the Spirit. One of the major blessings of the messianic Kingdom would be a liberal outpouring of his Spirit. Indeed, it was the Holy Spirit who would make God's Kingdom a living and present reality to his people.

Sad to relate, the apostles at first misunderstood Christ's teaching about the Kingdom of God and the Spirit of God. They asked (v. 6, NIV): "Lord, are you at this time going to restore the Kingdom to Israel?" Their question must have filled the risen Lord with grief and dismay; were they still as obtuse as that? As Calvin put it in his commentary on the Acts: "There are as many errors in this question as words." In his reply (vv. 7-8) Jesus corrected their mistakes and adjusted their perspective. He emphasized three truths about God's Kingdom.

God's Kingdom is spiritual in its character. To us a "Kingdom" is a territorial sphere (like the Kingdom of Jordan or the United Kingdom), but the Kingdom of God cannot be located on the map, for it is the reign of God in the lives of his people. By asking whether Jesus was about to "restore" the Kingdom to Israel, however, the apostles showed that they were still dreaming of a territorial Kingdom. They longed for Israel's liberation from the colonial rule of Rome.

But in his reply Jesus spoke of the Holy Spirit coming upon them to empower them to bear witness to him. In other words, the Kingdom of God to which Jesus referred was the divine rule in human hearts and lives in the power of the Holy Spirit. It would be spread by witnesses not by soldiers, through a gospel of peace not a declaration of war, by the power of the Holy Spirit not by force of arms or political dominion. Do not misunderstand this. In asserting that God's Kingdom is a "spiritual" Kingdom I mean that it is not to be identified with any political system or territorial jurisdiction. I do not mean that it is a purely internal experience in our hearts. On the contrary, this "spiritual" Kingdom has very material consequences. God's rule makes radical demands on the whole of our lives and all our relationships in the material world. It is spiritual in the sense that it is God's rule in our lives with all the consequences of that rule.

God's Kingdom is international in its membership. The apostles seem still to have had narrow, nationalistic aspirations. They asked Jesus if he was about to restore *Israel's* lost national independence, which the Maccabees had recovered for a brief intoxicating period. Jesus replied (v. 8) that the Spirit would give them power to witness to him not only "in Jerusalem and in all Judea," but far beyond the borders of Israel, first to despised Samaria and then to the Gentile nations throughout the whole earth.

Verse 8 is a kind of text or title for the Book of Acts. For in the following chapters we watch Christ's promise being fulfilled. In chapters 2 to 7 the gospel is preached in Jerusalem, and thousands believe and are baptized. In chapter 8 persecution drives believers out of Jerusalem, and those who are scattered preach the good news wherever they go. In particular Philip preaches to the Samaritans, and the apostles Peter and John later came down to endorse the bold step he had taken. In chapter 9 Saul of Tarsus is converted and appointed the apostle to the Gentiles. In chapters 10 and 11 the Holy Spirit persuades Peter to preach to Cornelius, who becomes the first Gentile to receive the Spirit.

Then with chapter 13 Paul's great missionary journeys begin. In the first he goes no further than central Turkey, in the second he crosses the Aegean Sea and reaches Europe, while in the third his three years' preaching in the capital city of Ephesus leads to the evangelization of the whole Roman province of Asia. Finally he is arrested in Jerusalem, and his dream of preaching the gospel in Rome is fulfilled as he is taken there as a prisoner at the Emperor's expense. As Luke takes leave of him at the end of the Acts, we see him welcoming everybody who visits him in custody, and telling them about God's Kingdom and about the Lord Jesus Christ "quite openly and unhindered" (28:30-31).

Thus within about thirty years what had begun as a small Jewish sect became a cosmopolitan Christian community which was established even in the capital city of the Empire. "We are so familiar with the march of the gospel from Jerusalem to Rome that it has ceased to surprise us. But this journey is so strange and unprecedented that it can only be explained by repeatedly pointing to the intervention of God himself" (J. Blauw, *The Missionary Nature of the Church*, Eerdmans, 1974, p. 94).

God's Kingdom tolerates no narrow nationalisms. It is an international Kingdom in which the barriers of race, color, nation and tribe are broken down. And when the Kingdom is consummated in heaven, as we saw when tracing the fulfillment of God's promise to Abraham, the redeemed community will include representatives "from all tribes and peoples and tongues" (Rev. 7:9).

God's Kingdom is gradual in its expansion. The apostles'

question was whether Jesus was going "at this time" to restore the Kingdom to Israel. Their earlier expectations had been destroyed by his death. So would he do *now* after his resurrection what they had hoped he would do earlier, and would he do it *immediately*? Jesus' reply was twofold.

First, "it is not for you to know times or seasons which the Father has fixed by his own authority" (Acts 1:7). Jesus forbade curiosity and speculation about dates and his prohibition has been scandalously disregarded by many ever since.

Second, Jesus indicated that between the Spirit's coming and his own coming again they were to be his witnesses in gradually widening circles. Indeed, the whole period between Christ's ascension and Christ's return (however long or short that period might prove to be) was to be filled with the Christian missionary enterprise. They were to be his witnesses to the end of the earth (v. 8) and to the end of the age (Mt. 28:20). They had no liberty to stop till both ends had been reached. In fact the two ends would coincide, as Jesus had taught earlier, for only when the gospel had been preached to all nations would the end come (Mt. 24:14).

This, then, was the substance of Christ's teaching between the resurrection and the ascension. He emphasized that when the Holy Spirit came in power, the long-promised reign of God (which Jesus had ushered in and proclaimed) would effectively begin. It would be *spiritual* in its character (in human hearts and lives), *international* in its membership (embracing Gentiles as well as Jews) and *gradual* in its expansion (beginning at once, and then growing until it reaches the ends of earthly time and space). This vision and this commission must have given direction to the prayers of the disciples during their ten days of waiting.

The waiting period began with the ascension which Luke describes in verses 9 to 11. I am myself naive enough (as I hope we all are) to believe that this story is literally and historically true. That is, Jesus left them by ascending into the sky before their very eyes. The reason for this visible ascension was not because Jesus needed to take a journey in space and should be acknowledged as the first cosmonaut, for presumably he could simply have vanished (as he had done on several previous occasions) and gone to the Father invisibly. No, he ascended visibly in order to show that he had gone for good. There would be no more resurrection appearances. They were not to wait around for the next, but to return to Jerusalem, wait instead for the coming of the Spirit and then get on with the proclamation of the good news. They would not see Jesus again with their eyes until the day of his visible and glorious appearing (v. 11).

Luke goes on to tell us in verse 12 that the apostles did return to Jerusalem and, with about one hundred other disciples, gave themselves to prayer, waiting expectantly for the promise of the Spirit's coming to be fulfilled.

Their only other recorded activity during the ten days of waiting was their appointment of Matthias as an apostle in place of Judas (vv. 15-26). The details cannot concern us now. We note simply that they were determined to be ready, when the Spirit came, to bear witness to the historic Jesus, and that one of the indispensable qualifications of the original apostolate was to have been an eye-witness, especially of the risen Lord (see vv. 21-22).

Thus the first chapter of the Acts focuses on the promise of the Spirit—a promise which Christ himself confirmed and which those early disciples were confident would be fulfilled.

On the Day of Pentecost: The Coming of the Spirit

As we turn from the promise to its fulfillment, we observe that Luke first gives his own description of the coming of the Spirit (vv. 1-13) and then adds the apostle Peter's explanation (vv. 14 ff).

Luke's description (vv. 1-13). The great event of the Spirit's coming is described by Luke in words of objective simplicity. His coming was accompanied by three supernatural signs—a sound "like the rush of a mighty wind," a sight like fire ("tongues as of fire, distributed and resting on each of them") and speech in "other" (that is, foreign) languages, "as the Spirit gave them utterance."

Luke goes on to tell how a crowd immediately gathered. They were Jews, Jews of the dispersion "from every nation under heaven" (v. 5), that is, of the then known world. At first they were bewildered by what they heard, and then amazed, for these Galileans were announcing God's mighty works neither in the sacred language of biblical Hebrew, nor in popular Aramaic, nor in common Greek (which all of them could have understood), but in their native languages of Asia, Africa and Europe.

Luke is at pains to emphasize the cosmopolitan nature of the crowd, for he lists fifteen areas around the Mediterranean basin. Nothing could have demonstrated more clearly than this the international nature of the Kingdom of Christ which the Holy Spirit had come to spread. Pentecost seems to have been God's deliberate and dramatic reversal of the curse of the Tower of Babel, as many commentators ancient and modern have suggested. At Babel human languages were confused and the nations were scattered. In Jerusalem at Pentecost the language barrier was supernaturally overcome, as a sign that the scattered nations would now be gathered together in Christ and in his international Kingdom.

Peter's explanation (vv. 14 ff). Having described what happened, Luke goes on to record Peter's interpretation. The phenomenon they had witnessed, he explains, was not intoxication (as a minority had supposed who for some reason could not understand the languages, vv. 13, 15), but rather the fulfillment of an ancient prophecy of Joel that in the last days God would pour out his Spirit "upon all flesh" (v. 17), and not upon Israel only, but upon Gentiles as well. Thus Peter declared that "the last days" had begun, which indeed is the unanimous witness of the New Testament. Jesus inaugurated the new age. And the final proof of this was that he had poured out his Spirit, for the outpouring of the Spirit was *the* promise of promises for the end-time.

Peter then went on to show how it was through Jesus that this Old Testament prophecy had come true. Notice how he begins his sermon proper (v. 22): "Men of Israel, hear these words: Jesus. . . ." I never fail to be moved by these words. His first word was Jesus, and Jesus must be our first word too. If we are asked what the Christian good news is, we have no difficulty in replying. The good news is Jesus! Nobody preaches the gospel who does not concentrate on Jesus. Jesus himself is the heart and soul of the good news.

But which Jesus? There are so many Jesuses abroad today. There is Jesus the myth and Jesus the revolutionary, Jesus the failed superstar and Jesus the circus clown. So we ask: Which Jesus did Peter proclaim? Our answer to this question is that he preached the objective Jesus of history and of Scripture, rather than the subjective Jesus of experience, let alone of speculation. I am not implying by this that there is no place for bearing witness to the Jesus we know today in our own experience, but only suggesting that we should concentrate on the objective, historical Jesus, as he is presented to us in the Bible, and use our contemporary experience of him to corroborate and illustrate the primary witness of the apostles. What Peter did was to give a rundown of the saving career of Jesus. He mentioned in turn his life, his death, his resurrection, his exaltation and finally his gift of the Spirit.

First, his life (v. 22). Jesus of Nazareth was a historical figure, indeed a human being. Sometimes we are so preoccupied with trying to prove the deity of Jesus that we make him out to be less than fully human. But he was "a man," though wonderfully attested by God with the signs and wonders which God did through him in their sight.

Next, his death. Verse 23 is very important because it attributes the death of Jesus equally to the wickedness of men and to the purpose of God. On the one hand they (Peter's Jewish hearers) had "crucified and killed" him "by the hands of lawless men" (the Roman executioners). But on the other he had been "delivered up according to the definite plan and foreknowledge of God." Peter does not elaborate this here, or at least Luke does not record any elaboration. But later the apostles Peter and Paul both describe Jesus as having been hanged on a "tree" (5:30; 13:29), which is a shorthand reference to his having borne our sin and curse when he died, since according to the law those hanged on a tree were accursed (Deut. 21:22-23; Gal. 3:10, 13; 1 Pet. 2:24).

Third, God had raised him from the dead, as the prophets had foretold in the Old Testament and the apostles had witnessed with their own eyes (vv. 24-32). Thus God had reversed men's verdict on Jesus, by raising him whom they had killed.

Fourth, God "exalted" him to his right hand (v. 33) and "made him both Lord and Christ" (vv. 34-36)—"Christ" the anointed King of Old Testament expectation and the "Lord" whose enemies would one day be his footstool. In other words, God gave him a position of unique and universal dominion.

And, fifth, from that position of supreme honor and executive power Jesus had poured out the promised Spirit whom the Father had given him and whose coming they themselves had seen and heard (v. 33).

If only our sermons were as full of doctrinal meat as that. Why Peter gives us the whole career of Jesus from beginning to end as the basis of our salvation. No wonder Peter's hearers could not possibly have missed the implication of what he was saying. He had begun by quoting God's word through Joel, "I will pour out my Spirit"; he ended by declaring that the Spirit had been poured out by Jesus. This, then, was who Jesus was—the Jesus whom they had crucified.

No wonder the crowd was "cut to the heart," as the outpoured Holy Spirit began his work of convicting sinners of the paramount sin of rejecting Jesus. "Brethren," they cried out, "what shall we do?" Peter's reply was that they must "repent." That is, they must completely change their opinion of Jesus and their attitude to him. Next, they must "be baptized . . . in the name of Jesus Christ." That is, they must humbly submit to baptism in the name of the very person they had hitherto repudiated. It would be a public token of their repentance and of their faith in him. Then they would receive two free gifts of God, "the forgiveness of your sins"—even the grave sin of rejecting Christ—and "the gift of the Holy Spirit" to make them new people and establish God's rule in their lives.

For they must not imagine, Peter continued, that the Pentecostal gift, the gift of the Spirit, was for the apostles alone, or for the one hundred and twenty disciples who had waited ten days in prayerful expectation, or for any élitist group, or even for that nation and that generation. On the contrary (v. 39), "the promise" (and evidently "the promise," "the gift" and "the bap-

tism" of the Spirit are interchangeable terms in Acts 1 and 2)
was for them also who were listening to Peter's sermon, and for
their children of subsequent generations, and even for "all that
are far off" (a technical term for the Gentile world), indeed for
"*every one* whom the Lord our God calls to him." Thus everybody whom God calls to himself through Jesus Christ, and who
responds to God's call in penitence, faith and baptism, receives
both the forgiveness of sins and the promised gift of the Holy
Spirit.

Three thousand people responded that day, so powerfully did
the Spirit confirm the word in Peter's hearers. They received
his word in penitence and faith (vv. 41, 44). They received baptism in the name of Jesus Christ. So there can be no doubt that
(in fulfillment of God's promise) they also received forgiveness
and the Spirit—although this time apparently with no supernatural accompaniments, for no mention is made now of wind
or fire or foreign languages.

After the Day of Pentecost: The Community of the Spirit

It is wonderful that the earliest Christian community multiplied
in one day twenty-six times, for it grew at a single leap from one
hundred and twenty people to 3,120. It was a community of the
Spirit. True, they enjoyed a direct continuity with the old Israel.
Yet at the same time they were a new creation. The church of
God had become the church of Christ, his body animated and
filled by his Spirit.

What did that first Spirit-filled Christian community look
like? It is important to be able to answer this question, for then
we shall know what evidence to expect today of the presence
and power of the Holy Spirit. Luke tells us that it had four marks.

First, its instruction: "They devoted themselves to the apostles' instruction" (v. 42). The very first thing we are told about
the community of the Spirit is that it was a learning, a studying
community. The Spirit of God moved the people of God to submit to the Word of God. They were not revelling in a mystical
experience which led them to despise their intellect, disdain
theology or suppose that instruction was superfluous. No, they
gave themselves up to learning from the apostles. And in so

doing they were submissive to the apostles' authority which was derived from Christ who had appointed them and was authenticated by miracles (2:43; 5:12).

Today the apostles' doctrine is to be found in the New Testament. It is here that, in its definitive form, it has been bequeathed to the church. And a church led by the Spirit will always submit to this authority. What is true of churches is equally true of individual Christians. One of the clearest evidences of a Spirit-filled Christian is his hunger for Scripture and his humble submissiveness to the authority of Scripture as God's written Word. But show me a person who claims to be a Christian yet is not devoting himself to the apostles' teaching, who rather neglects and even disregards it, and you give me cause to question whether he has received the Holy Spirit at all. For the Holy Spirit is the Spirit of truth (as Jesus called him). He is given us to be our teacher, and those who are filled with him have a keen appetite for his instruction.

Second, its fellowship: "They devoted themselves to . . . the fellowship" (v. 42). This is the first time the word *fellowship* (*koinonia*) occurs in the New Testament. But of course! Christian fellowship is essentially "the fellowship of the Spirit" (2 Cor. 13:14), our common participation in him. It is his indwelling presence in each of us that makes us the one body of Christ. So there could be no true "fellowship" before the Spirit came at Pentecost. When he came, however, he created the fellowship, so that immediately (v. 44) "all who believed were together." I do not think Luke is saying that they actually lived together, and that the first Christian commune was established in Jerusalem. But they were certainly aware that they belonged together. They were a family of brothers and sisters, who together had come to share in God's great gift of the Holy Spirit.

The word *koinonia* bears witness to something else. It expresses not only what Christians "share in" together, but also what they "share out" together. Hence the Greek word for "generous" is *koinōnikos*. The way they shared Luke tells us in verses 44 and 45. "They had all things in common (*koina* is an echo of *koinōnia*); and they sold their possessions and goods and distributed them to all, as any had need." Does this mean that every

Spirit-filled Christian will follow their example, realize his capital and give it all away? Well, all down the Christian era, some
Christians have thought so and done so. Personally, I do not
doubt that in every age Jesus calls some, like the rich young
ruler, to a life of voluntary poverty. But we cannot turn Luke's
description of the first-century Jerusalem church into a manda-
tory model for all churches at all times. The New Testament no-
where forbids private property. Even in the immediate post-
Pentecost period not everybody sold everything, for according
to v. 46 the Christians met "in their homes," indicating that
some had kept theirs. And later Peter told Ananias that his property both before and after its sale was his own and at his own
disposal (5:4).

Although we are not under obligation either to sell all our
possessions or to hold them in common, yet we are under obligation to be good and generous stewards of what we have, and
to care compassionately for those in need. For compassion and
generosity are Christian qualities which are repeatedly commanded in Scripture. I do not hesitate to say that every Spirit-
filled Christian has a sensitive social conscience. He cannot
turn a blind eye or a hard heart to human need in any form, and
still claim to be filled with the Spirit (see 1 John 3:17-18). The
early church set a fine example of a caring community. The two
principles which directed them are clearly stated: They distributed to all "as any had need" (2:45; 4:35) and "every one
according to his ability" (1:29)—two principles which were
later crystallized in the well-known socialist dictum (to which
Christians of every political persuasion should be able with a
good conscience to subscribe), namely, "from every man according to his ability, to every man according to his need."

So Christian fellowship is Christian caring, and Christian
caring is Christian sharing—not only of our money, goods and
homes, but also of our time, our sympathy and our service, and
that generously. Those early Christians loved one another and
expressed their love in sacrificial service, which is not surprising since the firstfruit of the Spirit is love (Gal. 5:22).

Third, its worship: The third mark of that early Spirit-filled
church is that "they devoted themselves ... to the breaking of

bread and the prayers" (v. 42). That is, their fellowship expressed itself in common worship as well as in mutual care.
And the definite article in both expressions suggests that the
reference is to the Lord's Supper on the one hand (though probably with a meal thrown in, v. 46) and prayer services or prayer
meetings on the other. Two features of early Christian worship
are specially noteworthy.

First, it was both formal and informal. According to verse 46
they were both "attending the temple together and breaking
bread in their homes." It is surely remarkable that they worshiped both in the temple and in their homes. It is almost certain that they no longer took part in the sacrifices of the temple,
for Jesus had himself fulfilled these in his death. But they did
continue to attend prayer services in the temple (see 3:1). So
they did not immediately abandon the institutional church, but
sought to reform it according to the gospel, and they also sup-
plemented the temple services with their own more spontaneous meetings at home. Today's young people, understandably
impatient with the inherited structures of the church, can learn
a valuable lesson here. The Holy Spirit's way with the institution of the church seems to be more the way of patient reform
than of impatient rejection. Meanwhile we too can supplement
the more formal services of the church with the freedom and the
informality of home meetings.

Second, early Christian worship was both joyful and reverent.
There can be no doubt of their joy. Luke writes of their *agalliasis*
(v. 46) or "exultation." They were overwhelmed with gratitude
at what God had done in Christ and given them through Christ.
So every worship service was a joyful celebration. For "the fruit
of the Spirit is . . . joy"—and often a more uninhibited joy than
some churches have witnessed for decades. It is right to be dig-
nified in worship; it is unforgivable to be dull!

But if joy is an authentic evidence of the work of the Spirit,
so is "fear" or reverence: "Fear came upon every soul" (v. 43).
That is, "Everyone was filled with awe" (GNB). God was in their
midst, and they knew it. So their joy, though great, was never
irreverent. They bowed down before the living God in deep
humility and wonder.

Fourth, its evangelism: "And the Lord added to their number day by day those who were being saved" (v. 47b). Although those early Christians devoted themselves to their instruction, their fellowship and their worship, they were not so absorbed in their own interior life that they forgot the outside world. Oh, no! The Holy Spirit is a missionary Spirit, always reaching out through and beyond the church to those still outside its fellowship. This is how Harry Boer puts it:

When the Church tries to bottle up the Spirit within herself, she acts contrary both to her own and to His nature. For it is the nature of the Church ever to be enlarging her borders, and it is the nature of the Spirit to transmit His life to ever widening circles. When the Church does not recognize this law of her being and of the being of the Spirit, the Spirit is quenched and He withdraws Himself, and the deposit of religiosity that is left becomes a putrefaction in the lives of those who have grieved Him. (Pentecost and Mission, Lutterworth, 1961, p. 210).

We can learn three important lessons from the early church's evangelism.

First, the Lord Jesus himself did it: "The Lord added...." There can be no doubt that he did it through their spoken witness and the example of their lives and their fellowship, for they were "having favor with all the people" (v. 47a). Nevertheless, it was essentially his work. Only Jesus Christ can save sinners and add them to his church. And in these man-centered, man-confident days it is urgent that we recover the God-centeredness of biblical evangelism.

Second, what Jesus did was two things at once: He added "to their number," that is, to the church, those who were being saved. Salvation and church membership belong together and should not be separated. On the one hand, there was no solitary Christianity in those days: Jesus did not save people without adding them to the church. But on the other hand he did not add them to the church without saving them. He did both together, and we must expect him to do the same in our day.

Third, he did it daily: "The Lord added to their number day by day...." Their evangelism was not an occasional or sporadic activity. They did not organize a mission every five years, and after each mission lapse into idle complacency for the next quinquennium. Their witness was as continuous as their worship. Both were "day by day" (vv. 46a, 47b). Their evangelism was the spontaneous overflow of hearts full of the Spirit of Jesus. As William Temple expressed it when commenting on John 7:37-39: "Where the Spirit is, he flows forth; if there is no flowing forth, he is not there" (Readings in St. John's Gospel, Macmillan, 1939, Complete Edition, 1945, p. 130).

Conclusion

Apostolic instruction, fellowship, worship, evangelism: these were and still are the marks of the Spirit's presence. A Spirit-filled church is a biblical church, a caring church, a worshiping church and a missionary church. And it seems to me that these four marks are exactly what young people are rightly looking for in the contemporary church. Many are deeply disenchanted with the institution and are voting with their feet. What is it they are looking for? (1) A biblical ministry, which is faithful to Scripture and relevant to the modern world, (2) a warm, loving, caring fellowship, (3) a worship which expresses the reality of the living God and joyfully celebrates his mighty works through Christ, (4) an outreach into the community that is bold, continuous and compassionate. Where these things are absent, it is no wonder that young people are absent too. But when they are present, the people are present too, for evidently the Holy Spirit himself is there.

six
The Christian Church Is a Missionary Church

John R. W. Stott

So far we have considered from the Old Testament that the living God is a missionary God, from the Gospels that the Lord Christ is a missionary Christ and from the Acts that the Holy Spirit is a missionary Spirit. Today we move on to the New Testament Letters in order to see that the Christian church is a missionary church.

Let's begin by remembering that the churches to whom the apostles wrote their letters were themselves the products of mission. To use J. B. Phillips' familiar expression, they were "young churches," newly brought into being by the gospel. Thus Paul wrote to the Galatians whom he had evangelized on his first missionary journey. Philippi, Thessalonica and Corinth, to whose churches he also wrote, he visited on his second missionary journey and Ephesus on this third.

In their letters, however, the apostles saw the churches not only as the *products* of mission, but also as the *agents* for further mission. Not that there is very much apostolic instruction in the Letters about evangelism. The apostles seem to have taken it for granted that an evangelized church becomes an evangelizing church. Certainly this was the case, and they say so in their letters. Thus, Paul thanks the Philippians for their "partnership in the gospel [that is, in promoting it] from the first day until now," and thanks God that the faith of the Roman Christians is "proclaimed in all the world" (Phil. 1:5; Rom. 1:8). He expects all Christians to "shine . . . like stars" (Phil. 2:15, GNB) and to wear as their shoes "the readiness to announce the good news of peace" (Eph. 6:15, GNB). He also says that because "the word of the Lord has sounded forth" from the Thessalonian church into the neighboring provinces, and because their "faith in God has gone forth everywhere," he even finds it unnecessary himself to add anything to their testimony (1 Thess. 1:8).

It is clear, then, that in those early days the gospel was being spread not just by the apostles but by the churches. A further truth also emerges: that the churches' witness was powerful not because they organized campaigns, nor even just because their members gossiped the gospel—though they did—but because the church itself was seen to be God's new society, the new community, the new creation of God.

The Church's one foundation
  Is Jesus Christ her Lord;
She is his new creation
  By water and the word.

That's what people saw. The very existence of the church, with the new life its members were living, was a standing testimony to the saving power of God's gospel.

In order to pursue this theme we are going to turn from Paul to Peter, who in his first letter (2:1-12) gives us one of the fullest and most vivid characterizations of the church to be found anywhere in the New Testament. He brings together five striking metaphors to illustrate different aspects of the church's being and consequent responsibility. Together these metaphors describe what Christ's people are by his appointment, and therefore what he wants them to be in their relationship to him, to each other and to the needy world outside. Unless the church can recover a true vision of itself in God's purpose (that is, what God intends it to be as his new society), and can then fulfill that vision in its everyday life, there is little or no prospect of its making any evangelistic impact on the world.

Newborn Babies

"So put away all malice and all guile and insincerity and envy and all slander. Like newborn babes, long for the pure spiritual milk, that by it you may grow up to salvation; for you have tasted the kindness of the Lord" (1 Pet. 2:1-3, RSV).

There can be no doubt why Peter likens his readers to newborn babies. It is, as he has written in 1:23, that they had been "born anew not of perishable seed but of imperishable, through the living and abiding word of God." In other words, the seed of God's word, the gospel (v. 25), had brought about their new birth. They were new people and must give evidence of their new birth in a new life.

In particular (v. 2), he expects them to "grow up." Nearly everybody loves babies and little children, but we don't want them to stay that way forever. On the contrary, we want them to grow up into maturity. It is the same in the Christian life. The kind of spiritual growth Peter has in mind he calls growth "into salvation," as the words at the end of verse 2 should be rendered literally. This puzzles many people. "Surely," they say, "I received salvation when I first trusted Christ, didn't I?" "Yes, indeed," we reply, "you did." "How then," they continue, "can I 'grow up into salvation' if I have already received it?" The probable answer to this question lies in the fact that "salvation" in the New Testament is a comprehensive word, including not only justification but sanctification, that is, not only acceptance with God (which we receive through faith in Christ) but also Christlikeness of character (into which we need to grow).

That this is what Peter means is clear from the contrast between verses 1 and 2. In verse 1 he begs his readers to "put away all malice [ill will towards people] and all guile [that is, deviousness, deceit and lying] and insincerity [or hypocrisy] and envy [or jealousy] and all slander ['insulting language,' GNB, or tittle-tattle behind people's backs]." We are to get rid of these things

entirely, he says, to purge them out of ourselves and our
churches. For, he implies, these things are babyish, and it is
high time that we "grow up to salvation."

But how shall we grow into spiritual and moral maturity as
Christians? Answer: by drinking "the pure spiritual milk." It
is not quite certain whether by his adjective *logikos* Peter means
"spiritual" milk as opposed to literal cow's milk, or "rational"
milk (milk for the mind rather than the body), or (in the well-
known AV rendering) "the milk of the word." Probably we do
not need to choose between these alternatives, for the "spiritual" or "rational" milk we need is, in fact, the "milk of the
word," of that "living and abiding word of God" to which he
has referred in 1:25. In that verse the word caused our new birth;
here it causes our Christian growth. So we are to "long for" it,
a strong verb expressing "the ardour of a suckled child" (E. G.
Selwyn on 1 Pet. 2:2). Have we not already "tasted" the Lord's
kindness (v. 3)? Then, having had a taste, we need now to get a
thirst.

It is not difficult to interpret Peter's metaphor. As babies need
milk regularly if they are to grow up, so we Christians need a
sustained diet of God's word if we are to develop Christian character. There is no substitute for the daily discipline of Scripture
meditation, hungering and thirsting for God through his Word.
This is the way to grow into maturity in Christ; we put away in-
fantile behavior like malice, jealousy and slander and instead
become like Christ. Certainly a church whose members behave
like children will never impress the world; the credibility gap
is too wide. But if its members are mature and loving and behave
like Christ, the world will be ready to listen.

Living Stones
The image changes from a biological to an architectural metaphor. We have been in a child's nursery, watching the child take
its milk; we now go out-of-doors and watch a building under
construction. It is a stone building. We have no difficulty in rec-
ognizing it as the church. For God is building his church, a
worldwide community of people from every nation. Secularism
may make inroads into some churches. And persecution may

drive others underground. But nothing can destroy God's church. It is growing. And it is indestructible. Even the gates of Hades (or death) will not prevail over it. Moreover, since Peter likens the church to a building, he refers to church members as stones in the building, "living stones," in fact.

How then does one join the church? "Come to him," Peter replies (v. 4), that is, to the Lord Jesus whose kindness he has mentioned in the previous verse. For Jesus Christ is the foundation stone of the building; he is "that living stone, rejected by men but in God's sight chosen and precious." It is, therefore, impossible to be a true member of the church without being personally related to Jesus Christ, just as it is impossible for a stone to belong to a building without being related to the foundation. In verses 6 to 8 Peter elaborates this thought by bringing together a chain of three Old Testament texts referring to rocks and stones. They point to Jesus Christ as the foundation stone or cornerstone of the building. Notice in passing that, although the apostle Peter is the writer, he does not think of himself but of Christ as the rock on which the church is built. He goes on to argue that everybody responds to Jesus Christ in one of two ways. Either Christ is the foundation stone on which we build (vv. 6-7) or he becomes a stumbling stone over which we fall (v. 8).

But what is the point of this whole picture which Peter develops of the church as a building, with Jesus Christ as its foundation and individual Christians as the stones of which the building is made? Surely this: We are to allow ourselves to be "built into a spiritual house." If babies need milk in order to grow, stones need mortar in order to be built into the house. The metaphor of the newborn baby is somewhat individualistic, each child taking its milk and growing up. But the living stones are all mortared into the building, each being firmly attached to the stone above it, beneath it and on each side of it, and no stone can get away from the building. As I visualize the building, I cannot see any stone suspended in midair. No, the stones belong to each other in the building and cannot escape from each other. Thus if the baby metaphor speaks to us of the necessity of growth, the stone metaphor speaks of the necessity of fellowship.

The church of Jesus Christ urgently needs better quality mortar! Too often the mortar crumbles and the stones fall away from each other, until the building itself sometimes seems in danger of collapsing.

One of the reasons why Urbana 70 stands out in my memory is that during it some friends and I asked for and were granted an interview with Dr. Hobart Mowrer. Dr. Mowrer is Emeritus Professor of Psychiatry in this University of Illinois. He is a well-known critic of Freud, especially in his insistence on our taking guilt seriously, and he has expounded his thought in several books. By his own confession he is not a Christian. When we asked him why, he told us that the church had failed him when he was a teenager and continued to fail his patients. When we asked him what he meant, this was his reply: "Because the church has not learned the secret of community." It is perhaps the most damaging criticism of the church I have ever heard. For the church is a community; it is the new community of Jesus Christ. If it has not learned the secret of community, it is contradicting its very being.

Now I think Professor Mowrer was exaggerating, for there are undoubtedly some churches which have "learned the secret of community" and which are models of mutual love and care. Or perhaps Professor Mowrer's own experience of churches has been particularly unfortunate. Yet I think there is enough truth in what he said for all of us to feel extremely uncomfortable. Where is the fellowship? Where is the community? Young people everywhere are searching for authentic relationships of love. And the one place where they ought to be infallibly certain of finding them (the Christian church) is the one place they often don't even bother to look for them, so certain are they that they will not find them there. But if the church is ever to draw people to itself and so to Christ, it will do so only by the almost irresistible magnetism of a fellowship of love.

Holy Priests
A third time the metaphor changes. We are still in the building, but now Christian people are likened not to the stones which are built into it but to the priests who minister in it, indeed (v. 5)

who "offer spiritual sacrifices acceptable to God through Jesus Christ," that is, who offer God the spiritual sacrifice of their worship.

Now, if one may slightly oversimplify things, the Jewish priests in Old Testament days were granted two particular privileges which were denied to the lay people. First, they enjoyed access to God. Herod's temple had a "court of the priests" immediately surrounding the temple, which only they might enter. They were also allowed into the temple itself, while the high priest was given the unique privilege on the annual day of atonement of passing through the veil into the inner sanctuary or holy of holies, in which the symbol of God's presence (the Shekinah glory) was seen. But the people had to stay out, on pain of death.

Second, the priests had the privilege of offering the sacrifices to God. They shed and sprinkled the sacred blood, and they performed the rest of the sacrificial ritual. This was their prerogative; nobody else might share in it.

But now, through Jesus Christ, these two distinctions between priests and people have been done away. Of course there is still a "pastorate" in the church, but there is no sacrificial "priesthood." For now all Christian people, pastors and people equally, enjoy direct access to God through Jesus Christ and "have confidence to enter the sanctuary by the blood of Jesus" (Heb. 10:19). Now too all Christian people, pastors and people together, offer to God our spiritual sacrifices. To be sure, there are now no atoning sacrifices to be made, for on the cross the Lord Jesus "offered for all time a single sacrifice for sins" (Heb. 10:12). Yet although there are no offerings for sin today, there are still offerings of praise. Indeed, the whole church is "a holy priesthood" (v. 5) or "a royal priesthood" (v. 9), appointed to offer to God the continual sacrifice of worship. This is the "priesthood of all believers."

This too is relevant to the church's mission. All of us are familiar with the contemporary quest for transcendence. Today's young people are dissatisfied, and rightly so, with scientific materialism. They are convinced that there is more to reality than can be confined in a test tube or smeared on a slide for microscopic analysis. There is another dimension to life, a missing transcendence. So they seek it through mind-expanding drugs or sexual adventures or transcendental meditation or yoga or other psychological techniques. And what they seek Christians claim to have found. Indeed wherever Christians gather together in the name of Jesus, he stands among them, the transcendent is in their midst, they touch ultimate reality. Only a worshiping church can be an evangelizing church because only a church which meets and knows him in its worship can make him known in its witness.

A Chosen Race

"But you are a chosen race, a royal priesthood, a holy nation, God's own people, that you may declare the wonderful deeds of him who called you out of darkness into his marvelous light. Once you were no people but now you are God's people; once you had not received mercy but now you have received mercy" (1 Pet. 2:9-10).

In verse 9 Peter applies four epithets to the people of God. "But you," he affirms, over against those who stumble over Jesus Christ and reject him (v. 8), "but you are a chosen race, a royal priesthood, a holy nation, God's own people [margin, 'a people for his possession']." What is particularly interesting is that Peter did not invent those expressions himself; he found them in Exodus 19:4-6. There God told Moses to say to the people of Israel, just after he had rescued them from Egypt and just before he made his covenant with them at Sinai, "You have seen... how I ... brought you to myself. Now therefore, if you will obey my voice and keep my covenant, you shall be my own possession among all peoples; ... and you shall be to me a kingdom of priests and a holy nation." Similarly, in Deuteronomy 7:6: "You are a people holy to the LORD your God; the LORD your God has chosen you to be a people for his own possession." Thus God made his people Israel "a holy nation," "a royal priesthood," "a chosen people," "a people for his own special possession." Then Peter, with the audacity given him by the Holy Spirit, finding these descriptions of the children of Israel, transferred them to the Christian church. You are today, he wrote to his

Christian readers, what Israel used to be. Indeed, you are the true Israel, God's chosen, holy, priestly, special people, his peculiar treasure.

But why did God choose Israel? And why has God chosen us? Mysterious as God's purpose of election remains to our finite minds, it is important to see how Scripture answers our questions. Election is with a view to witness. God chose and appointed his servant Israel to be "a light to the nations" (Is. 42:1, 6); not just to receive and guard his revelation, and certainly not to monopolize it, but to spread it through the world. So Peter continues, "But you are a chosen race, . . . God's own people, *in order that* you may declare [or proclaim] God's wonderful deeds."

And what are God's "wonderful deeds" which we are to announce to the world? They are the deeds "of him who called you out of darkness into his marvellous light." We were in the darkness of sin and guilt; he has called us into the light of his forgiveness. We were in the darkness of ignorance; he has shone upon us the light of his truth. We were in the shadow of death; he has brought us out into the light of life. No wonder Peter calls it "his marvellous light." Are we going to keep it for ourselves?

Then he goes on: "Once you were no people but now you are God's people; once you had not received mercy but now you have received mercy" (v. 10). This is a direct allusion to the symbolic names which God told Hosea to give to his second and third children. His second child was a daughter. "Call her name 'Not pitied,' " God said, "for I will no more have pity on the house of Israel, to forgive them at all." Next came a boy. "Call his name 'Not my people,' " said God, "for you are not my people and I am not your God" (Hos. 1:6-9). Later, however, God relented and promised that after a period of judgement Israel would be restored: "In the place where it was said to them 'You are not my people,' it shall be said to them 'Sons of the living God.' " And again, "Say to your brother 'My people' and to your sister 'She has obtained pity' " (Hos. 1:10; 2:1). In these promises the apostle Peter (like the apostle Paul) was given to see a deeper significance than the restoration of Israel, namely the inclusion of even Gentile believers in the true Israel of God.

Applying these verses to ourselves, we can at least begin to appreciate the wonder of God's saving grace to rebels like us who deserve nothing from his hand but judgement. We were in darkness, but now we enjoy God's marvellous light. We were "no people," for we were alienated and astray, but now we are God's people; he has found us and brought us home. We were unpitied, guilty and without mercy, but now God has had pity on us and we have received mercy from him. Before there was darkness, alienation and rejection; but now there is light, fellowship and mercy. These are the "wonderful deeds of God." He has enlightened us, adopted us, had mercy on us. How can we keep these things to ourselves? No, we must announce his wonderful deeds to the world; it is for this, and not for selfish enjoyment, that he has made us his people.

Aliens and Exiles

At first sight it must seem strange that, having just declared our alienation to be over, Peter should immediately describe us as "alienated" again. But of course these are two different kinds of alienation. We were alienated from God; now, having been reconciled to God, we find ourselves to some extent alienated from the world. What did Peter mean?

An "alien" is a foreigner without rights of citizenship. An "exile" is a foreigner who is away from home. Of course Peter's readers were literally "aliens and exiles." In the first verse of this letter he describes them as "the exiles of the Dispersion." He is writing to the Christian diaspora, scattered through the Roman provinces of Pontus, Galatia, Cappadocia, Asia and Bithynia. But what they were physically they also were spiritually. All Christian people are "exiles and aliens" on earth, and this is because of our new birth. We have been born again into God's family and kingdom. Heaven has become our home. In consequence, we are strangers, even refugees, on earth.

Now this is very dangerous teaching. And if we are not careful we can twist Scripture into saying something it never intended to say. Some Christians use this "aliens and exiles" talk as an excuse to opt out of their social responsibilities. "We are only pilgrims," they say (which is true); "on earth we have no continuing city" they add (which is also true), "so we have no responsibilities to society," they conclude (which is criminally false). To me it is one of the many evidences of the beautiful balance of Scripture that this very passage which declares us to be only "aliens and exiles" on earth goes on to lay down our earthly responsibilities. Thus, we are to "maintain good conduct among the Gentiles" (1 Pet. 2:12). We are to "be subject for the Lord's sake to every human institution" (v. 13). We are to "honor all men. Love the brotherhood. Fear God. Honor the emperor" (v. 17). As Christian people we are citizens of two kingdoms, and each kingdom lays upon us duties of citizenship. It is true that our citizenship of God's Kingdom has primacy and in a sense makes us "aliens and exiles" on earth; but this fact must never be used as a cloak for social irresponsibility, or as an opium for the people to drug them into acquiescing in the injustices of the status quo by promising them justice in the sweet bye and bye.

Why, then, does Peter remind us that we are "aliens and exiles"? In general, because to remember this alters our perspective on everything. Earthly possessions, affluence, luxuries, sorrow, suffering and death all look quite different in the light of eternity. In particular, a remembrance of our alien status will affect our attitude to "the passions of the flesh that wage war against our soul." There is an obvious contrast in this expression between the "flesh" and the "soul." Aliens and exiles recognize that it is the soul which is travelling home to God, and that therefore all those "passions of the flesh" which impede its progress or "wage war against" its true welfare are to be strenuously resisted and ruthlessly disowned. Holiness or Christlike character becomes important to us only when we remember that we are travelling to an eternal destiny. For Christlike character endures. It is one of those "treasures in heaven" which Christ told us to store up; it cannot be destroyed by any pest or pesticide. We are back, you see, in the dimension of transcendence and eternity. And Christians ought to live as people to whom these things are significant; they are much more important than the transient trivialities that fill so much of our life and ambition.

Lift up your eyes! You are certainly a creature of time, but you are also a child of eternity. You are a citizen of heaven, and an alien and exile on earth, a pilgrim travelling to the celestial city. Lift up your eyes!

I read some years ago of a young man who found a five-dollar bill on the street and who "from that time on never lifted his eyes when walking. In the course of years he accumulated 29,516 buttons, 54,172 pins, 12 cents, a bent back and a miserly disposition." But think what he lost. He could not see the radiance of the sunlight, the sheen of the stars, the smile on the face of his friends or the blossoms of springtime, for his eyes were in the gutter. There are too many Christians like that. We have important duties on earth, but we must never allow them to preoccupy us in such a way that we forget who we are and where we are going. On the contrary, it is precisely when we do remember that we are aliens and exiles on earth, and heirs of eternity, that we perform our earthly duties with the more conscientious care. A Christian who forgets himself and behaves like a secular humanist who believes that man is on his own and this life is everything, does not commend the gospel of Jesus Christ.

Conclusion

Here, then, are Peter's five metaphorical pictures of God's people. Each describes what we are (by God's intention) and what in consequence we should be (by our own intention). To begin with, on account of our new birth, we are "like newborn babies," and therefore we have a duty to "grow up to salvation." Next, we are "living stones" in God's building, the church, with a responsibility to cleave to one another in love. We are also "a holy priesthood," charged to offer to the living God the "spiritual sacrifices" of our worship. Then we are "a chosen race" and "God's own people" in order that we may declare his glory to the nations, proclaim the wonderful deeds of the God who has given us light and identity and mercy. And finally we are "aliens and exiles," with an obligation to abstain from all those "passions of the flesh" which hinder our spiritual progress and militate against our true welfare.

Growth, fellowship, worship, witness and holiness: These are the five marks of the people of God. And all of them relate to our the five marks of the people of God. And all of them relate to our mission in the world. Central to them is the affirmation that God has chosen us and made us his special people, in order that we may spread abroad his excellencies. But we cannot do this credibly unless we are, and are seen to be, the people of God, God's new people, the true alternative society or Christian counter culture—growing up into Christlikeness, caring for one another and supporting one another in the Christian fellowship, worshiping God and abstaining from sin, that is, unless the living God is the supreme reality of our lives. It is when we truly know God, and when people know that we know him, that then and only then we can effectively make him known.

part II

Declaring the Glory of God

seven
Declare His Glory among the Nations

Edmund Clowney

"Ladies and gentlemen, our national anthem!" Network television zooms in on the pop singer crooning about the dawn's early light under the artificial noon of the stadium arcs. The camera shifts to assorted embarrassed athletes standing more or less at attention. The baseball greats of the Red machine shift their wads of chewing tobacco—or is it bubble gum? There is Pete Rose, actually *singing* the national anthem. Then the whole stadium cheers. Patriotic fervor? No, the game is about to start.

Well, ladies and gentlemen, it is my privilege to announce our *international* anthem. No one has asked me to sing it—for some reason, no one has ever asked me to sing anything—but I have been asked to present it. It is not the "Internationale" of world communism; it is the doxology of the new mankind. One day the redeemed from every tribe, tongue, people and nation will sing the song of Moses and the Lamb on the other shore of the sea of fire (Rev. 15:2-3). But today God calls us to sing it here at Urbana:

"Declare his glory among the nations, his wonders among all the peoples" (Ps. 96:3).

His glory, his wonders—the anthem of missions does better than make the all-time top ten. Here is heaven's Hallelujah Chorus, number one in eternity. Maybe you came to God singing, "Just As I Am," but you are sent to the nations singing, "How Great Thou Art!" What does it mean to declare the glory of God? From the two great themes of the Psalms we find the two stanzas of our international anthem: Praise God for what he has done; praise God for who he is. To declare God's glory among the nations we number his marvelous works (v. 3) and bless his name (v. 2).

Stanza One: Sing His Mighty Works!

The Lord is King! The cymbals clash, the people shout God's holy name. Psalm 96 is a psalm of acclamation. The ancient Babylonians enthroned their god Marduk in a ritual New Year festival. But Israel shouts for him whose throne is established forever. One living God is the King of the nations because he is the God of creation. "All the gods of the peoples are idols; but the LORD made the heavens" (v. 6). Israel calls the nations not to better worship of the gods, but to worship a better God—indeed the only God.

Ancient heathen hymns are full of descriptive praise telling the gods how great they are; a man with a large pantheon, like a man with a large harem, must be unusually convincing to the immediate object of his devotion. But the psalms of Israel ring with declarative praise, glorifying God for what he has done, beginning with his works of creation.

The Apostle Paul stands on the rocky knoll of the Areopagus just beneath the Acropolis of Athens. In the shadow of the world's most beautiful temples he declares, "The God that made the world and all things therein, he, being Lord of heaven and earth, dwelleth not in temples made with hands" (Acts 17:24). Not Zeus or Athena, but the God unknown to Greek wisdom is the Creator and the Judge of the world.

"Praise him, ye heavens of heavens, and ye waters that are above the heavens. Let them praise the name of the Lord; for he commanded and they were created" (Ps. 148:4-5). "Fire and hail, snow and vapor; stormy wind, fulfilling his word; mountains and all hills, fruitful trees and all cedars" (Ps. 148:8-9). Descend with Jacques Cousteau to behold God's wonders in the deep; ascend with the astronauts and read the Genesis account in space. "O Lord, our Lord, how excellent is thy name in all the earth, who hast set thy glory above the heavens!" (Ps. 8:1).

Job's complaints were turned to adoration when God challenged him to consider the constellation of Orion, the thighbone of the hippopotamus and the scales of the crocodile (Job 40—41). But you do not need a telescope, a microscope, or even a trip to the zoo to find wonders from God's hand. Here you are, men and women, made in God's image. Before the vastness of the galaxies the psalmist may cry, "What is man, that thou art mindful of him?" (Ps. 8:4). But you are called to rule the earth; more than that, you are called to walk on earth with God your Maker. How beautifully the Bible describes man's creation— God quickens the work of his fingers with the breath of his lips. The breath you draw to shout God's praise is his gift who made you for himself.

We need not hold our God-given breath while a landing craft on Mars turns over rocks looking for life. We know that we are not alone in the universe, and we have better companionship than anything that can crawl from under Martian rocks. "Know ye that the Lord, he is God: It is he that hath made us, and not we ourselves"; "Come, let us worship and bow down; let us kneel before the Lord our Maker" (Ps. 100:3; 95:6).

Praise is more than our duty; it is our humanity. Men have climbed Everest, they tell us, because the mountain is there. How much more must we climb God's holy hill in worship because God is there, revealing his glory to man made in his image!

The God of the Psalms is Ruler as well as Creator. When the psalmist tells us that the world is established, that it cannot be moved (Ps. 96:10), he is celebrating God's works in controlling both nature and history. The nations rage, but God has only to speak and the earth melts (Ps. 46:6).

Every proud empire stands under God's judgement. Long after World War II there still stood in a West Berlin park a memorial from World War I. A bronze sculpture showed two German soldiers carrying a wounded comrade from the field of battle. The fury of the battle for Berlin in the second war had pocked the base of the statue with bullet marks. A more bizarre freak of battle made the sculpture a grotesque monument to the absurd. A shell had carried away the bronze head of the wounded soldier. The two heroes now labored to carry off a headless corpse. What a macabre monument to the ruin that Hitler's demonic genius brought upon Germany! As every earthly empire must, Hitler's thousand-year Reich came under the judgement of Almighty God.

God breaks the arrows of the bow (Ps. 76:3), burns the chariot in fire and is terrible to the kings of the earth (Ps. 76:12). God is terrible in justice. He hears the cry of the poor and oppressed from the barrios of earth; not one act of exploitation will go unavenged. "Vengeance is mine; I will repay, saith the Lord" (Rom. 12:19, AV; Deut. 32:35). God's justice delayed is not justice denied. God is coming to judge the earth. The last judgement is not convened by a military tribunal protecting privilege or by a people's court seeking revolutionary vengeance; it is summoned by the righteous King of all the nations.

Declare the glory of the coming Judge. God's song for the nations thunders from the storm-cloud of God's wrath against wickedness. Paul preached the day of judgment to Athenian idolaters; missionary messengers must today be prophets of God's righteousness.

But is the anthem of missions accompanied only by the crescendo of God's trumpet, summoning the nations to God's work of judgement? No, the psalmist hails God not only as the King of the nations but as Savior: "Sing unto the Lord, bless his name; show forth his salvation from day to day" (Ps. 96:2). If God came only in wrath who could stand before his holiness? We may call down fire from heaven upon the sins of others, but how shall we escape when our own sins are judged?

Praise God, the cloud of glory is bright with mercy. Declare the glory of his saving acts—the glory of the fire that filled the bush in the desert but did not consume it, the glory of the "I-am" God who called to Moses from the fire to promise deliverance to his people groaning under the lash.

Declare his glory—the psalms sing of God's mighty acts in Egypt; they echo the song of Moses on the shore of Reed Sea: "I will sing unto the Lord, for he hath triumphed gloriously : The horse and his rider hath he thrown into the sea. The Lord is my strength and song, and he is become my salvation" (Ex. 15:1-2).

What glory Israel can sing! Pinned against the sea by the war chariots of Pharaoh's striking force, the people saw the cloud of God's glory become a wall of darkness and fire to restrain the enemy, and then a pillar of cloud to lead them through the parted sea (Pss. 77; 78; 105; 106). The psalms sing, too, of God's wonders in the desert when he led his flock like a Shepherd, fed them with bread from heaven and satisfied their thirst with water from the rock (Pss. 78; 105; 106; Neh. 9:17). The God of creation is the Lord of salvation.

But God's glory cloud did not just lead his people out of slavery. He brought them out that he might bring them in. At Sinai God said, "Ye have seen . . . how I bare you on eagles' wings, and brought you unto myself" (Ex. 19:4).

"Unto myself!" On Sinai God came down in glory to establish his covenant with his redeemed people, to speak to them the words of his law. Through the mediation of Moses God gave Israel his law and his sanctuary. The glory that dazzled their eyes as it was reflected from the face of Moses filled the tabernacle, for God came down to dwell among his people.

God's exodus deliverance became a triumphal entry. The glory of God led his people into the promised land and up the height of his holy hill. There his glory filled his dwelling place in Zion. Indeed, this is the picture in Psalm 96. The Chronicler quotes the psalm in the context of King David's establishment of the service of praise after the ark of the Lord had been brought to Jerusalem (1 Chron. 16:23-33).

"God is gone up with a shout, the Lord with the sound of a trumpet" (Ps. 47:5). "Lift up your heads, O ye gates; even lift them up, ye everlasting doors: and the King of glory will come in" (Ps. 24:9).

The God of salvation is King in Zion. His trumpet sounds, summoning the nations to worship at his holy hill. Israel's shout of praise echoes to the islands of the sea.

For a moment God's glory did rest on Zion. Solomon's temple was filled with glory. The kings of the earth and the queen of the South came to Jerusalem to hear the wisdom of God's anointed, to see the blessing God had poured out on his chosen people (1 Kings 4:34; 10:6-9).

But Solomon turned from wisdom to folly, the kingdom was soon divided and God's blessing was turned to judgement. Where the cloud of glory had rested on God's house there arose the smoke of burning as invading Gentiles put the torch to the cedar of the temple.

Is Psalm 96, then, part of an ancient hymnbook to be found only under the charred remains of a gutted temple? No, Psalm 96 is the word of God, the saving God who remembers his promise to Abraham and the nations. Psalm 96 is a new song: God's mighty deeds of the past will be fulfilled in his great deliverance in the future.

Isaiah takes up again the song of Moses to celebrate a second exodus: "The Lord, even the Lord, is my strength and song; and he is become my salvation" (Is. 12:2; Ex. 15:2). But what hope of glory can remain when Jerusalem is ruined and God's people are scattered among the nations? Ezekiel sees the glory of God departing from the temple; he sees the people of God—dead and decomposed, dry bones scattered in the valley. "Son of man, can these bones live?" (Ezek. 37:3).

Only One can bring life from death and glory from destruction. God himself must come in the power of his Spirit and the wonder of his presence. Man's plight is too hopeless for any other deliverer and God's own promises are too great for any lesser fulfillment.

The new song is an advent hymn: "Prepare ye the way of the Lord; make straight in the desert a highway for our God. . . . The glory of the Lord shall be revealed, and all flesh shall see it together" (Is. 40:3, 5, AV).

Wonder of wonders, God will come not just to save his people from their captors but to save them from their sins. God will come not only as the King of glory but as the Lord our righteousness (Jer. 33:16). Not only will he tread the enemy underfoot; "he will tread our iniquities underfoot; and thou wilt cast all their sins into the depths of the sea" (Mic. 7:19).

The Lord will come and the Servant will come. He is the Branch of Righteousness (Jer. 33:15), the Son of David, called to sit at God's right hand (Ps. 110:1). He is the root of Jesse, "To him shall the nations seek" (Is. 11:10). When God's judgement hews down the cedar of Israel's pride he does not utterly destroy his people. No, there is a remnant; a tiny shoot springs up from the stump of the fallen tree. Here is the Christmas tree of the prophet. God's shoot, God's branch, grows to become a great mast on the mountain, a standard to which the nations are drawn.

That shoot from the root of David is the Lord's Messiah. By him and to him the nations are gathered. But the mystery of God's salvation lies in the Messiah's work. To redeem his people God must blot out as a thick cloud their transgressions and sins (Is. 44:22). The kings of the earth are astonished when they see the face of God's Servant. Torn and scarred, he is inhuman in the anguish of his suffering (Is. 52:14). He is despised as a shoot out of dry ground. Yet "surely he hath borne our griefs, and carried our sorrows; . . . he was wounded for our transgressions, he was bruised for our iniquities." His soul was made an offering for sin. "He poured out his soul unto death, and was numbered with the transgressors: yet he bare the sin of many, and made intercession for the transgressors" (Is. 53:4-5, 10, 12).

Now we see him who is raised as an ensign above the nations —he is lifted on a cross. "And I, if I be lifted up from the earth," said Jesus, "will draw all men unto myself" (Jn. 12:32). John explains, "But this he said, signifying by what manner of death he should die" (v. 33).

"Declare his glory among the nations." What wonders are the nations to hear? That the God of glory, the King of the nations has come to save. The Lord has come as the Servant. Heaven's glory drives darkness from the fields of Bethlehem. An angel announces, "Unto you is born this day in the city of David a Savior, which is Christ, the Lord!" But shepherds, not the nations, see the glory, and the sign they receive is a child lying in the feed bin of a stable.

What wonder silences us before the mystery of God's coming

in Jesus Christ! Yes, the glory has come, for he has come. "Arise, shine; for thy light is come, and the glory of the Lord is risen upon thee. . . . Nations shall come to thy light, and kings to the brightness of thy rising" (Is. 60:1-3). The magi follow his star from the east and worship him; old Simeon holds the infant Jesus and blesses God for the salvation "prepared before . . . all peoples; a light for revelation to the Gentiles, and the glory of thy people Israel" (Lk. 2:31-32).

Indeed both John the Baptist and Jesus come preaching the Kingdom of God: the message of the coming of God the King taken from these royal psalms and the good news proclaimed by Isaiah. The mighty works of God the King celebrated in the Psalms are wrought by the Lord of Glory in the midst of his people: He feeds the hungry, makes the lame to walk, the blind to see, the deaf to hear. He stills the roaring of the seas (Ps. 65:7), he speaks life to the dead and gathers his remnant flock as the true Shepherd (Ezek. 34:11).

But he does not bring the judgement of God's justice, and John the Baptist sends from prison an anguished question: "Art thou he that cometh?" (Lk. 7:19). Can this be the Lord whose reward is with him and his recompense before him (Is. 40:10)?

John is blessed if he is not offended with Jesus. Christ did not come to bring the judgement but to bear it. The song of praise in the Psalms is found most often in the vow of the sufferer to render thanks to God for delivering him from the depths. Jesus Christ is the royal sufferer who cries in abandonment as he drinks the cup of wrath, but who sings in resurrection triumph as he goes up with a shout to the Father's right hand. The agonizing Savior could count all his bones as he hung on the cross, but in his triumph he will count his Father's blessings. In Psalm 22, the psalm of his agony, he utters his vow of thanksgiving: "In the midst of the congregation will I sing thy praise" (Ps. 22:22; Heb. 2:12b).

The angels sang at Christ's birth, "Glory to God in the highest," but it was the shepherds who returned from the stable, "glorifying and praising God for all the things they had heard and seen" (Lk. 2:20).

Brothers and sisters, the new song, God's missionary anthem, is our song. Not the holy angels but redeemed sinners sing it on planet earth, and we sing it with Jesus. Yes, Christ now sings his missionary triumph among the Gentiles. "For I say that Christ hath been made a minister of the circumcision for the truth of God, that he might confirm the promises given unto the fathers, and that the Gentiles might glorify God for his mercy; as it is written, Therefore will I give praise unto thee among the Gentiles, and sing unto thy name" (Rom. 15:8-9).

When we sing God's glory among the nations, we sing with Jesus. How Paul the apostle thrilled to hear the Gentiles with one mouth glorifying the God and Father of our Lord Jesus Christ (Rom. 15:6).

The wall of partition that shut out the Gentiles from God's altar has been broken down. The Gentiles who were afar off are now brought near, and the spiritual sacrifice of their bodies is acceptable to God (Rom. 12:1-2). The song of Moses has become the song of the Lamb, the international anthem of the redeemed who are no more strangers or aliens, but fellow-citizens with the saints, joined to the commonwealth of Israel, of the household of God (Eph. 2:11-22). Only now the mountain for our festival of praise is not Sinai with its fire and smoke or even Zion where Solomon's temple stood. Rather, it is the heavenly Zion where the saints and angels are gathered, and where Jesus is, who has sprinkled the mercy-seat of heaven with his blood.

Our generation has a new perspective on this planet. We have seen its beauty, marbled with clouds, photographed from the moon. Christ's church needs a new perspective on the nations, gained not from the moon but from heaven—from that assembly where Jesus leads the song of redemption.

Stanza Two: Sing His Glorious Name!

Praising God's works of salvation always means praising his name as Redeemer. The very name "Jesus" blesses God the Savior. He is the "Wonderful Counselor, the Mighty God, Everlasting Father, the Prince of Peace" (Is. 9:16). Jesus taught us to pray, "Hallowed be thy name!" He poured out his life's blood to make that prayer our song. We declare the glory of that holy name that is made our name in Jesus Christ. Remember, you are baptized

not into your own name but into God's name: the name of the
Father, the Son, the Holy Ghost.

Does the very name of God bring joy to your heart and praise
to your lips? Do you remember the ten lepers sent by Jesus to
show themselves to the priests at Jerusalem to be pronounced
clean? Obedient, but lepers still, they set off on the long journey.
What risk if they were to near the temple as lepers! But as they
walked they were healed. One of them, a Samaritan, spun about.
Shouting "Glory to God!" he rushed back down the rocky path
to Jesus, fell headlong at his feet and gave thanks to the Savior.
Jesus said, "Were not the ten cleansed? but where are the nine?"
(Lk. 17:17).

"Where are the nine? Why, Jesus, they are on the road to Jerusalem. They are going where you sent them—to the priest who
can pronounce them clean. Jesus, you said nothing about coming back. They are doing their duty!"

Duty? Yes, but what obedience is this that knows nothing of
the joy of salvation, the praise of God's name! A sinful woman
bursts unbidden into the Pharisee's dinner to wet the feet of
Jesus with her tears; Mary of Bethany lavishes upon Jesus the
extravagant spikenard of her devotion.

Glory to God! Paul the apostle, once Saul the inquisitor, was
stopped short in his persecuting rage by the glory of the Lord.
He heard from his Savior's lips the name of Jesus. Ever after he
rejoiced in God's amazing grace. Reflecting on the profound
depths of God's sovereign will in salvation, he cried, "For of
him, and through him, and unto him, are all things. To him be
the glory forever. Amen" (Rom. 11:36).

Praise his name, we are called to doxological evangelism:
Salvation is of the Lord! Let that song die and we have nothing
to sing to the nations. They don't want to hear those old patron-
izing songs of missionary colonialism and they don't need our
help in learning the chants of revolutionary violence. But when
the people of God sing his praises, then the nations listen.

Praise his name, our God is glorious in wisdom. Kings came
to learn of the wisdom of Solomon, but a greater than Solomon
is here: Jesus Christ! From the cloud of glory on the mount the
disciples heard the Father's command: "This is my Son, my

chosen: hear ye him" (Lk. 9:35). Jesus said, "Take my yoke upon you, and learn of me" (Matt. 11:29). "If ye love me, ye will keep my commandments" (Jn. 14:15). The words spoken by Jesus have been confirmed by those that heard (Heb. 2:3); we are to remember "the words which were spoken before by the holy prophets, and the commandment of the Lord and Savior through your apostles" (2 Pet. 3:2).

To declare his name we must be taught by his Word. The nations must hear of the real Jesus, the biblical Jesus. God speaks to us in his Son and commands us to listen. We cannot stand under the name of God and over the Word of God. Indeed, God's name is in his Word, for God speaks to us to reveal himself. The mystery of God's name is reflected in his Word. How soon we are beyond our depth! Yet only then can we know with Paul what it means to be lifted up with praise on the towering wave of divine wisdom.

My friends, we do not declare among the nations an empty mantra, a name that means everything and nothing. We declare the riches of God's truth, the whole counsel of God, the glory of Jesus Christ in whom are hidden all the treasures of wisdom and knowledge (Col. 2:3).

Praise his name! We sing the glory of his power, too. God's name is hallowed in majesty in Jesus Christ our King.

Who is the King of glory? Once he rode through the hosannas and the palm branches to Jerusalem so that he might climb the hill of Calvary to die. But now he has ascended another hill. "Lift up your heads, O ye gates, even lift them up ye everlasting doors and the king of glory shall come in." The Lord mighty in battle has triumphed over the powers of darkness, and he ascends to his Father's throne. The Son, the brightness of the Father's glory says, "All authority hath been given unto me in heaven and on earth. Go ye therefore, and make disciples of all the nations" (Matt. 28:18-19).

Christ's heavenly glory is not just a reservoir of power, an energy source to be used in discipling the nations; no, Christ's glory is the Lordship to which they are discipled. If we do not praise his name, we do not preach the gospel. We baptize into the name of the Father, Son and Holy Ghost those who confess that Jesus Christ is Lord. Christ now rules over history and walks among the heavenly lampstands as the Judge of his church. Our gospel is "the gospel of the glory of Christ, who is the image of God" (2 Cor. 4:4).

Strange as it may seem to us, we proclaim his glorious name not in the posture of conquering heroes but as ministering slaves. Sometimes, like James and John, we begin to fantasize about becoming princes at Christ's right hand, or at least riding as a Rose Bowl marshall in the parade of Christ's kingdom. If that's what you have in mind, you have the right parade but the wrong place. Paul, the bondslave of Jesus Christ pictures his ministry not as though he were riding in Christ's triumphal chariot, but as though he were a chief captive, chained to the chariot of the victorious king (2 Cor. 2:14). We carry the treasure of Christ's glorious name in earthen vessels. Pressed, perplexed, pursued, knocked down, the apostle bears in his body the dying of Jesus, knowing that he will also be raised with Jesus (2 Cor. 4:8-14). He was made a spectacle, widely regarded as trash by the world. But what about your position? "I beseech you," writes Paul, "be imitators of me!" (1 Cor. 4:16).

Yes, the name of Jesus, the King of glory, was nailed above the cross. His name is glorious in wisdom and power and it is glorified in love. The wisdom of God is foolishness to men; the power of God is weakness to men; the love of God is an offense to men. Yet we bear before the nations God's name of love.

In the shadow of the cross, Christ's soul was troubled. He cried, "What shall I say? Father, save me from this hour?" (Jn. 12:27a). That was the prayer of the afflicted psalmist, the cry of the Lord's anointed for deliverance. "But for this cause came I unto this hour" (Jn. 12:27b). Jesus came as priest and sacrifice, to give his life a ransom for many. What shall he say? What prayer but this: "Father, glorify thy name!" (v. 28). Jesus, who taught his disciples to pray, "Hallowed be thy name," now prays that the Father will hallow his name at the cross. The Father in heaven replies, "I have both glorified it, and will glorify it again" (v. 28). How will the Father now glorify his name?

Will he glorify it with the glory of legions of angels? With the glory of the cloud on the mount? No, the Father will glorify his name by lifting up his Son on Golgotha.

What glory is this? The shame of nakedness, the agony of tor-
ture, the bitter wine of mockery, the doom of abandonment.
Does the elect Son glorify the Father's name when he cries, "My
God, my God, why hast thou forsaken me?"

Yes, never was God's name so glorified. The eternal song of
the seraphim cannot so lift it up. The devotion of the Son is fulfilled. In love to the Father he drinks the cup; in love to his own
he offers his soul for sin. And the infinite love of the heart of
the Father burns in the darkness. "God commendeth his own
love toward us, in that, while we were yet sinners, Christ died
for us" (Rom. 5:8). "For God so loved the world, that he gave his
only begotten Son" (Jn. 3:16). The price that Abraham did not
have to pay when Isaac was spared at the altar on Mount Moriah,
that price God the Father paid when he spared not his only-be-
gotten Son, but delivered him up for us all.

Declare among the nations the name of the God of Calvary,
the glory of the love of God that sealed salvation at the cross.
You may be called to sing the psalms of glory in a prison cell of
affliction. Paul did that at Philippi. His bleeding back was too
raw, his feet too numb in the stocks to find rest in sleep, so he
found refreshment in praise: "The Lord reigns; . . . the Lord is
great; . . . holy is he!" Is it surprising that those who glory in the
cross are called to take the cross and follow Christ?

What do you seek here at Urbana? Is it the glory of your Lord?
Lift up the Lord's great name in the praise-offering of your lips
and with the thank-offering of your life. Present your bodies a
living sacrifice of praise, holy, acceptable to God (Rom. 12:1).

The first question for you is not where among the nations the
Lord may call you nor even how among the nations your lips and
life may declare his glory. The first question is, have you seen
the glory of the Lord? Have you heard the voice of the Son of
God calling from Calvary?

Yes, here at Urbana you may learn of Christ the King of glory
whose power will judge the warring nations, of Christ the
prophet of glory whose Word is truth for the erring nations, of
Christ the priest of glory whose sacrifice is the only salvation
for the rebellious nations. But to proclaim his name among the

nations you must first bless his name in your heart.

Cry to him in repentance, call upon his name in faith and sing with these thousands the glory of Jesus Christ your Savior. Like Jehoshaphat's army of old, the church goes out to the spiritual battle singing the praises of the Lord. Jesus sang in the upper room with his disciples. Now he leads the praises of his people. Sing with Jesus his international anthem, the song of the Lamb! Hallelujah!

eight
Declare His Glory in a Suffering World

Samuel Kamaleson

The problem of suffering is too large for anyone to answer finally. Nonetheless, within the family of man, personal knowledge of suffering is universal. So my effort here is not to propose a definitive answer but to find the relevance of life in Christ in the midst of a suffering world.

Within the human family a Christian member is called to declare the glory of Jesus Christ contextually. But before we can understand this contextualized declaration of his glory, we need to discuss three things.

First, other people who have looked at God from different standpoints have taken a keen, deep look at suffering, and they have come up with some propositions. We must at least have some knowledge of their proposals. Second, we must know about the meaning of suffering by listening to Jesus Christ. This is what discipleship and life in Christ is all about. Third, when we have heard the Master tell us the meaning and the message of suffering, we need to declare this meaning in the idiomatic language that makes sense to us as well as to those who have not yet known the glory of Jesus Christ.

Some Views of Suffering

There are many views of suffering. Some have termed it as part of Karma—you suffer because of wrong done in this present existence or in some existence prior to this. Your evil acts will somehow search for you and find you out. But once you accept this viewpoint concerning suffering, it saps the very springs of personal compassion within you. If everyone who suffers is somehow paying for the deeds that he has done in the past, why interfere with his suffering? Let it have its full sway. Then again, if all the good that I do in this existence is in order that I may not come into another existence after this, then the motivation, being steeped in selfishness, eats up my real desire to alleviate suffering.

Within this school of thought, there is also speculation as to how many times a soul has to come back to be recycled. Some have said it will take over eight million transmigrations. But if the memory is a faculty related to the body and if souls have no memories, then when my soul leaves my body and puts on another body it has no capacity to recall. What good does it do to undergo punishment for something I can never know the root cause for? How can I repent? Where is there hope?

Others, after a serious look at the problem of suffering, have concluded that if a person can achieve an actionless, passionless state, he will not be touched by suffering. Desire is the root of passionate action. When the root of desire, including the desire for life itself, is cut, then the state of nirvana results. The result is a pronounced and devastating No against life itself.

This becomes escapism par excellence. Because its core is nothingness, this rationale is the end of faith in a personal God. It is a spiritual way to deny the very existence of God himself. If you want to be a spiritual atheist, this is the way to go.

Still others accept a personal God and attribute to him more than ninety-eight different names, the most important of these names being "Inexorable Will." Here nothing can be prayed for or sought after. That which must happen inevitably happens. Hence, the whole discipline is called submission. The stifling and stunning fatalism this leads to is obvious.

In Luke 7:11-17 we read about a most unusual happening. A widow's only son had died. Jesus and his disciples, on their way to Nain, met the funeral procession coming out of the city, and Jesus watched this woman cry.

If someone other than Jesus had been there, he might have said, "Woman, do not weep. Your son is more alive now than before. The seen and the felt and the tangible world is 'Maya' [illusion]. Seek consolation in that thought." And he would have gone on.

Another might have said, "Woman, desire is the cause of your pain. Desire not and you will hurt not." Yet another might have said, "Woman, resign yourself to the will of the Inexorable Will. Then you will find relief from your sorrow."

But none of these characters were there. The Son of God himself was there. He saw her agony, he addressed her personally and then he went into action on her behalf. He turned to the funeral bier, stopped the procession and spoke to the dead man, "I say to you, arise." And the dead man sat up. Jesus turned him back to the woman and walked away. There must be a way that he interpreted suffering that you and I ought to be keenly interested in.

The problem of suffering produced two basic viewpoints within the Old Covenant. First, the righteous will be exempt from the normal suffering that comes to the wicked (Ps. 91:8-10). This does not mean that the righteous will not undergo pain, nor does it mean that the righteous will not undergo physical death. It means the righteous (those who have accepted the moral law that God has written into the very basic construction of man and who do not break it) will not be exposed to the kind of heartache, the kind of brokenness, the kind of disgusting disappointment that comes to the wicked. But still the righteous get sick. They die. They suffer pain like other people.

The second viewpoint under the Old Covenant is found in Habakkuk 3:17-18. Dr. E. Stanley Jones used to say that this statement comes closest to the New Covenant tradition.

Suffering in Christ

What is the New Covenant tradition? One phrase occurs repeatedly in the New Testament: "in Christ." The rationale for suffering that comes through in this New Covenant view is impossible if you take your position outside Christ.

In Christ, what is the rationale? Christ himself is the New Covenant for me because he is the wisdom, the righteousness, the sanctification and the redemption. And Jesus Christ suffered: "Although he was a Son, he learned obedience through what he suffered" (Heb. 5:8). Hebrews 12:6 says that Jesus suffered because he was the Son of God. Because we are sons of God in him, the same measure of love is meted out to you and me. Where personal suffering is not interpreted in Christ, the possibility of declaring his glory in a suffering world ceases.

We cannot glorify him in a suffering world if we interpret human suffering through man-made philosophies. It is impossible. In Christ the Christian accepts God as a Father who loves him. He has no question about it. No one likes pain. No one wants to suffer. If I have a headache, I immediately resort to the "four ingredients doctors recommend most." When I have a soul-pain, I have a temptation to think about God as an aspirin.

But it doesn't work that way. In the intensity of the pain that will not go away, I decide that I am not loved. And I further conclude that I am unlovable anyhow. If God has given up on me, there is no hope for me. The cold fear that God himself doesn't love me creeps in. Then I go into the tailspin of asking for proofs of his love. Invariably, the proofs that I ask of him have to do with success and pleasure—relief from pain as I would have it, not as he would have it. And the norms that determine my likes and dislikes are the norms of the world around me. Yet this is the world to which God has called me to declare his glory.

Now if I do not arrive at the conclusions he wants me to arrive at, I do not declare anything but the fact that my aspirin has failed. This is crucial. If we miss it, we miss the whole point.

What is the basic understanding in the New Covenant? God, who is the Father of Jesus Christ, and who is my Father now that I am in Christ, loves me. He loves me so much that he did not spare his own Son in expressing this love. Because of that same love, he will not permit me to deceive myself now. He will work through the situation that I call agonizing pain and suffering and enable me to discover what his Son discovered. Only in this discovery will I find the possibility of glorifying his own Son.

If there was a patron saint of India, his name would be Sadhu Sunder Singh. You ought to read some of his writings. He underwent a great deal of pain and rejection, humiliation and persecution because he had chosen to stand in Christ Jesus. In thinking about his experiences afterward, he said:

> Whenever I had to suffer for our dear Savior... it gave me such a wonderful joy that I could not find anywhere else.... Suffering was suffering before I became a Christian, for at that time I had no peace. That was suffering in the real sense of the word; I felt as if I were in hell. But after my conversion I had no suffering at all. (The Cross Is Heaven by A. J. Appasamy, p. 46)

From his biography, however, we discover that this man suffered intensely after his conversion. Yet somehow he seems to think that this was not suffering compared to what he underwent prior to his stand in Christ. What is this? You have got to get "in" to know what this is. And unless you get in there is no possibility of declaring his glory in a suffering world.

Within the New Covenant, I affirm the love of God and so come into a new understanding of the motives and discipline of love which invites me into its experience. Christ's sufficiency now becomes my true self-sufficiency.

We are part of a technocratic age. Technology has taught us to remove obstacles that impede movement toward intended goals. How does a technocratic man handle obstacles in his own personal life? In his spiritual life also he wants to try "spiritual technology" to devise "sure-fire methods for removing obstacles. If the solution doesn't work, it is back to the drawing board for another technique, as in any technological endeavor" (Fr. Francis Martin, "The Mystery of Suffering," The New Covenant, April 1976).

An obstinate obstacle, then, can lead to very limited options as conclusions. I have to say to myself, "I'm not doing the thing right, and God will not help me to correct myself." Or "God simply doesn't care for me." And I wander back into the agony of meaninglessness. Fr. Francis Martin has said that "only when we are humbled by our inability to remove obstacles, real obstacles not just spiritual trials, only then can we understand Jesus Christ," only then will we understand what the New Testament calls the discipline or the education of God. If I do not understand Jesus Christ, I cannot declare him among the suffering.

The term "in Christ" illustrates the discovery of true self-sufficiency as being Christ's sufficiency. "In-Christ" existence is the true spirit existence. Paul states this condition in Galatians 2:19-20. This status of transcendence is offered to us in documented form in the New Testament as the authentic experience of not only the individual but also the community.

To check this out, read Acts 8 where the community was suddenly stripped of all the permanency in their life. Chased out of Jerusalem, they had no land or property, no wealth. Even the degree that they had from Jerusalem University was not recognized outside Jerusalem! They were chased out with nothing. And yet when they left the city, they proclaimed Jesus Christ. They seemed to have everything although everything was taken away from them. Notice also that they had what the world was looking for. Although they had been stripped of all their possessions, life still had meaning because they knew Jesus Christ as the risen Lord. The world sought them for that one message, and there was great joy in Samaria because of their presence.

In Acts 11:19-26, God used the same community again to transcend the known, established laws in society—relationships with people, the trade laws, the inseparable separation of Greek and Jew. All these things came tumbling down because there was a community that had the courage to say, "We look upon all things only as in Christ." They had to give them a new name, and so they called them "these Christ folk."

In Acts 13 we pick them up again. Notice that they have now transcended racial, linguistic, geographic, cultural and economic barriers. The only commonality they discovered was Jesus Christ. And when they discovered this commonality, they were declaring the glory of God inside a badly mangled, suffering world. They made no reference to their personal agony. But somehow in the discipline of God's love, about which they had no question whatsoever, they discovered the capacity to declare the glory, and the glory radiated.

Dr. E. Stanley Jones used to say, "Jesus transforms suffering by using it: The victim becomes the victor; a test is turned into a testimony." Historically, those who belong to him have illustrated this over and over again.

Sadhu Sunder Singh speaks about the martyr Kartar Singh. He came from a very famous, well-to-do family in the land of Punjab, in the northern part of India. When he came to Jesus Christ, his family turned him out with not even a strip of clothing on him. Suddenly he had to work to earn his own clothing and his food. He did it cheerfully, says Sadhu Sunder Singh.

Then he ended up in Tibet preaching the gospel. The Tibetans said unless you leave us, we'll have to exercise our law on you. He said that's all right, go ahead and do it. So after his refusal, they passed sentence on him—the sentence of death. It was a gruesome death. They took the skin of a yak—that is an animal that bears burden in Tibet—sewed him tightly in that skin and set him out in the blazing sun so that the skin would tighten and crush him to death. Three days this man was agonizing. On the fourth day when liberation was close, he asked for release of one hand and for a pencil to write. These are his words:

He gave me life, but given life was His own still. The truth is this, that I have not in any sense repaid Him. The full acknowledgment would be if I sacrificed myself to the glory of His dear name. I will ask from God not one but a hundred thousand lives. A hundred thousand times I may die for my Friend's sake. I pray that my love for him may not be less than the Hindu woman who burns along with the corpse of her dead husband. When for the dead husband, whom she may not hope to meet again, she does so much, how much more should I not do for a living Lord, who is moreover the Lord of Life? It is a shame for me to do less than a Hindu woman would do.

Sunder Singh said he related this story one day on the platform of a railroad station in Patiala. A neighbor was eagerly listening and he queried him and found out that he was the father of Kartar Singh. Through the witness of the glorious death of his son, the father became a believer also.

To declare his glory in a suffering world, we must understand Calvary as the ultimate model for living itself. The Word became flesh is the word that we repeatedly use. God, through Jesus Christ his Son, said Yes to you and to me. And now in turn he expects us to repeat this Yes to him. Will we turn around and say to God, "Through him we say Yes to you"?

In one village in India pressure was put on the so-called outcasts, who were Christians, by the majority of citizens of that village. They burned their homes. When a YMCA secretary heard about this atrocity, he became very angry. So he called the people together and found out what kind of injustice had been done. He discovered that when one of the men went to put out the blaze his hands were cut off because he tried.

This infuriated him even more. And so he began to gather money to go to court to fight for his cause. The man who had lost his arms came to this learned YMCA secretary and said, "Iyya, you taught me the Christian gospel, and the Christian gospel teaches us to love our enemies and pray for those who despitefully use us and persecute us. Now you are telling me something else. You are telling me to prosecute. How can I? You introduced me to Christ, and he teaches me to forgive. I am sorry, I cannot take the money." E. Stanley Jones says, "The handless Christian took the hand of Jesus and walked into the future with his head up and his heart up in victory. I can never forget him."

To Declare His Glory
Let me introduce you to two Scripture passages and tell you what they mean to me, and then I will move to my conclusion. Matthew 16:13-20 speaks about the identity of Jesus of Nazareth. Inside the city of Philippi, Jesus asked his very humble looking band of disciples, "Who do men say that the Son of man is?"

What about the city of Philippi? It was a city with a cafeteria of gods; you could pick and choose any you wanted. From the ancient Babylonian gods to the most recent fad of Caesar worship, everything was available. Jesus in effect said, "Look around. Shop around. Then decide what identity you will bestow on me."

After they had spoken about the world's identification of him, he turned to his intimate disciples and asked, "But who do you say that I am?" Simon Peter said, "You are the Christ, the Son of the living God." And Jesus immediately said, "Flesh and blood has not revealed this to you, but my Father who is in heaven."

What did he mean? Did he mean that the rational should not be used to come to this conclusion? No. He meant that a truly rational person will know that to know his true identity he needs help from beyond his own reason. That's a rational conclusion, because Jesus transcends all known human categories; you cannot call him apostle, you cannot call him just a good man. Simon said, "You are . . . the Son of the living God." Jesus said, on this confession I will build my church, and the gates of hell shall not prevail against it.

What kind of gate of hell am I thinking about tonight? The hell of fear. The gate that slams shut between good intention and good action. Most of us are moved with compassion when we think about the world that is suffering, but we are kept away from action because something tells us that poverty is contagious like leprosy. It can jump on me. We've been taught that way. We've been told ever since we were young that to be poor is to be subhuman.

Then I look at the one in the city of Philippi. He didn't wear a doubleknit suit, not even one from Montgomery Wards. He wore a homespun robe. And he stood there and all the power in the world could not take away from his majesty. If I am in Christ, that capacity is given to me. The gates of hell cannot slam shut on me. I am not afraid of the contagion because he has given me a humanity that nothing in this world can ever take away from me. Poverty, agony, pain, suffering—nothing can remove this humanity. He has given it to me, never to be pulled back.

Charles Wesley's hymn "And Can It Be" expresses this fearlessness delightfully:

Long my imprisoned spirit lay
Fast bound in sin and nature's night;
Thine eye diffused a quickening ray:
I woke; the dungeon flamed with light!

My chains fell off, my heart was free,
I rose, went forth, and followed Thee.
When God has so broken the chains you need not fear poverty
or suffering any more. The humanity God restored to you cannot
be cut off.

Now let us move on to the freedom of the spirit that the Christian enjoys. Let me illustrate this with a story taken, with gratitude, from HIS magazine. It is about the coming of Christ.

There was a revolt up in heaven. A small band of people got
into a huddle and they said, "The one who is in charge here
doesn't know what's happening down below. How can he ever
properly govern it. We ought to go and talk to him." And they
began to talk about things he did not know.

One said, "He doesn't know what poverty is."

Another said, "He doesn't know what it means to be in a refu-
gee camp in Bangladesh."

Another said, "He doesn't know what injustice is."

And then a small man who had been silent until then suddenly jumped up. He was the kind of character who finds words inadequate to give vent to emotion. Every time he spoke his nos-
trils punctuated his emotions by dilating. He spoke emphat-
ically, "Does God know about death? What does he know about
the threat of non-existence?"

So they said, "We'll go and talk to him."

As they began to move, a little child came close to a very tall,
beautiful woman, clad in a lovely sari. And she pulled at the end
of the sari and when the woman bent down to listen, the child
whispered, "I'm too small and too young to talk to God. But
when you get there would you ask him a question for me?"

And the beautiful woman said, "What do you want me to talk
to God about?"

"Would you ask him if he knows anything about being ille-
gitimate?"

The beautiful woman in the beautiful sari was considered a
"fallen woman," so she bent down and picked up the little girl
and said, "Honey, I'll carry you. You ask God."

So they went to the presence of God. And God said, "What is
it that you want?"

And they said, "God, you don't know anything about what's going on on earth. You don't know what it means to suffer. You don't know what pain is."

And the little girl jumped up and said, "God, do you know what death is? Do you know what illegitimacy is?"

God said, "What do you think I ought to do?"

They said, "You should spend at least a week in Bangladesh."

And God had a friend on earth whose name was Isaiah. He called him and said, "Isaiah, proclaim it." And this is how Isaiah proclaimed it:

For unto us a Child is born; unto us a Son is given; and the government shall be upon his shoulder. These will be his royal titles: "Wonderful," "Counselor," "The Mighty God," "The Everlasting Father," "The Prince of Peace." (Is. 9:6, LB)

Why do we have a message to declare within the suffering world? Because we have that kind of God—a God who knows every degradation that people experience today and yet restores the full dignity of humanity.

But this incarnation of God creates a very great and scandalous concreteness. It is one thing to say God came near, but it is another thing for him to expose himself to all the problems of this nearness. Let me illustrate with a fictional story. Neil Armstrong is a household name, even in India. If Armstrong were to visit us in Madras, we would roll out the red carpet to receive him. Millions would turn out. Was he not the first man on the moon? Should we not treat him with respect? And I would be there among the millions.

In this sea of humanity, my little boy standing at my feet says, "Daddy, where is this man who landed on the moon?" So what do I do?

I lift him up above my shoulder and then ask him, "Do you see that big, black limousine way out there?" We have a strange notion in India that if a dignitary is coming we have to get a big black limousine to put him in.

"Yes, I see it."

"Do you see the man who is the chief minister of the state?"

"Yes, I see him."

"Do you see that speck beside him?"

"Yes, I do."

"That is the man who landed on the moon."

My son will have no problem about his identity. Why? Because people who have gone to the moon must be way out of the reach of ordinary people. You shouldn't be able to get near them. They are beyond human, don't you see?

I go home that evening feeling satisfied that I have seen him. I can't be sure what gender he is, but I am absolutely satisfied.

Let's say, then, that that same afternoon I get a splitting headache. So I go to the corner drug store. This is now my turf. This is my area of Madras. Everybody knows me and I know them. I ask the druggist, "Hey, can you give me a packet of Anacin?" And he gives me a packet of Anacin.

While I'm about to put it in my mouth, a very nice-looking friendly American in a short-sleeved shirt, tails hanging out, comes up, smiles and says, "Hey, I want the same thing. But he couldn't understand my accent. Could you get one for me?"

"Sure," I tell him. (I haven't been to the United States for nothing.) "I'll get it done for you." So I speak the word and the man gives it to him.

As I give him the Anacin, I turn to this man and say, "Hey, your face looks very familiar. Did anybody ever tell you you look like Neil Armstrong?"

He smiles from ear to ear and says, "I am Neil Armstrong."

Do you think I'll believe him? No, sir. You know why? Why would Neil Armstrong walk around barefoot? Maybe he wants to see the city of Madras. That's true. But there are more beautiful parts of the city that he could go to than my neck of the woods. All right, he comes to my part of the world, why does he come to my drug store? You tell me. Or if he came to my drug store, a man who has been to the moon, will he ever get a headache? It blows my theory to pieces. I have one more question: If the man who has been to the moon gets a headache, will they not prescribe something more romantic than Anacin for him?

Is this not the scandal of the Incarnation? Is this not the problem of the Word becoming flesh? He didn't drive around in an Oldsmobile, but then he says the Father judges all things by him. He says he is the measurement of the coming order. Then he tells me that in the coming order they pave the road with things like gold. Nobody kills another while robbing asphalt from the streets of New York.

What a drastic difference. But why did he ever become flesh? And if he had to become flesh, should he become flesh like this? Every Christian must face this issue. But if I accept it, he gives me the right to become a son of God. Liberated. No gate of hell can hold me back.

You say, "All right, Sam, give me some creative handles. How can I work it out? I want to." It looks like an impossible task. What do you do when 600 million people compose one nation, and eighty per cent of those have never known what a full, satisfying, nutritionally programmed meal is? Do you give up? We can't afford to. The day of small beginnings will never end as long as there are disciples of Jesus Christ. What about the 17,000 at Urbana? Because this Word has become flesh and lived among us in this fashion we must do something. What can we do?

What We Can Do

Three simple things all of us can do. First, we can decide not to squander or waste. This includes mother's admonition that we ought to eat the helping of spinach because people in India were dying without it. We could very readily tell her, "Please let them have it, I don't want it." But I mean another thing beside that: There is waste in overindulgence: We eat when we know we don't need to eat. A huge helping satisfies our ego, but is too much for our stomach. Will you courageously refuse to waste like that?

Second, refuse to try to satisfy your spiritual hunger by going on a buying spree. How often the advertising agencies know our inner, spiritual anxieties and prompt us to buy promising, "If you buy this, you'll be satisfied." But you never will be. A $1,000 stereophonic system will never satisfy the inner hunger you have for Jesus Christ. A perfectly acoustic room will never satisfy the need you have to listen to the voice of God. Will you and I have the courage to refuse to be sucked into this? When there is a spiritual need, I go alone to him and let him meet the need.

Third, what you have saved by steps one and two, take to the Lord and say, "Lord, what do you want me to do with it?" In *What Do You Say to a Hungry World?* Dr. Stanley Mooneyham, the president of World Vision International, tells of an ethics professor who spoke to his class in Long Island about the basic ethical problem all humanity faces. He asked if they would place a $5.00 value on modern man. Not $6 million, but merely $5.00. Most of them said that even with inflation it is possible to value man at $5.00. Then he asked, "When you hear about the suffering, the hunger, the poverty in other parts of the world or next door to you within your own city, will you be willing to evaluate human beings at $5.00 a head and do something about it?" There was silence in that classroom. That is a job for the government, they agreed; we are not involved.

But the 17,000 at Urbana cannot do that, can they? Why? Because the Word became flesh. And embarrassingly he became *that* kind of flesh. As long as I look upon human suffering as something that can "catch" on me, I will never give dignity to the one whom I go to serve. I will always be condescending in my compassion, and that is not Christian compassion. But if, as Mother Teresa says, I see the Lord himself in the suffering, then it is not the wounds of that suffering person that I'm binding, but the very wounds of the Lord. In this way I somehow restore dignity not only to the one to whom I go but to myself. Declare his glory in a suffering world.

Some will hesitate when called to action: "You know I've done this several times before, but I'm not able to sustain myself in this kind of commitment." And they will withdraw.

But that is sad, for Jesus said, "I'm the good shepherd. . . . I lay down my life for the sheep." We can trust him to keep us to our commitment. Sheepdogs are ingenious in the ways they keep sheep from straying. They will bark at them. They will pretend to bite them, but they never injure the sheep. All they want is to corral the sheep in a safe area. If a sheepdog knows enough to keep sheep straight on the path, how much more capable is the Savior, who died and now lives for us?

What kind of a God do we serve? Can we trust him to keep us straight in our commitment? What kind of a commitment is called for tonight? A Yes to end all Noes. If Jesus Christ is God's Yes to me, then he is my Yes to God tonight. And what am I saying in that Yes? I am saying, "God, if I'm ever tempted to say No, I give you the right to turn me every way but the wrong way. And don't let me sit on my No. Move me out of it. I trust in you implicitly."

Our world is a suffering world. That is no secret. The God to whom I belong is faithful. He will fulfill that for which he has called you and me. And then we will be declaring his glory contextually.

The Ethics that Document Freedom

[The material which follows is the final section of Samuel Kamaleson's manuscript. Because he did not have time to include it in his Urbana address, Mr. Kamaleson requested that it be included in the Urbana 76 compendium—Ed.]

The Macedonian Christians "first gave themselves to the Lord and then to us by the will of God" (2 Cor. 8:5). The paragraph within which this verse is found speaks about the response of those who knew what poverty was to those who were now suffering in poverty. They first gave themselves to the Lord. And their response became the will of this God because he is that kind of God.

After all, if they were to know the power of his resurrection they had to share the fellowship of his suffering. And he suffers where his people suffer.

In Luke 10:25-37 we read about the Samaritan. There are three different laws in operation here. The law of the jungle operates when the bandits get what they want by brute force. The law of diplomacy expresses itself when the religious pass by and get by rationalization the apathetic indifference they want. But the law of love gets what it wants by self-giving, because love must always give.

It is this love that liberates man from inhibiting, paralyzing fear. Fear is never without its own rationale. In the Samaritan story there are at least three strong roots for this rationale—the root of irreconcilable race distinctives and discriminations, the irresistible drive to retaliate and hate, and the economic impossibility of repayment. But Calvary love liberates from these fears. In Romans 8:2 this rationale is called the "law of sin and death."

As the warrior proves himself in the battle, the Christian enacts his claim and perfects it in martyrdom. It happened in Uganda on June 3, 1886. More than a hundred young men walked nine miles carrying the wood that eventually would be used to burn them to death. They were page boys in the court of Kabaka Mwanga. They were Christians. They had found it necessary to take a strong stand on moral issues. The Kabaka interpreted this as a challenge to his authority. So the options were plain—submit or die.

They walked nine miles under the pressure of these options. They made their choice. During the final hours these young men, who were in their late teens and early twenties, sang their way to victory.

The axe cuts the wood. But when sandalwood is cut, it imparts a fragrance to the cutting edge of the axe.

The young men did not die in vain. Virtually hundreds, who had been waiting for an evidence of this kind of liberation, now saw the light. And their chains fell off. And there was a mass movement to Christ triggered by the choice of those young men.

I know a lady in South India. All day with a curved knife she cuts grass to sell in order to make a living. Even under inflated prices her whole day's earnings may not be more than 75 cents. But she tithes this every day and contributes to missions.

Some years ago I knew of a student in the university in Jakarta, Indonesia. He considered himself more fortunate than others because while he was in school he had the opportunity of a job. He earned much more than others were capable of making so he sat down and calculated his earnings and his needs. He restricted his needs and found an extra amount in his hands. This he shared prayerfully and lovingly with those on the campus who had none.

The ethic that endorses spiritual freedom is not what we do to save ourselves, but it is what results from the assurance of our personal salvation. And just as salvation is the ongoing relationship with Jesus Christ, so the expression of it also increases in understanding and depth and confidence.

Let me retell another story from HIS magazine. A long time ago there was a king. He invited all his subjects to a feast. A beggar wanted to go, but when he read the small print in the invitation, he was disturbed. For the king's all-inclusive invitation demanded that the guests be properly dressed. How can a beggar ever be clothed properly for the king's table?

So they ushered him into the presence of the king and he made his complaint vocal. The king heard his case patiently. Knowing the contradictions that validated the rationale of the beggar's complaint, the king decided to do something about it. He called his son, the crown prince, and sought his help.

The prince obeyed his father. He took the man to his room and offered him a choice of any one of his princely robes. The beggar (who was a beggar like me) could not bring himself even to imagine such a possibility.

So the prince himself made the choice and fitted the beggar in a purple suit (the beggar was a beggar like me). He bent down to pick up his rags, which he had now shed, and carefully bundled them up.

"Oh," the prince said, "you won't need them. The suit of clothes you wear is miraculously made. It is mine. It will never wear out!" (But the beggar was a beggar like me.) He couldn't believe it. After all, all the clothes he had ever owned eventually wore out. Why shouldn't this suit do the same? He begged to retain his bundle of rags. He said he would feel more secure and comfortable! Just in case! And the prince had to let him go.

Everyone in the village laughed at the beggar, who, though robed in purple and princely robes, still carried a bundle of filthy rags! What a fool!

The day of the dinner arrived. Everyone including the beggar was there. He gained admittance and sat at the table with a bundle of rags on his lap. Every time a delicacy came by, he received the plate with one hand and with the other he held on to his bundle of rags so it wouldn't slip off his lap! Since he didn't have a third hand, he *saw* the food, *smelled* the food, *watched* others being fed with the food, but, unable to help himself, he sat there, lean and hungry, holding onto his rags.

He left the dinner at the king's table more hungry than he had been when he came in. But he still had his rags!

One day word went round that the beggar was dying. The king said, "He is my friend and I should visit him." When the royal visitor bent down to enter the humble hut, there was the beggar in his last moments, laid out on a torn mat on the floor. He was still robed in the princely robes. They were as new as on the day when he received them. But, at his head and close beside him, he still had the bundle of rags.

The king wept! He wept for what *could have been* and was not.

The ethic that documents freedom is not our effort to work out our Karma. It is the result of the salvation that he has already given to us.

To the one who is so liberated in spirit, the practical ways of expressing such an ethic are unending. The innovating Spirit opens them up to us contextually.

Today, in almost every nation of this world, there are those who belong to the witnessing community. They too want to declare his glory among the suffering. They know the context. But their resources are limited. And this is part of their ache. The demands of love and the need are unlimited.

The same Lord whose resources are placed under our control is also Lord of the almost limitless need. When we find the ethic of obedience, he relates the resource to the needs. Since it is the risen Lord who relates the resources to the needs, they who are contextually declaring his glory among the suffering are no longer under bondage to any mere human whim and fancy that would like to have the controlling patronage. The expression of love now is theirs. They must think it through. They must act it out. And it must be the expression of their compassionate love. That is the only way that the declaration of his glory can be contextualized.

But we must go further. We must go beyond declaration. In Romans 8:22-23, 26 (AV) we read about three "groanings." Creation is groaning because the awaited new order is coming into being. It is like childbirth pangs. The new order is Jesus Christ. But until the fruition of all known human relationships, the groaning of the old created order continues.

The children of God who are the first fruits of this new order also groan. They groan when they perceive the tension between what is and what is yet to be. They groan because what is *already actualized* in themselves leads them to plead for what is *yet to be actualized.*

But then, within this creaturely groaning, the Creator also groans. This groaning of the Holy Spirit gives direction. He groans creatively and contextually.

William Wilberforce heard this groaning in the eighteenth century and obeyed. Mother Teresa has heard it and is obeying. Today can be a historic day for you and me. Could God be saying something to us about the extreme injustice of wastefulness? Could he be saying something to us about the rat race of trying to quench spiritual hunger by mere material means? Could he be speaking to us about creative channeling of resources—personal and material—to those who have need of them, who suffer and have been rejected, who have been beaten down, robbed and left to die (1 Jn. 3:17)?

To declare his glory among the suffering does not mean to prove that pain and suffering are palatable. It means rather that in Jesus Christ pain can become purposeful, because in him all things become purposeful. Dr. E. Stanley Jones used to say, "Yourself in your hands is a pain and a problem. Yourself in Christ's hands is a power and a possibility."

In the old days of the Sultans, there was a man called Jaffer. He was a good man. Everyone loved him. But the Caliph became jealous of his popularity. One day he found a reason to have Jaffer executed and ordered it. He also proclaimed that within his kingdom nobody should even mention the name Jaffer again.

An Ethiopian slave whom Jaffer had set free at one time stood up in the marketplace that same day and prayed for Jaffer. The soldiers of the Caliph caught him. Standing bound in chains, the Ethiopian slave was challenged by the Caliph to give an answer for his absolutely stupid behavior. The slave lifted his hands and jingled his chains and said, "Oh, Caliph, from chains worse than these Jaffer set me free."

And the Caliph thought, "What a brave spirit. I must win him for myself."

So he called his bodyguard and asked him to cut the slave loose, and give him one of the crown jewels while he walked into his new freedom. "Let the dog know to whom his gratitude now belongs," said the Caliph.

They cut the slave loose, gave him the jewel, and thought he would now praise the Caliph. But the former slave lifted up his head and raised the crown jewel in his hand toward heaven and, in the presence of the court and the Caliph, said, "Jaffer, even this I owe to you."

nine
The Glory of God's Will

Elisabeth Elliot Leitch

High in the mountains of North Wales in a place called Llany-mawddwy, lives a shepherd named John Jones with his wife Mari and his black and white dog Mack. I stood one misty summer morning in the window of their farmhouse watching John on horseback herding the sheep with Mack. A few cows were quietly chewing their cud in a nearby corner while perhaps a hundred sheep moved across the dewy meadow toward the pens where they were to be dipped. Mack, a champion Scottish collie, was in his glory. He came of a long line of working dogs, and he had sheep in his blood. This was what he was made for, this was what he had been trained to do, and it was a marvelous thing to see him circling to the right, circling to the left, barking, crouching, racing along, herding a stray sheep here, nipping at a stubborn one there, his eyes always glued to the sheep, his ears listening for the tiny metal whistle from his master which I couldn't hear.

Mari took me to the pens to watch what John had to do there. When all the animals had been shut inside the gates, Mack tore around the outside of the pens and took up his position at the dipping trough, frantic with expectation, waiting for the chance to leap into action again. One by one John seized the rams by their curled horns and flung them into the antiseptic. They would struggle to climb out the side and Mack would snarl and snap at their faces to force them back in. Just as they were about to climb up the ramp at the far end John caught them by the horns with a wooden implement, spun them around, forced them under again, and held them—ears, eyes and nose submerged for a few seconds.

I've had some experiences in my life which have made me feel very sympathetic to those poor rams—I couldn't figure out any reason for the treatment I was getting from the Shepherd I trusted. And he didn't give me a hint of explanation. As I watched the struggling sheep I thought "If only there were some way to explain! But such knowledge is too wonderful for them—it is high, they cannot attain unto it." So far as they could see, there was no point whatsoever.

When the rams had been dipped, John rode out again on his horse to herd the ewes which were in a different pasture. Again I watched with Mari as John and Mack went to work, the one in charge, the other obedient. Sometimes, tearing at top speed around the flock, Mack would jam on four-wheeled brakes, his eyes blazing but still on the sheep, his body tense and quivering, but obedient to the command to stop. What the shepherd saw the dog could not see—the weak ewe that lagged behind, the one caught in a bush, the danger that lay ahead for the flock.

"Do the sheep have any idea what's happening?" I asked Mari.

"Not a clue!" she said.

"And how about Mack?" I can't forget Mari's answer:

"The dog doesn't understand the pattern—only obedience."

There are those who would call it nothing more than a conditioned reflex, or at best blind obedience. But in that Welsh pasture in the cool of that summer morning, I saw far more than blind obedience. I saw acted out exactly what I want to talk about tonight. I saw two creatures who were in the fullest sense "in their glory." A man who had given his life to sheep, who loved them and loved his dog, and a dog whose trust in that man was absolute, whose obedience was instant and unconditional, and whose very meat and drink was to do the will of his master. He never stopped wagging his tail. "I delight to do thy will," was what Mack said, "Yea thy law is within my heart."

My topic is "The Glory of God's Will." My husband used to say that a speaker has four speeches: the one he prepares, the one he actually delivers, the one the audience thinks it heard, and the one that gets reported in the newspapers the next day—and there isn't necessarily any similarity between them. In an effort to bring what I want to say into closer alignment with what you hear me say, I'm going to tell you what it is, then I'm going to try to say it, and then I'll tell you what I've said.

One: The glory of God's will for us means absolute trust. Two: It means the will to do his will. And three: It means joy.

Now what is this thing called trust? Did Mack's response to John's commands hinge on the dog's approval of the route his master was taking? Mack didn't know what the shepherd was up to, but he knew the shepherd. Have you and I got a Master we can trust? Do we ask first of all to be allowed to examine and approve the scheme? The Apostle Paul never said, "I know what God is up to." He said, "I know whom I have believed."

We start, then, with the recognition of who God is. He is our Creator, the one whose spoken Word called into being the unimaginable thing called space which scientists tell us is curved, and the equally unimaginable thing called time which the Bible tells us will cease. He set the stars in their trajectories and put the sliding shutter on the lizard's eye—this is the God who dreamed you up, thought of you before light existed, created you, formed you, and now calls you by name. He says, "Fear not, Susan." He says, "I have redeemed you, Steve."

When the Apostle John was an old man in exile on an island called Patmos "on account of the Word of God and the testimony of Jesus," he was granted a vision of "One like a Son of Man"—eyes like a flame of fire, a voice like a waterfall, his face shining like the full strength of the sun—and in his hand he held seven stars. Old John, who had known and loved Jesus, was overwhelmed. He fell at his feet as one dead. And then the hand that held the seven stars was laid on him, and the voice that was like a thundering cataract, said, "Fear not, I am the first and the last, I died, I am alive, I have the keys. Now write what you see." What John saw turned out to be the Book of the Revelation, the most abstruse of all the books of the Bible, full of bowls of wrath and bizarre beasts, of lightning and harps and smoke and seas of glass and rainbows of emerald. The courage it took to put all that down in writing for other people to read came from the vision John had had of who it was that was asking him to do it.

It is this same One who asks you and me to do what he wants us to do. The God of creation who's got the whole wide world in his hands. The God who in the person of Jesus Christ "for us men and for our salvation came down from heaven and was made man and was crucified." Those hands that keep a million worlds from spinning into oblivion were nailed motionless to a cross —for us. That hand that held the stars—laid on you. Can you trust him?

Two thousand years ago Paul said that the Jews were looking for miracles. The Greeks were seeking after wisdom. Not much has changed, has it? People are still looking for instant solutions, chasing after astrologers and gurus and therapists and counselors, but Christianity still has only one story to tell—it's an old, old story: Jesus died for you. Trust him.

Karl Barth was once asked to sum up in a few words all he had written in the field of theology. This was the sum: "Jesus loves me, this I know, for the Bible tells me so."

If you can trust that kind of God, what do you do next? You do what he tells you. You obey. This was the second thing I saw when I watched the shepherd and his dog. If you know your master, you will to do his will.

This world is his show, he's running it. Do we think of it as under our management? Created for the service of our own desires? "Do your own thing," they tell us. They even say, "If it feels good, do it." Have you ever heard a more idiotic piece of advice? Is it our world, a sort of make-your-own-sundae proposition, with the will of God just a nice, creamy squirt of earthly

success and heavenly approval that goes on top? The will of God
is not something you add to your life. It's a course you choose.
You either line yourself up with the Son of God and say to the
Father, "Thy will be done," or you capitulate to the principle
which governs the rest of the world and say, "My will be done."

Harry Blamires has said, "From the human race today goes up
one mighty prayer of praise and one tremendous shout of defiance against the loving rule of God. At every moment, and in
every act or thought, we swell the volume of that hymn of praise,
or else of that cry of blasphemous rebellion."

We identify ourselves with Christ or we deny him. Jesus chose
a path, and went down it like a thunderbolt. When we say as
Christ did, "I have set my face like flint to do his will," we are
baptized into his death, and like the seed which falls into the
ground and dies, we rise to new life. "We have shared his
death," Paul wrote to the Romans. "Let us rise and live our new
lives with him. Put yourselves into God's hands as weapons of
good for his own purposes."

That's hard, clear language: put yourself. Obedience to God is
action. I can't find anything about feelings in the Scriptures
that refer to obedience. It's an act of the will. "Our wills are
ours," wrote Tennyson, "to make them Thine." God gave us this
precious gift of freedom of the will so that we would have something to give back to him. Put yourself in his hands. Choose.
Give yourself. Present your bodies a living sacrifice. Until you
offer up your will you do not know Jesus as Lord.

There are many men and women here tonight, I'm sure, who
have made this choice and said the eternal Yes to God, "Thy will
be done." But you are wondering when I'm ever going to get to
the part about how you can know what it is that God wants you
to do. If you can just figure out what the orders are you are willing to obey them. You wish with all your heart that it was as
clear to you as the pillar of fire to the children of Israel or the
little metal whistle to the collie dog. You high school seniors
don't know which college to go to. You college freshmen wonder what you're going to major in. A lot of you came to Urbana
perplexed about a missionary career. Are you called or not?
And it's just possible that there are a dozen or so here who would

like to get married. How can you possibly know?

Let me tell you a story. When the author of *Christ the Tiger* was a small boy he used to pull out of the cupboard the paper bags that his mother saved and spread them around the kitchen floor. This was permitted on the condition that he collect them and put them away when he finished playing. One day his mother (who also happens to be my mother) found the bags all over the kitchen and Tommy in the living room where his father was playing the piano. When she called him to pick up the bags there was a short silence. Then a small voice said, "But I want to sing 'Jesus Loves Me.' " My father took the opportunity to point out that it's no good singing God's praises while you're being disobedient. To obey is better than sacrifice.

To will to do God's will involves body, mind, and spirit, not spirit alone. Bringing the body under obedience means going to bed at a sensible hour, watching your weight, cutting out the junk food, grooming yourself carefully (for the sake of others). It means when the alarm goes off your feet hit the floor. You have to move.

Some of you remember hearing of Gladys Aylward, a remarkable little London parlor maid who went to China as a missionary. She spent seven years there of happy single life before an English couple came to work nearby, and as she watched them she began to realize that she had missed out on something wonderful. So she prayed that God would choose a man for her in England, call him and send him straight out to her part of China and have him propose. Then as she told me this story she leaned toward me on the sofa where we were sitting, her bony little index finger pointing in my face, and said, "Elisabeth, I believe God answers prayer. He called him. But he never came." It's a little like the alarm clock. The call to duty. But you have to put your feet on the floor.

So much for the obedience of the body. Bringing the mind under obedience means, for example, doing that reading your professor has assigned. The will of God for a student is to study. You don't need to do any praying about *whether* you should study. The will of God for a Christian is to be a witness. You *are* the light of the world, my witnesses, Jesus said. You don't need to pray about whether this is your job or not, but bringing the spirit under obedience entails plenty of praying for understanding and for guidance about the how, when and where. The Bible won't tell you whom to marry or what mission field to go to but I believe with all my heart that as you seek honestly to do the things you're sure about, God will show you the things you aren't sure about. We might as well admit that most of our difficulties are not with what we don't understand, but with what we do understand.

In preparation for writing a book on the guidance of God, I read through the whole Bible to find out how he guided people in those days. I found that in the overwhelming majority of cases it was not through what we'd call "supernatural" means —voices, visions, angels or miracles—but by natural means—in the course of everyday circumstances when a man was simply doing what he was supposed to be doing, taking care of sheep or fighting a battle or mending fishnets, that his guidance came.

Just before he issued the Emancipation Proclamation a group of ministers urged Abraham Lincoln to grant immediate freedom to all slaves. "It is my earnest desire to know the will of Providence in this matter," Lincoln wrote. "And if I can learn what it is, I will do it.... I suppose it will be granted that I am not to expect a direct revelation. I must study the plain physical facts of the case ... and learn what appears to be wise and right. The subject is difficult and good men do not agree."

Lincoln sets for us a sane and humble example. There is no reason to assume that divine guidance is a purely spiritual matter or an inward impression. If we belong to the Lord lock, stock and barrel—body, mind and spirit—why should we expect him to employ only the spirit?

Lincoln said, "I must study the plain physical facts of the case." If the case happens to be the matter of becoming a missionary you have to believe that God has something to do with your even considering such a career. What brought it to your attention? How come you're here at Urbana? Think of all the things that had to fit together to get you here at all: You heard about it, friends talked about it, you couldn't see giving up your Christmas vacation to go listen to a bunch of missionaries or preachers, you didn't have time, you didn't have the money. But here you are.

You asked God to speak to you. You look at a particular need and you see that you could in fact fill that need. The timing is right. "My times," said the Psalmist, "are in thy hands." You have certain gifts—"Oh, but mine aren't any good, I mean like you know I can't do what she does," you say. I'm not talking about what she does. Consider the gifts God gave you.

Circumstances may point the way. Even your own desires could be sanctified and used for God's purposes. Study the facts: need, timing, gifts, circumstances, desires—the clear command to witness. Use your head. Don't overspiritualize. Trust the Shepherd to show you the path of righteousness, and remember that nobody can steer a car that's parked.

One week before I graduated from college I learned that a young man named Jim Elliot was in love with me. For months I had been hoping this would happen but kept telling myself that it would be fatuous to imagine that he could ever look twice at me. He was what we used to call a BTO—Big Time Operator— while I was a TWO—a Teeny Weeny Operator. And I was sure that every little sign that he might be interested in me was only my desperately wishful thinking. But no, he told me he loved me.

My heart turned over and then sank like a stone when he went on to say that he hadn't the least inkling that God wanted him to marry me. He was going to South America, I thought I was going to Africa, each of us had just been through months of heart searching in an attempt to accept the possibility of life as a single missionary. We believed we had reached that point, and then, wham—there we were in love.

How do you discern the will of God when your own feelings shout so loud? We prayed the prayer of Whittier's hymn:

Breathe through the heats of our desire
Thy coolness and Thy balm,
Let sense be dumb,
Let flesh retire,
Speak through the earthquake, wind, and fire,
O still voice of calm."

We prayed Amy Carmichel's prayer:

I pray thee hush the hurrying, eager longing,
I pray thee soothe the pangs of keen desire,
See in my quiet places wishes thronging,
Forbid them, Lord, purge, though it be with fire.

And work in me to will and do thy pleasure,
Let all within me, peaceful, reconciled,
Tarry content my Wellbeloved's leisure,
At last, at last, even as a weaned child.

And one evening as we talked about what was at stake, we agreed that it was really too big for us to handle. God's call to the mission field was strong. Our love was, if anything, stronger. There seemed to be only one thing to do—put the whole thing back into the hands that made us and let him do what he wanted with it. If he didn't want us together, that would be the end of it. If he did, "No good thing will he withhold from them that walk uprightly." We had to believe that promise. Some of you know the end of the story. We waited five years. Then God gave us to each other for two years. Does this make the will of God even more scary?

Let me go on to the third lesson. You've forgotten the first two by now—the shepherd and his dog reminded me that the glory of God's will for us means, first, absolute trust, it means, second, the will to do his will, and it means—believe me, young men and women—it means joy. It can't mean anything less from the kind of God we've been talking about. He made us for glory and for joy. Does he ask us to offer up our wills to him so that he can destroy us? Does he take the desire of our hearts and grind it to a powder?

Be careful of your answer. Sometimes it seems that he does just that. The rams were flung helplessly into the sheep dip by the shepherd they had trusted. God led the people of Israel to a place called Marah where the water was bitter. Jesus was led into the wilderness to be tempted by the Devil. The disciples were led into a storm. John the Baptist, the faithful servant, at the whim of a silly dancing girl, and her evil scheming mother, had his head chopped off. Nearly twenty-one years ago five Ameri-

can missionaries attempted to take the gospel to a group of
jungle indians who had never heard of Christ. On the eve of
their departure they sang together that great hymn by Edith
Cherry from the Inter-Varsity hymnal,
  We rest on Thee, our Shield and our Defender,
  We go not forth alone against the foe.
  Strong in Thy strength, safe in Thy keeping tender
  We rest on Thee and in Thy name we go."
One of the men was Jim Elliot, my husband by that time, who
had written in his diary when he was a junior in college, "Father, take my life, yea, my blood if Thou wilt. . . . It is not mine
to save, have it Lord." Months of preparation went into the effort to reach the Auca Indians of Ecuador. The men prayed,
planned, worked, dropped gifts from an airplane and believed
at last that God was clearly showing them that it was time to
go. They went, and Jim's prayer was answered far more literally
than he envisioned. They were all speared to death.

Five men who had put their trust in a God who represents
himself as our shield and our defender were speared. They were
speared to death in the course of their obedience. Now what
does that do to your faith? Does it demolish it? A faith that dis-
integrates is a faith that has not rested in God himself. You've
been believing in something less than ultimate, some neat program of how things are supposed to work, some happiness-all-
the-time variety of religion. You have not recognized God as
sovereign in the world and in your life. You've forgotten that
we're told to give up all right to ourselves, lose our lives for his
sake, present our bodies as a living sacrifice. The word is sacrifice. In one of Jim's love letters—and his were different from
most I can assure you—he reminded me that if we are the sheep
of his pasture we are headed for the altar.

But that isn't the end of the story! To get back to the question
as to whether God grinds our hopes to powder. The will of God
is love. And the love of God is not a sentiment in the divine
mind; it's a purpose for the world. It's a sovereign and eternal
purpose for every individual life.

"Everything that happens," says Romans 8:28, "fits into a
pattern for good." There is an overall pattern. When my second

husband was a boy he always visualized God sitting up there surveying a huge chart. He got this idea from the Lord's Prayer: "Our Father 'Chart' in Heaven."

Last year my daughter and I had tea with Corrie ten Boom. As she talked about her own experience and that of my husband Jim, she took out a piece of embroidery which she held up with the back to us—just a jumble of threads that made no sense at all. She repeated for us this poem:

My life is but a weaving betwixt my God and me,

I do not choose the colors, he worketh steadily.

Oftimes He weaveth sorrow, and I in foolish pride,

Forget He sees the upper and I the underside.

She then turned the piece over and we saw that it was a gold crown on a purple background.

The dog doesn't understand the pattern, only obedience. As George McDonald put it, "Obedience is but the other side of the Creative will."

I have two more things to say about why the will of God means joy. It is redemptive and it transforms. It is redemptive for it means joy not only for me as an individual but for the rest of the world as well. Did it ever occur to you that by your being obedient to God you are participating with Christ in his death, and then in his redemptive work? Paul told us this. He said, "We have shared his death . . . we are weapons of good for his own purposes." Your response helps all the rest of us. Obey God, I say to you, for his sake, first of all. Obey him for your own sake. If you lose your life, remember he promised you'd find it. But obey him too, for my sake, for the sake of all of us.

There is a spiritual principle here, the same one that went into operation when Jesus went to the cross. It is the principle of the corn of wheat. The offering up of ourselves, our bodies, our wills, our plans, our deepest heart's desire to God is the laying down of our lives for the life of the world. This is the mystery of sacrifice. There is no calculating where it will end. This is what I mean by transformation. The bitter water, the wilderness, the storm, the cross are changed to sweetness, peace and life out of death. God wills to transform all loss into gain, all shadow into radiance. I know he wants to give you beauty for ashes.

He's given me the oil of joy for mourning, the garment of praise for the spirit of heaviness.

Jim Elliot and his four companions believed that the world passes away and the lust thereof, but he that doeth the will of God abideth forever. Another translation says they are "part of the Permanent and cannot die." In Jim's own words, by giving up what he couldn't keep, he gained what he couldn't lose. Jesus had to go down into death, the corn of wheat had to be buried and abide alone in order to bring forth life.

I told you what I was going to say. I've said it. The glory of God's will means trust, it means the will to do his will, and it means joy. Can you lose? Certainly you can. Go ahead and lose your life—that's how you find it! What's your life for? "My life," Jesus said, "for the life of the world."

ten
Responding to God's Glory

Billy Graham

Let us begin by reading from the first chapter of John's Gospel. We have heard it repeated so often at Urbana 76 that you probably have already memorized it. Two verses (vv. 14-16) are especially valuable for us now: "And the Word became flesh and dwelt among us, full of grace and truth; we have beheld his glory, glory as of the only Son from the Father. (John bore witness to him, and cried, 'This was he of whom I said, "He who comes after me ranks before me, for he was before me." ')" I would like to share three things from this passage. First, this passage tells us that God has declared his glory; second, it reminds us that we have beheld his glory; and third, it challenges us to declare his glory to the nations.

God Has Declared His Glory

"And the Word was made flesh." The people of Israel in the wilderness had a tabernacle or a tent where they worshiped God.

There the glory of God was actually seen. Located in the Holy
of Holies was a glorious light. It was called the Shekinah, and
it was the symbol of God's presence with his people. It reminded
them that God was not simply the invention of their imagination, but was the sovereign, glorious and holy God of the universe. And they were his people.

Now we've just celebrated Christmas, full of stories of the
angels and the shepherds and Bethlehem and the star and all the
rest of it. In the New Testament the glory of God was no longer
seen in the Shekinah light. The glory of God was summed up in
the Incarnation, the coming of the Son of God to earth.

"The Word was made flesh and dwelt among us." The phrase
literally means "the word was made flesh and tabernacled
among us." In a far greater sense than in the Old Testament, God
has taken up residence with man by being born in a stable
among animals.

But who is this Jesus who was born in the most humble circumstances imaginable? We've heard a great deal about him
today and yesterday and the day before. Who is this Christ that
demands that I give him everything I've got in 1976? Who is this
Christ that demands that I follow him into 1977 and give him
the rest of my life? Who is this Christ that demands that I surrender my will totally and completely to him? Who is this Christ
that demands that I come to him and ask him to help me choose
a life's mate? Who is this Christ that asks me to change my life-
style? Who is this Christ that makes such tremendous demands
upon me as he did upon Elisabeth Leitch or upon Helen Roseveare or upon others we've heard here?

Is he just a revolutionary hero? Was he an evil man, a glut-
tonous man, a winebibber? Did he have a devil as they said he
did? As we stand on the threshold of 1977, I cannot help but
ask the question that Saul asked on the road to Damascus two
thousand years ago: Who art thou Lord? Who are you? Who is
this Christ? Who is this Jesus? Plays, books, operas, movies are
being made about Jesus. A blasphemous movie is being attempted in England at the moment.

First we know that he was a man. The Word became flesh.
The Logos became flesh. And we know that he was hungry and

thirsty and tired. We know that he had friends, we know that he felt lonely at times and we know that he wept at the tomb of a loved one.

The Scripture says that in every respect he was tempted like as we are. Yes, he was tempted. Tempted like you. Do you mean to tell me that he was ... ? Yes, he was. Just like you.

But he was more than a man. He claimed to be the unique Son of God. He said, "Before Abraham was, I am" (Jn. 8:58). "I Am that I Am" (as in Ex. 3:14). And when he said that, he set himself apart from every other man who ever lived. No other one ever said that.

Paul writing to the Colossians declared, "He is the image of the invisible God, the first-born of all creation; for in him all things were created.... He is before all things, and in him all things hold together" (Col. 1:15-17). There is a stickum that holds this podium together. Throughout the whole world what is it that holds the world together? The Lord Jesus Christ. If he ever took his hand off of it, it would explode. Incredible. Impossible. But that is what the Scripture teaches: He is the image of that invisible God who created those one billion galaxies and in every galaxy a billion stars and planets and beyond that infinity. And we have no instruments that can go there. And back of it all is this Jesus Christ.

He was fully man, but he was fully God. That's the mystery and the wonder of the Incarnation. "The Word became flesh and dwelt among us." He made the blind to see and the deaf to hear and the dumb to speak. He fed the hungry and he had compassion upon us. He has the hairs of our head numbered and he sees the sparrow fall. That's the Jesus that's making the demands upon us tonight.

There was only one man who ever lived a sinless life, the Lord Jesus Christ. And on the cross he, the righteous, holy Son of God, took upon himself your sins and my sins. "These words spake Jesus and lifted up his eyes to heaven and said, 'Father, the hour has come; glorify thy Son that the Son may glorify thee' " (Jn. 17:1). He was talking about Calvary, about the cross. This was not the hour of his ascension, but of his descension into hell.

The only mention of the atonement in the Apostles' Creed is

the phrase "descended into hell." That is the reason we leave it in. He took your hell, your judgment, your sin. He was made to be sin for us. And we usually do not think of that as glorification. He said, "Father, the hour has come; glorify thy Son that the Son may glorify thee."

He looked upon the crucifixion and the descent into hell and the bearing of your sin as glorification. The greatest glory of God this universe has ever seen is our Lord Jesus Christ on that cross, dying for you and for me, that by some incredible way God took your sins and your guilt and mine and laid them on Jesus Christ, and he became the cosmic scapegoat. He bore our sins, and now God can say to you, "Your sins are forgiven."

God remains just and at the same time the justifier. You become justified in the sight of God as though you had never committed a single sin. Think of going to bed tonight and knowing that every sin is totally, completely, forever forgiven—just as though you'd never committed it. It goes beyond forgiveness.

The world is in desperate shape today—international tension, domestic problems. I heard a man say today that this may be the last Urbana. We don't know, but we do know that the world is rushing at this moment toward some sort of climax. I personally think that climax is what Festo Kivengere is going to talk about—the glorious coming again of our Lord Jesus Christ, this time as King of kings and Lord of lords, to take charge of this planet. There is no possible solution to all of our problems apart from him.

It's very interesting to study the life of our Lord. He only had three years of public ministry and he did not heal everybody. He had the power to do it, but he didn't do it. He didn't feed everybody. He had the power to take those stones and turn them into bread and feed the world, but he didn't do it. And when he came to the end of his life, do you know what he said? "Father, I have finished the work that thou hast given me to do" (Jn. 17:4). He didn't go thrashing around madly.

I heard Dr. Donald Barnhouse once say from this Urbana platform, "If I only had three years to serve God, I'd spend two of them in preparation and one out preaching." We must recognize there is a sovereign God. Nothing takes him by surprise. He has not lost control. Satan is not going to win. The forces of evil were defeated at the cross. The devil is a defeated bug.

I was in the Senate dining room some time ago and Senator Magnuson called me over to his table and said, "Billy, we're having an argument over optimism and pessimism. Which are you, an optimist or a pessimist?" I said, "Well, I'm an optimist." He said, "Why are you an optimist?" I said, "I've read the last page of the Bible and God's going to win."

They took him down from the cross, buried him and said we're finished with him. But God spoke. And on the third day he rose again from the dead. And tonight we are not talking about a dead Christ. We are talking about a living Christ who sits tonight at the right hand of God the Father interceding for you and me. Our great High Priest is coming again to be crowned King of kings. It sends cold chills up and down me just to think of it.

You know right now *The Omen* has probably made as much money as almost any picture that has ever been made, and so at this moment every major studio in Hollywood is making from two to five motion pictures on the devil and the antichrist. We are going to be flooded in the next two or three years with scores, maybe hundreds, of pictures about the devil and the antichrist. They don't know that they're depicting a defeated foe. He was defeated at the cross, defeated at the resurrection and will be absolutely shorn of all power at the coming again of the Lord Jesus Christ.

"The Word became flesh and dwelt among us": This is our message to a dark and lost world. People without the good news of the gospel—what do they do? We see in the art world, in philosophy, the trouble, the despair, the nihilism, the emptiness of it all. What a contrast to the hope and the joy and the thrill and the glory that we have found in Christ!

I feel like that man they used to tell about—it was a true story —who was on his way to the gallows. The chaplain in England was trying to talk to him about Christ. Suddenly the man turned to the preacher and said, "If I believed what you're saying, I'd crawl across England on broken glass to tell every person in England about this Jesus." That's exactly what God may be calling some of us to do. This is the message we proclaim to a broken, despairing, bleeding world.

In Africa we were reminded time after time by speakers that this is a bleeding continent. America too is a bleeding country, but not in the same way as Africa. Psychological pressures and the pressures of modern life are driving eleven million of us to become alcoholics, others to become drug addicts, driving us into escapisms of every kind, just to get away from it all.

We Have Beheld His Glory

We have seen the glory of God. "We have beheld his glory, the glory of the only Son from the Father." Many people of Jesus' day did not see the true glory. The masses saw him as a provider of bread and a possible revolutionary. But when he refused to conform to their selfish expectations and began to talk about a cross and self-denial, they said, "Oh, no. I thought you were going to set up a kingdom, Lord, right here on earth. You were going to be the king and we were going to be the cabinet. I didn't know that you were talking about denying self and going to a cross." The cross was the symbol of execution, the same as taking your electric chair, taking your gallows, with you. "Lord, we didn't count on that. Count us out." That eliminated about ninety per cent of his crowd.

The religious leaders saw him as a potential threat to their position and demanded his death. Judas did not see the glory of God in Christ. Pilate didn't see it. The impenitent thief on the cross didn't see it. And many people today do not see it.

We live in an age of massive, all-pervasive, crushing secularism in America. We see the television set, the one-eyed monster. We bow to it and have our devotions in front of it; we have our family time in front of it; it becomes our god. And we're guilty of a new idolatry. A new medium has come into our homes, bringing education, yes, but bringing other things as well. A man who has talked to a top television producer told me today, "We are going to have to change the presentation on television because we are not able to depict violence as violent as what is happening in the country. We're going to have to get worse in order to be real."

God has never promised that Christians would be anything other than a minority swimming against the stream of this world's materialistic thinking. Jesus warned about a narrow gate. If you want to follow Christ, you've got to go through a narrow gate: "The gate is narrow and the way is hard, that leads to [eternal] life, and those who find it are few." Those who really mean business are few.

It's tough to be a Christian. In the last few years we have gotten into an idea of easy discipleship and easy following Christ. We were told it's like taking a drug and getting on a high and Jesus would keep you on this great big high all the time.

My life hasn't been that way. I have had a lot of lows in my life. And we heard about some of them today, and we heard about some of them last night. Just read the Psalms. I read five psalms every day, and that takes me through the book of Psalms every month. The psalmist was up and down, up and down, up and down, up and down—so discouraged that at times he was like a pelican in the desert, like an owl in the wilderness.

Have you ever felt that way? You look at other people and they are full of joy and happiness and seem to be on top of it all the time. I heard Dr. Norman Vincent Peale say one time, "Boy, when I wake up in the morning I jump out of bed and I say 'Praise the Lord, another day.' " I don't always do that. Sometimes I do, especially at Urbana. But sometimes I grumble my way out of bed.

We Must Declare God's Glory

Because God has declared his glory and because we have beheld his glory, we must declare his glory to the nations of the world. We must respond. Look at John the Baptist: John bore witness to him (Jn. 1:15). John knew the glory of God and he couldn't keep silent. Many people mocked him, but he did all he could to point others to the coming Christ.

How do we respond to the glory of Christ? Three words I want you to remember: *conviction, commitment, conduct.* That's how we respond.

First, conviction. There is a conviction that Jesus Christ is who he claims to be, the Son of the living God. Do you believe that?

Second, a Christian will have committed himself to Christ as Lord and Savior, totally without reserve, holding nothing back. That's why the Scripture places so much emphasis on the heart and not just the outward actions. This involves the total man—the emotion, the intellect, the will, all of it. Are you willing to be his man and his woman regardless of what he might want to do with you in the future? How are you going to answer that tonight?

Third, there must be conduct. We must live what we believe. Jesus said that we would be known by our fruit. And the greatest fruit is love. Do we really love this world for whom Christ died? Are we acting upon that love? "By love serve one another," as John Stott reminded us today. He didn't come to be served, he came to serve. We have to become servants.

You say, "Billy, we see pictures of you with this person and that person, playing golf with Arnold Palmer. (I did that just once.) And how can you serve anybody? You speak to big crowds of people, but you don't see the little crowds."

You don't see the empty seats; we don't show that on TV. And you don't see us at home. We are servants.

We are to serve one another in love. If these things are a part of your life and you are seriously considering God's will for your life, you cannot help but take with complete seriousness his call to serve. His commission is inescapable: "Go therefore and make disciples of all nations" (Mt. 28:19). "You shall be my witnesses in Jerusalem and in all Judea and Samaria and to the end of the earth" (Acts 1:8).

We cannot escape his Great Commission text. That is what drove that group forty years ago. They read those Great Commission texts. They took them seriously and literally, and they went out. Tonight we are here because some people dreamed a dream that the world could be evangelized in this century. The Student Volunteer Movement believed that, and they almost turned the world upside down.

We may have a short time or a long time; no one knows. But we had better work while it is day because the night comes when no man can work. You know, Jesus somehow tied the proclamation of the gospel to the nations with his coming again, because he said, "This gospel of the kingdom will be preached throughout the whole world, as a testimony to all nations; and then will the end come" (Mt. 24:14).

Today, we have the technology to carry the gospel to the whole world, and no iron curtain or bamboo curtain or any other kind of curtain can keep the gospel out. But I warn you, as you have already been reminded so graphically and dramatically, it is going to cost you. Jesus said, "If any man would come after me, let him deny himself and take up his cross and follow me" (Mt. 16:24). Christ asks you to renounce your plans.

One of the first things Christ said to me when I came to him was "You've got to give that girl friend up." I was in love. It was puppy love, but it was real to the puppy, let me tell you. She wouldn't make the commitment. So I went over to her house to tell her—it took me four hours. And I cried all the way home. I was doing it just for Christ's sake.

I am sure people laugh and smile at that little thing, but that was the first step. God was testing me. He was changing my plans to conform to his plans. Are you willing to do that? Are you willing to make his goals your top priority? He asks that your ambitions and your motives be his. Are you willing to do that?

We might as well forget missions until first of all you have surrendered totally to the Lordship of Jesus Christ. In the New Testament the word Christian is used only three times—in Acts 11:26, 26:28 and 1 Peter 4:16. On each of those occasions the idea of suffering and persecution was in the background. Christ does not promise that all is going to be easy and trouble free for us.

We have been living in a very abnormal situation in America in the last few years. By and large, the totally committed Christians throughout history have been suffering people, persecuted people. If you really commit yourself to do the will of God, whether it be missionary or some other type of service in this country, what are they going to do to you?

Consider what Christ told his disciples in Matthew 10. First, he said that they will deliver you up. This type of opposition is seen throughout the book of Acts. Second, he said, they will scourge you. Christ himself was scourged. Many of his followers were scourged.

In modern America there can be psychological scourging at a university campus when they see you going to a prayer or fellowship group or when they see you with a Bible. Some of the kids in the dormitories will scourge you with their tongue and their smart remarks. But let me tell you, they will watch you and respect you because they are searching for what you've got and they are waiting to see if it's real in your life. The people who put up the biggest fights against Christ are people who really want you to convince them by the way you live and the way you talk and act. They want to see if somebody really believes it, if somebody really lives it. That is why people like Moon and the other messiahs get a big following. That is the reason a little 16-year-old guru could get a crowd around him.

We have the message that can change the world. And we ought not to be ashamed of it. Jesus is worthy of our sacrifice. He is worthy of our utmost for his highest. The wonder of it is that we are not alone.

God has promised us full resources in the battle. Christians would retreat, deny and fall under the attacks of the world, the flesh and the devil if they did not have resources superior to the forces of evil. The Scripture says, "he who is in you is greater than he who is in the world" (1 Jn. 4:4).

What are these resources? First, God will give you the gift of speech. Did you ever think about that? The how and the what of our defense will come supernaturally. The Scripture says, "What you are to say will be given you in that hour" (Mt. 10:19). This happened to Peter and Stephen and Paul, and it's happened to you and to me on occasion.

Second is the indwelling of the Holy Spirit. The early Christians were equipped by the Holy Spirit in their defense.

Third is perseverance. The endurance unto the end does not mean that our salvation is contingent upon our own endurance. Our salvation does not rest upon our works or our money. It depends upon the grace of God. The Scripture says, by God's power they are "guarded through faith for a salvation ready to be revealed in the last time" (1 Pet. 1:5). God is at work in you, both to will and to work for his good pleasure" (Phil. 2:13). And while God holds us as far as our salvation is concerned, we are to persevere and be faithful in the midst of suffering and persecution. How long? To the end.

Fourth—this one will surprise you—there come times when we are to flee, to run. Did you ever think about that? There are times when we must flee for protection. Moses did it. Jacob did it. David did it. Paul did it. He was let down in a basket to get away. And many others throughout the Scripture. The Lord doesn't ask us to risk our lives unnecessarily when we face evil men bent on our destruction. Luther's flight to Wartburg was justified by the sinister threats on his life.

Once I was invited by the Communist Party to address them in Maracaibo. I don't know how it happened; I think they made a mistake. But anyway I got up and I started talking about Christ. And while I was talking about Christ, truckloads of soldiers unloaded outside. I could see them through the windows. Suddenly, while I was speaking, bullets began to pour into the place. Now I noticed that they were hitting high up. I don't think they were meant to hit anybody. But I didn't quite know that. The fellow that introduced me pulled his coat back and there were two pearl-handled pistols, and he pulled them out. He said, "Follow me." When Newsweek magazine reported it, they said that Billy Graham got under a table and was praying the Lord's prayer. I was not praying the Lord's prayer. I was running.

I remember too one night in Soho in London. An Anglican chaplain had talked me into coming down there and preaching at midnight. When I arrived there were lights and television cameras and a giant crowd and police everywhere. I knew that I shouldn't be there, but I got up on top of a car and started to preach with a bull horn about the Lord Jesus Christ.

Then I saw out of the corner of my eye something beginning to happen. I saw a girl, handed from one man to the other, being pushed toward me. And I knew what was coming. The Holy Spirit spoke to me. I found out later she was paid to do it. She was on drugs and she was going to come and unzip and stand there nude with me and pictures were going to be taken. Well, I saw that, and I said, "See you at Earl's Court tomorrow night.

God bless you." And I jumped in the middle of the policemen. There come times to flee. And that was one of them.

Fifth is the coming of the Son of Man. This is the ultimate hope, our ultimate escape from the sufferings of this world. The sufferings we endure here will be only for a moment, nothing compared to the glory that is to be ours there. As André Crouch has written, "It won't be long." And as Bill Gaither says, "Because he lives, I can face tomorrow."

The Christian must always remember that he must expect the same treatment from a hostile world as his Lord received. But he also knows that Christ is with him and God's full resources are available no matter where he is. Do you know the lordship of Christ? Are you ready for all of this? Are you willing to pay the price?

In 1519 Cortez outfitted some ships in Cuba to explore the coast of Mexico. After the landing, he ordered his men to have all the yardage and the sails and the metal fittings and cannon removed from the ship. Then he ordered the ships to be burned so there could be no retreat. It was a terrible sight to those men standing on a hostile beach and a mysterious continent to their backs watching their ships burn. They would probably never see home again.

Are you willing to burn those ships in your life and say, "No retreat. It's all for Jesus. My life, my plans, my goals, my ambitions, my heart, my mind is his. Lord, I'll go where you want me to go and I'll be what you want me to be, whether it's to be a nurse or a doctor or a social worker or a preacher or a Bible translator."

During the Korean War, the North Koreans moved into a peaceful farm village in South Korea. Sometime before this a faithful missionary had brought the gospel of Christ to this village. Those who were converted were soon witnessing to friends and it wasn't long before most of the people in the village had turned to Christ.

One day the North Korean soldiers made all the people of this particular village gather in the village church. They told them that they would have to renounce their faith in Christ or face certain death. The soldiers jerked a picture of Christ off the wall, threw it on the floor and ordered every person in the church to go by and spit on the picture. The first one to walk by was a deacon. Looking shamefacedly and frightened, he spit on the picture of Jesus. So too the second man, the third, the fourth.

The fifth was a teenage girl. She walked by. She stood there looking for a minute, tears streaming down her cheeks. She picked up the picture, took her skirt and wiped off the spittle. Then she said, "Shoot me. I'm ready to die for Jesus."

A soldier raised his gun but he couldn't fire it. They ordered everybody out of the church except the four men who had spit on the picture. The people heard four shots. The men that did the spitting were killed because the soldiers said, "If you will renounce Christ so easily, you will renounce our ideology just as easily." Are you ready to take your stand tonight with that teenage girl in Korea?

God right now on every continent is quietly preparing his heroes. When they are needed, they will appear and the world will wonder where they came from. They are being prepared tonight. And God says, "I searched for a man who would make up the hedge, fill the gap, and I didn't find one." Tonight I believe throughout the world on every continent in the last few years God is preparing tens of thousands of students everywhere —and I include the Soviet Union and China as well. His heroes are being prepared. And one day they may have to pay a price. The glory is theirs and tomorrow belongs to them. Tomorrow belongs to us. Jesus is asking you to join him, be his, to surrender.

eleven
The Triumph of God's Glory

Festo Kivengere

"The Triumph of God's Glory": What a tremendous topic! It makes me feel terribly inadequate because its dimensions can make angels clap, let alone men. It is the very heart of your salvation and mine.

The triumph of God's glory climaxes in the Second Coming of the Lord Jesus. But we cannot get excited by beginning there. We have to begin where the triumph begins; we have to begin where we are. It is the triumph of God's glory in daily experiences in America today, in Africa today, all over the world, which leads to the tremendous excitement of his coming to take the kingdom.

By the way, I was really scared when I considered this topic. I had butterflies all over. I remembered when I was preaching in the Solomon Islands years back, a young man was affected by this glory of Jesus Christ, his holiness. One hot afternoon in the church on the Island of Maleta, without any invitation this young man of about 20 got up excited and came forward. This is what he said: "Brothers, me love Jesus too much. Me try speak about him other people. Me shake shake too much. But me now know him better; me shake shake no more." What beautiful pidgin English!

I now want to tell you here at Urbana that when I saw this glorious triumph of the glory of God, me shake shake too much. But as I look at you and as I catch the heartbeat of your experience and your eyes and the glow, me shake shake no more.

We will begin with Jesus' words in John 17:22 and 24. The Lord Jesus is about to go to Calvary, to the grave, the resurrection and ascension. These are his words when he is about to leave the flesh: "And the glory which thou hast given me [he is speaking to his Father for you and for me] I have given to them."

Who? You mean these believers at Urbana, Lord Jesus? Do you mean that girl and that boy and that young man and that African preacher trying to express himself? Or do you mean angels? Who are these whom you have given that glory which your Father actually gave you?

Those who believe in my name: "Father, I desire that they also whom thou hast given me, may be with me where I am." The purpose is that they may "behold my glory" which you have given me because you loved me before the universe came into being, before time began. So here is Jesus praying to his Father, almost lifting ordinary, simple people into an unspeakable, incredible kind of experience.

What is this exciting glory? Do we understand what it is all about? Is it an angelic experience? Is it in the third heaven which St. Paul experienced? Do we then sit so far below that we sit back in despair? What is this glory?

According to the Bible, glory means the radiant character of the living God. And that radiant character is love, for John says, "God is love." It couldn't be simpler or more profound. It is so profound that it will pick a believer from wickedness and usher him into glory.

So when Jesus says, "I have given you the glory," he means, "I have given you God's radiant character, the image which you lost when you fell into sin. It is a complete restoration of what you lost through Adam, but it is more than that. For Adam only received the image. Jesus is the very image of God."

God's Glory in the Old Testament

What was that radiant character in the Old Testament? According to the Old Testament, this radiant character of God, the shining excellence of his moral standard, always hit men and women who had been given the privilege of growing nearer to God. God said to Abraham, "Look here, Abraham, I am the almighty God. You walk with me." And Abraham trembled and shook and hid his face. That was the image of the glory. It was shining, attractive, but always formidable, unapproachable, a consuming fire.

Fire is very attractive, isn't it? Its light attracts. Its heat attracts, particularly at Urbana in December! (I come from Africa where we don't have below zero weather.) Fire attracts, too, because of its strength. But at the same time, it refuses to be played with. Get too near, become too familiar, and you are burned. That was the holiness of God according to the Old Testament. Abraham, the old man, the friend of God, trembled.

Moses was a man looking after sheep on the mountains. He had lost his vision of recovering the humanity, the human dignity, of God's people. They had become slaves almost forever, 400 years. Utter despair. And Moses had given up. He was alone looking after the sheep. Then God came in the burning bush. The bush in the desert became aglow with strange fire which never consumed. Moses turned to look and a voice said, "I am the God of Abraham, God of your Fathers. Take off your sandals. They are too dirty to approach." Moses hid his face, trembling with fear, because God's glory, although attractive, was still formidable, unapproachable, threatening.

Later Moses led God's people, and they fell into sin and worshiped idols. There was a catastrophic experience in the camp. Moses went into prayer, hungry and thirsty, that there might be renewal and revival. He cried, "God, please show me your glory, your radiant character for these brokenhearted people." And God said, "All right, I'll give you permission. I am willing. I'm the God of grace. I am going to declare my name to you so that you may know me as I am. But Moses be careful. You can see only my back parts. My face you can't see, for no man shall see me and live." So men saw glimpses of God's glory in the Old Testament.

Take Isaiah, the wonderful prophet, full of zeal and fire, proclaiming the corruption of his country. One day he went into the temple and the glory of the Lord filled the temple. The angel proclaimed, "Holy, holy, holy." And Isaiah trembled. His sinfulness was exposed. He discovered that he was not what he should be. And he cried, "Woe to me for I am undone. For my eyes have seen the glory of the King." Then a live coal from the fire, from the altar, touched the lips of the prophet; the lips which had pronounced judgement were made sensitive. The heart which was hard, judgemental, melted with compassion. And the prophet was set on fire.

"Whom shall I send?" God said.

"Here I am, send me," Isaiah responded, liberated to move.

God's glory was actually threatening. God was a consuming fire and no one could dare approach with familiarity. Men and women were attracted into that radiance, but they were afraid. The bridge had not yet been revealed.

And yet that formidable glory which made people tremble was a liberating glory. Triumphant. Abraham lost the weaknesses of age. He began to praise God. He began to count the stars. He became a man with a tremendous, exciting vision. The glory liberated him. Isaiah spoke the evangel, the good gospel, and in Isaiah 53 he discovered the Messiah. Moses was the same. Eighty years old, he led his people from slavery into freedom. We could go on. But let us move on to the fullness of the glory.

God's Glory in Jesus Christ

Now the glory has come. Jesus Christ, the One whom God particularly sent as the visible image of the invisible God has come, and now people no longer need be frightened by the glory. They will, of course, have a sense of awe; they will be reverent. But they will no longer be threatened, because the distance has been removed. The glory of God in Jesus Christ triumphed over distance. No distance is left.

Where does Jesus begin? Pre-existent time. Jesus says, "God, I have a greater desire. I want those who believe to be with me where I am. I want them to see the glory which you gave me because you loved me before the foundations of the world." God overcomes the distance between eternity and time. The Eternal One has moved to where men in their finite experience are.

Then came his birth. John says, "The eternal word became a human being." What a coming! Can you imagine God becoming a baby so that he may pick us in our weakness? Can you imagine God who is almighty putting such limitations around himself? Condescending to be like you and me, in utter weakness? In so doing he removed the barriers between the perfect God and broken humanity. He picked up the pieces, put them together, and out of those broken pieces of men and women in Africa, in America, in Asia, he created a new man.

Because he became a human being, no longer can we accept any external differences. He gives my Africanness a completely new value. You simply cannot play with me any longer. No longer can anyone sit down on another unless he wants to sit down on the Lord Jesus. Poor and rich, those categories are irrelevant. Man in his humanness is given an intrinsic value, precious because Jesus came.

Apart from Jesus, human beings are broken up, fragmented, bits and pieces, hating one another because they hate themselves. No wonder. They are men and women with a civil war inside, and therefore battles and wars go on all the time—broken homes, tribal wars, racial tensions, conflicts everywhere, until he comes.

Jesus became one of us in order to make us what we should have been. Glory triumphed over our disintegration. That is a remarkable experience. What a beautiful, wonderful Savior! What an almighty God!

Then Jesus grew. Not only was he born, not only did he become one with us, but he became with us. Emmanuel: God present with us. Isn't that tremendous? Have you discovered the glory of God triumphing over loneliness in a university dormitory? Those miserable rooms. You sit alone and you become so lonely that in the end you speak to pictures on the wall. And they don't answer back. Jesus comes—Emmanuel, God with us —and accepts our infirmity. He puts my weaknesses on his humanity, and he becomes my brother. And the experience is that I'm no longer lonely and strained because he is there. I can whisper into his ear. This is salvation triumphing over loneliness, isolation, meaninglessness. No wonder people who have no Jesus are disciples of nihilism. What can they do? Life is empty. It is lonely. It is a forest of strange experiences.

Jesus has come and he is with you. You weep with him. And you laugh with him and he understands your pain. You fail the exam and he holds your hand and says, "Take it easy. I'll be with you next time as I was in the last experience." Because he is there, nasty experiences which break men and women become redeemable. He overcomes those because he is present with us.

The glory of God picked up all the things which broke humanity, all the nasty experiences of our sinful nature, all the accumulated guilt, and he put them on the shoulders of the God-man, steadily, firmly, like a rock. Oh what a life! Jesus moved into Gethsemane. He moved to the hill of Calvary. He lifted that wood on which he was going to hang and he died.

Now you may say, Is there any glory in death? Indeed, that is the essence of the glory of the New Testament. There is no Christianity if you remove the essence of the death of Christ. I am not lifting up death but love. The death of Christ is the climax of love. God is love. His radiant character is his love, and love shines more when it is willing to die for the beloved. There is nothing beyond that love. This love so loved broken humanity that it took all the judgement and all the burden and went on the cross and hanged there like a criminal.

Now some men say, "Well, what is beautiful about that? What is glorious about a criminal hanging?" He was not a criminal. He accepted human criminality. He lifted it on his mighty shoulders, upon his heart, and he triumphed over it for you and me.

What happened on the cross? Two criminals were hanging —between them, in the center, the glorious Jesus. His face was marred beyond recognition. One man on one side became angry and bitter and rejected Jesus in utter despair. The other fellow?

His eyes were opened, his heart was melted when he heard, "Father, forgive them for they don't know what they're doing." Immediately the man who was dying as a criminal was ushered into the presence of glory, liberated from despair, removed from darkness.

You know what he did? He sang the Hallelujah Chorus. He said, "King, when you come back in your kingdom, please remember me." What a discovery! You mean this man who is hanging on the cross is a king? The cross is his throne? The thorns the crown? A shattered body a kingly body? A naked body covered with robes of a king? What a discovery!

Glory overcame the despair of this criminal, the triumphing glory of God. Love overcame the barrier, and the man was ushered into the presence, and the king said, "Don't you wait for long. Today you and I are going to share paradise." That was victory, the greatest victory, the climax of the glory. And it is because of this we talk about his return with glory.

If this were removed, his return would be a terrible threat. Humanity would be consumed like dry grass in a fire. But because of what happened on the cross of Calvary, you can lift your eyes and your head and you look in the face of the eternal King and say, "King, when you come back, remember." And he does remember, for you have been engraved in his palms, says the prophet Isaiah. Your names are all there, no matter how weak you are. You are there.

And then the procession moves on; the triumph takes you in. Jesus was buried and he was resurrected. Jesus' death overcame the sin and the guilt and the separation. Jesus' resurrection conquered death, the last enemy of mankind. It makes men tremble. It makes clever men weep. It is a point of despair, a point of departure, the dead end of the road. And Jesus entered the realm of death, three days in battle. Down there in grip with the terrible enemy of mankind he killed death, disarmed it, opened the grave. He changed the whole nature of death so that for the Christian, death is not a departure but an arrival, no longer a dead end but the beginning, no longer darkness but the dawn of a new life.

Jesus came out of the grave triumphant, glorious. Do you

think he came alone? Not at all. He came with you. The head came out and the limbs came with him. You are there.

I know you despise yourself. You say, "Bishop, look, I am not that type." I know you are not that type. God knows you are not that type. But Jesus too knows very well, for he died for that type. He died for your kind of you, with all the things which make you tremble, with all your limitations, with all your reported failures. Jesus took you when he arose from the dead because, when he died, he gripped you. Now you are in him as a limb, part of the body. The head climbs from the grave, and you are there.

Paul says we have been given the same seating position in Christ Jesus. We are seated in heavenly places with him. You are there. He goes and you go with him. He enters into the presence triumphantly, and he sits on the right hand of God, the triumphant King of glory.

What happens then? You look in and you see your brother and your brother is the King of glory. He still has a glorified body, but it is your body. So your body is given that capacity. We don't know exactly what it's going to be like, but we know that when he appears we shall be like him, because we shall see him as he is. What a beautiful experience!

And then having been seated on the right hand of power, the glory reaches a climax. And the King says, "I am going to prepare a place for you. There are many places in my Father's house. And because I am going to prepare a place, I am coming back to take you to myself so that where I am you may be there" (Jn. 14:2-3).

The Return of the King

So the return of the King, Jesus Christ, what is the value of that? The coming back of Jesus means the completion of redemption. What you know in part you will know perfectly when he comes back. Now you love in part; then you will love in full. Now you praise and get tired after four days at Urbana; then you will praise eternally without feeling tired.

Oh, my dear friends, it will be a wonderful experience. When Jesus comes, all the hang-ups will be hung up. Nothing will be left. You will be gazing on the eternal King, and you will be lost in wonder and praise when he comes to complete our redemption. The decay will be taken care of, and we shall be given bodies not of corruption but of incorruption, a glorified body given as a gift by the risen King.

I am not talking about escapism. There is no escapism in Christianity. I am not talking about mere triumphalism, the triumphant kind of experience where you look up, look up, look up, when all the time you are looking down. I am talking about the reality of the King of glory who established the foundation upon which you can base your triumph.

You are all in the procession when the King returns to give men the completeness of the image of God, that glory. St. Paul says, "Now we see darkly in a glass. We can't see quite clearly. There are hindrances. When he, Jesus, comes, we shall see as we are seen." We shall see each other as we are seen. We shall see *him* as we are seen. We shall discover the depths of mercy and grace, and then the King comes back to take his kingdom.

He died and rose again in order that he might come back and take the universe. Not only men and women who are born again, but the whole of humanity and the whole of the universe, will be under his feet and you will come with him.

Do you know what that does to history? History for a Christian is no longer a monotonous cycle, like a Buddhist's prayer, which makes you feel tired and get bored. There is no boredom. History has a direction, and the direction is toward Jesus Christ. He is the goal of history because in him all things are completed. It is he who fills all things with himself, everywhere, when he comes back.

The King comes and you come with him. He takes his throne and men and women bow before him in praise; others because they rejected him, are inevitably condemned. It is sad but it is biblical and true. If you reject him, the Prince of glory, then you become the child of dust. Because he is the glorious One, to reject him is to reject the glory. Because he is a Prince of light, to reject him is to reject light. Because he is the completeness of what God means, if you reject him, he becomes a stranger, life becomes just a disappointing experience, a dead end. When he comes, then you believers are caught up with him.

The Courage to Declare God's Glory

What does that do to you as a believer, to discover that he has overcome death, that he has overcome sin, that he has overcome estrangement, that history has got a destiny, that the glory now is dawning and the end is no longer threatening but it is attractive and beckoning? It means that you can stand up from Urbana and can face this redeemable world. It is still redeemable, you know. It is not yet given up. And as the world looks at you, thousands of you—my heart beats fast—can the world despair when disciples, 17,000 of them, are in tune with the King of glory? Tune up, will you? Get your attention focused on Jesus Christ and his coming back to take his kingdom.

What is your part in that kingdom? Some of you are trembling. This triumphant glory makes weak men strong, makes cowards into warriors. I know that happened.

Let me tell the story of three children in Uganda, the oldest 15 and the youngest 11, who died as martyrs in 1885. They stood before an angry non-Christian king and said, "We love to serve you, your majesty, but we can't serve if it offends our King, Jesus." The king was furious. Mobs of non-Christians came; the boys were put in prison and were given a chance to recant, but they refused because the Spirit of Christ, the Spirit of glory had completely captivated them. Those three boys were led from the palace of the king, hands tied behind them, into the place of execution like the Master. Four miles away the little boys were tied and put in dry grass and burned. And they died singing, "Oh that I had wings like angels, I would have flown and been with Jesus." They died and the church began.

Do you call that human courage? Who prepared them? Their fathers were not Christian. When the glory penetrates your heart, that is the best preparation. Then suffering becomes a privilege. Then you can stand not on your poor little feet but on the eternal rock, Jesus Christ. When a Christian has found that glory, he becomes invincible.

May God bless you as you open your heart not to defeat, not to stumblings, not to endless discussion, but to the eternal completion of grace which is glory. Let the Spirit of God usher you into the presence. Then the wars of fear and the clouds of hesitation give room to the brilliant person of Jesus Christ. Then you can put your hand in the hand of the triumphant King. Then you can look Satan in the face and say, "Demon and all your spirits, I want to challenge you and tell you I am no longer a victim under your dominion. I belong to the King of glory. He is triumphant. No ideology can stop him. No weakness can stop him. He comes to reign and will reign eternally."

Get ready. Get tuned up. Get refocused. And then get on the move. It is exciting to be alive in America today. Move on. If you've got a word to say, say it. If you have a banner to wave, wave it, even if you are trembling. And if you've got a sin to repent, it can be forgiven too.

When we meet there at his feet, what will happen? You think we are going to ask for the words? The words are in him because all the fullness of God is in Christ and you are complete in him. That is the glory of the triumph of God. That is what the world desperately needs. That is the glorious hope: Christ in you, the hope of glory. As you leave Urbana, go singing.

As you use all the tools that God has given you, the Spirit will remind you of one important thing: He, the King of glory, is triumphant, over America, over communist Russia, over China, over Africa, with its conflicting elements, over the church with its wickedness. I am in the procession. Are you there?

If you are in the procession and you see where you are in Christ and what is coming, then you cannot speak about things which hold you back. The chain has fallen down and the heart is liberated in order that it may now tune up to sing the glory of the King. So we are going to end the conference, not with applause, but with reverence. Our hearts indeed are going to burst into song and hallelujahs but to the King not to the speaker.

If I wanted you to clap I would say, "All of you stand up and applaud the returning King of glory." Then I would say, "Yes, that is it. More, more. Clap till you get your wings put on."

Jesus is coming back. Signs are here. But we are not just enjoying prophetism. We are enjoying Jesus' words: "Father, I desire that they also, whom thou hast given me, may be with me where I am, to behold my glory which thou hast given me in thy love for me before the foundation of the world." The glory that God has given Jesus he has given us. Have you received it? He gave, you receive. And because you receive, you become responsible.

Many Christians make a mistake. They say, "I have received wonderful experiences. The King is coming back." And they forget that that is a burning fire. You can't sit on Christian experience. It burns. If you think you are going to take all the truths from Urbana and make them into pillows to sleep on, you've made a mistake. This is fire. You put your little head on it. It burns you and then you move on.

Christianity is like that. It is a fire, dynamic. Let us move. Come to Africa. Go to India. Go to China. As ambassadors of the glorious King. Speak without hesitation because he is coming to take the kingdom. He is triumphant. Hell knows it. Satan knows it. The demons know about it. They cannot do anything about it. Take heart.

Let us in reverence bow to worship the King of glory. If you are one of those who say, "I don't know," will you tell the Spirit, "Please, Holy Spirit, make it clear that I may see the glory of my King." If you have things which have stood in the way, clouds which have hindered you from seeing the glorious King, will you repent? Will you ask for forgiveness? The King has the precious blood. The Holy Spirit will show you so that you may go on to be a liberated Christian, waiting for the King.

part III

The Glory of God among His People

twelve
Declare His Glory on the Campus

Lemuel Tucker

As I began to think about "declaring God's glory on the college campus," I was a little confused. I had always thought of missionary work as something that happens "over there." It has been hard for me to think that the "over there" of missionary work could happen in the "over here" of the student center and the locker room. But the gospel is to be spread, our Lord tells us, beginning from Jerusalem and then to Judea, and then Samaria, and then to the uttermost part of the world. And it seems that there—the uttermost part, the outer corners of the world—is where the gospel should be preached. That's a much better place than, say, the student center or the locker room. But, as Christ tells us, the task of declaring his glory must begin in our own Jerusalem. You will receive the training for your missionary trip to France as you take your first missionary trip to the fraternity house.

As I thought about declaring God's glory on the campus, I

thought of it in three ways: the task, the scope and the agenda.

The Task of Declaring God's Glory

First of all, what is the task of declaring God's glory? We must begin by understanding the biblical "why" of Christian witness. We ought to be a model of the heavenly community, a paradigm of paradise. We witness because of what God has brought about, because of what he has accomplished for us in Jesus Christ, because this Word came and dwelt among us. We witness because Jesus, who is the perfection of the eternal community, took on human flesh and became himself our solution by paying the price for our pollution.

John the Baptist proclaimed the wrath to come because he knew both the sinfulness of man and the holiness of God. He knew that if the heavenly Messiah were to come, it could only mean one thing for the earth—a total baptism in fire. And the Messiah did come. Yet not to judge by law, but to save by grace. This is what John 3:16 is really all about. God's giving love for the unlovably lost.

This is the "grace and truth" in Jesus the Messiah that Christians possess. It is ours. We really possess that grace. We know that Christ has ransomed us from the judgment which we have so rightly earned. It is this grace that has given us our place as new creatures in the new creation. We have been called out of the old order, this perverse and passing world, and now have been commanded to live according to our call—as sons of the new creation, as sons of the living God.

We must learn to think of our lives in terms of our *status* before God and not our *performance* for God. When Christ says, "You will be my disciples," he doesn't mean you *will* become my disciples if you do this or that. He means that, because he has made us a part of his family, we *have already* become his disciples. We are his witnesses. That is what makes us witnesses. We belong to him.

Just think of your own family situation. You are a representative of your earthly family whether you feel like it or not, or even whether you are good at it or not. You can't use the excuse that you don't know enough, and you can't use the excuse that you haven't been in it long enough. You have your family last name.

In the same way we are witnesses, no matter how faithfully or unfaithfully, because we are disciples. You are not his witnesses because of the number of souls that you may have saved or won to the Lord, or because you have been a Christian for ten years or for two days. You are his witness because you belong to God. You and I have God's last name; we are in Christ. So the task of declaring God's glory is first of all the recognition of who we are in God's glory.

I think you can see how defining our task primarily as being rather than doing changes the way we think about success in our ministry. When we speak of successful campus witness, we must think first of success in God's eyes. Success is not how much you are able to score big in different projects of campus witness. Too often we judge success by the world's standard. We have too much of an eye toward the quantity and not the quality: Success is not evaluating how well we did in our campus witness in terms of how many people came to a program.

Another way we judge success by the world's standards is with regard to suffering. We live in a society which praises success and looks at suffering as a sign of defeat. We Christians, unfortunately, think too much like this as well. Computerized and programmed models for successful ministry rarely, if ever, include failure and suffering. As our brother Samuel Kamaleson told us last night, God may desire to use your suffering for great witness to his glory and to his sovereignty. And as Paul Little has said, there are times when there is a real struggle in committing ourselves to the will of God; dying to ourselves is never pleasant. It is excruciatingly painful. But there is a paradox: In that pain comes the deepest satisfaction this side of heaven.

The Scope of the Task

If the task of our campus ministry is to be his disciples, what then is the scope of that task? To whom do we declare our witness? What kind of people are there? What kind of place is the American or Canadian campus today? It's a place of the new-found gurus, Hare Krishna, Baha'i, Sun Moon, the palm readers, the TM Maharishis. It's a place of great psychic search, what

Time magazine has called the new narcissism. People are turning inward. No longer is there *student* power, like that of the 60s; the search is now for *inside* power. A men's clothing commercial with an in-vogue male voice shows how self-centered this shift can be. It goes like this: "You know, five years ago my biggest problem was how to save the world—peace, love, the whole bit. Today, my biggest problem is how to do the hustle and the bump without splitting my pants." Or as another student has more seriously put it, "We do not care . . . about the movement of history any more. We want to experience inside power." The search for inside power has led many students on the campus to suicide—the number-one killer of college students. Despite the unprecedented wealth and education of our student generation, students are perplexed, disconcerted and looking for a way out. Or should I say looking for a way in?

Most students introduce themselves today by their first name. I think they are saying, "Know me as me; no more impersonal structures, please." They are asking for the personal touch. They want to be known as persons.

When we look at the classroom and its curriculum, we are told that it is completely neutral, completely objective and completely scientific. Yet when we look behind these liberal arts labels, we see the presuppositions of Freud, Hegel and Darwin. The consequence of this devalued and compartmentalized system is that students have to do the integrating of all the brute facts themselves. So students then become the center of their whole education. They become the arbiter of the facts, the captain of their academic souls.

False views, the use of lies arrived at by such a self-integration process, invariably become self-centered. In fact, all self-made ideologies can be nothing more than idolatries. As one student said, "I just take courses . . . nothing seems to fit." The modern university is the world's greatest fact machine. It can give you the beads but nothing to string them on. It can tell you how to build a hospital or bomb but not which of the two is more important. It can teach you how to psychoanalyze people and their problems but not whether being homosexual is wrong. It can tell you how to legislate to save the eagle, but not whether saving an unborn baby from abortion is a still higher moral premium.

So Jesus, in Matthew 28, commands us to be his witnesses among the nations. Now when he used the word *nations* he was not referring exclusively to a geopolitical entity the way we might define a nation in the twentieth century. Instead, it seems more precise to say that the word *ethnos*, from which comes our English word *ethnic*, means all the distinct groups of non-Christians, all the homogenous social units of unbelief. These are the nations. And therefore the college community, the college campus, the island community that it is, is very much to be viewed as a nation. That means, as well, all the nations within the campus community, all the distinct groups of non-Christians, all the sororities, all the fraternities, all the athletic teams, the blacks, the social cliques, the whites, the international students, the down-and-outs, the up-and-ins—all the nations. That's the commandment. And so this is the scope of our mission on the campus. This is the nation to which we go.

There is, I would propose, little use in thinking about the call of God to Asia or Latin America if we are not thinking about the call of God to the College of William and Mary or the University of Iowa. As someone has put it, bloom where you are planted. Bloom where you are planted. For we will not be ready to witness everywhere until we are ready to witness somewhere.

Agenda for Declaring God's Glory

Having examined our task of declaring God's glory on the campus and having looked at the scope of that task, let us begin to formulate finally our agenda for declaring God's glory. Our agenda may be thought of in two parts: What is our commitment to worship, and, flowing from this, what is our commitment to witness?

The worship agenda includes corporate worship in the church, fellowship and individual worship. We must be committed to the enterprise of spiritual holiness. Holiness is the characteristic the Bible ascribes to the people of God. As Peter says, "But you are a chosen race, a royal priesthood, a holy nation, God's own people, that you may declare the wonderful deeds of him who called you out of darkness into his marvelous light" (1 Pet. 2:9). The unity we have with Christ is to be expressed in the community we have with other Christians.

It is here, my brothers and sisters, that I find the church characterized by less than total holiness. Peter says we are to be the people of a holy nation. And yet as I see the church today, it seems to be divided into at least the two peoples of the black and white nations. As I see how Christ prayed for the unity of the church, I often weep that the unity we have to offer the world is reflected in the telling question, Why is Sunday morning at 11:00 a.m. the most segregated hour in America? I love the church, and yet it is within the church that I have encountered so much racism. We cannot believe that unity without community is the expression of a biblical Christianity.

How does this fit into our agenda for campus ministry? It fits because it is on the college campus that blacks and whites will mix. We will have to deal with this question of spiritual commitment to holiness. For good insights into the whole problem of racism in America, I recommend *The Autobiography of Malcolm X*. But as you deal with this problem, remember that the values and prerogatives of spiritual holiness must come first.

Commitment to spiritual holiness also means we all should be involved in the local body of the church. I would encourage you all in addition to the normal life of the church, to avail yourself of relationships with older members of the body. I reflect on the several such relationships that I had in college with the local pastor, families in the congregation and Christian faculty. It was a very sustaining and profitable time in my life, so please don't cut yourself off from the church.

Being committed to other Christians on the college campus is also part of our personal commitment. Simon and Garfunkel were wrong when they sang, "I am a rock, I am an island." God has called you to a community, and as such you can function effectively only through the body. In principle, you should always be experiencing this body life in your home congregation. It is from such a base that you should be applying similar principles in your Inter-Varsity groups.

One last area for our agenda of worship is the development of our personal habits of worship, meditation and memorization. We must begin to develop an effective prayer life of confessing, thanking, petitioning and praising. This is what we need for our personal worship. But building an effective prayer life is not an overnight thing. For some juicy insights on prayer, read Walter Trobisch's pamphlet *Martin Luther's Quiet Time*. It may be helpful for you to keep a prayer list with a pen in hand when you pray. Be honest with your prayers, for what will severely hinder worship through prayer is not what you don't know about prayer but that you won't be honest about what you do know. And don't get caught up in half-truths by telling everyone you are praying for them. Learn to be obedient within the daily routine of prayer.

The agenda for worship becomes the agenda for witness when our walk with the Lord is directed toward other people. Just as the essence of worship is being with the Lord, so the essence of witness is being with men. Jesus is our model for this, for he is the incarnate One and he was God's personal touch to us. As others see him in you personally, it will mean much more than all the perfectly planned and engineered programs you can put together.

But this may call for a lot of sacrifice. The personal touch is not a matter of investing time, money and energy into programs in order to fatten people up for the slaughter which you then accomplish by browbeating them into the kingdom. It is not a slaughter engineered by man that we are after, but rather the harvest planned by a personal God. People do not respond to know-it-alls, but rather to those who come as did their Savior, clothed in humility and with love for the lost.

Personal attention will always be creative. We must be creative in our witness within the bounds of God's Word. Don't let your creativity get trapped and ensnared in the ordinary. Francis Schaeffer says it is the Christian whose imagination should go beyond the stars. This is true for us who are on the college campus declaring God's glory.

Let me give you some quick examples. Say at freshman orientation you put up a sign to the weary, weak and heavy laden:

Free lemonade. But then in addition pass out announcements about when you have your meetings or your small group Bible studies. Also, a booktable several times a year in strategic places will serve as channels of the personal touch. Ask the campus librarian as well as the student center director about having several HIS subscriptions delivered throughout the year.

Another key area of personal contact is the dormitory. Here you have a chance to spend a lot of time—even if you do go to all your classes. For example, one thing you might try is to go around at the beginning of the year and get to know everybody in your section. Get their names and tell them where you're living so they can stop by. Take the initiative. You will need to do that. Or start an evangelistic Bible study. I once put up a sign that was like a math equation: "The Bible ÷ life = (a) ∅ (the null set), (b) ∞ infinity, (c) none of the above, (d) interested in a rap over coffee & donut?" Then I added the time and my room number.

The classroom is also a key area for witness. Here particularly we need the armor of God. For each of your courses ask, What has God said about this subject? This insight might cause you to redefine your usual approach to the standard curriculum labels. For plenty of information about this, read the HIS Guide to Life on Campus (IVP).

Conclusion

Let me reiterate the task, the scope and the agenda for declaring God's glory. The task is to be his disciples, the scope includes all nations and the agenda calls for worship and for creative and biblical witness. This is to be our task, whether for another three and one-half years on campus, or just for another semester.

Declaring God's glory is not a matter of just being in college. It's not a matter of a curriculum for college. God is preparing us for life; for us the campus is our training ground, our field of labor, our turf for testimony. It is there we have been planted and there we must bloom. It is there we must make known the name of our Lord. But first we must make sure that his declaration meets with holy accord in our own lives.

If we do not know the greatness of our king, how can we share this greatness with others? How can we tell of his glory? Because we have seen his greatness and his mercy extended down from the cross, because we have been stirred to a radical discipleship by this vision, we are filled with praise and the determination to do his will. When we learn to be amazed at the work of God's grace in our lives, when we are set to wonder by this love, then we will be able to declare God's glory on campus.

thirteen
Declare His Glory in the Community

John Perkins

I am thankful that there are thousands of us here this day gathered around our Lord Jesus Christ, coming to ask how he might live through us to declare his glory. This gives me a great sense of the beauty and the power of God's universal body of Christ. It is true, God walks among his worldwide church today. Our gathering together is just a token of the harvest already reaped across the earth, just a glimpse of how broad our body really is.

But I am most thankful because I believe for the first time in recent history, more of us than ever before are a part of, and are struggling to be, the body of Jesus Christ in our local setting. In our hometowns, on our campuses, in cities, rural areas, in the ghettos and in the suburbs, I believe more of us than ever before are wrestling with what it means to be feet and hands, arms and legs, eyes and ears to each other in the same location under the headship of Christ. For that reason I believe that we are in a unique position to proclaim God's glory in the community.

Called to Mississippi

In 1957 God first began to call me to declare his glory in the community. That was the year of my conversion. We were living in California at the time, and after coming to know Jesus Christ as my Lord and Savior, I became involved in child evangelism, learning how to use flannelgraphs and Bible stories to reach young people with the good news. A group of us formed what we called the Fisherman's Gospel Crusade and began to witness to people in our city of Monrovia.

Then I began a ministry that was to change the direction of my life. A group of Christian businessmen asked me to go with them to speak to the young men in the juvenile detention camps that are located up in the San Bernadino Mountains of Southern California. I went and quickly began to see why my white Christian brothers had asked me to come. Here in the camps a high percentage of the prisoners were black. And as I shared Sunday after Sunday, and as kids came forward with tears in their eyes, the Lord began to burden me with the call to return to my home in Mississippi.

You see, I wasn't born in California. I was born in Mississippi. But I had left Mississippi in the forties after my brother was killed by our local policeman in a "racial incident." I came to California, never having heard the central truth of the gospel: that Jesus Christ can come and live out his life through a person and save that person. I had never heard that while I served in the army; it wasn't until 1957 that that message was made clear to me.

In the prison camps, the Lord showed me kids just like myself, many from the South. I could hear Mississippi and Alabama in their voices, and I knew that they were just like me, coming up without much education and without any understanding of or exposure to the gospel. They had come to the big city to make it, just like me. Somehow I had made it. They hadn't. They had stolen a car or something and ended up in jail.

What God was showing me was that maybe the problems among black people in the cities and in the ghettos were really the unsolved problems of the South. I thought of my people back home and the churches and the religion. One night I was preaching on the Apostle Paul. I was over in Romans 10 where Paul is talking about the great zeal and yet the great ignorance of his people, the Jews. I could say with Paul about my black people, "My heart's desire and prayer to God for them is that they may be saved." God was telling me that, "I bear them witness that they have a zeal for God, but it is not enlightened." This may be hard for you to believe, but the black community still represents one of the largest untouched mission fields in the world today. Only in the last few years has there been anybody committed to a comprehensive strategy of reaching blacks with the gospel.

So in 1960 God called us to move our family back home to Mississippi. This was a tough calling. We were comfortable in California. Both my wife and I had good jobs. We had just bought a big twelve-room house. We had five children. When we arrived home, the people were almost embarrassed to see us. They knew we were making it in California, but they also knew that their community had nothing to offer us. I had to work picking cotton the first couple years. It seemed like we had moved backwards.

But the Lord had work for us to do. He began to open doors to teach his Word in Sunday-school classes, in vacation Bible schools, and finally in the public schools—this was before integration. With our Child Evangelism materials we were eventually speaking to about 10,000 children each month.

It was a tough calling because of the conditions in and around Mendenhall—the physical, educational, economic poverty that trapped so many of our people. At this time the civil rights movement was just coming to Mississippi.

Before the movement, God taught us that real evangelism takes you to the point of standing face to face with the real needs of a person and then reaching out to help meet those needs. The need was so great for mothers to work that they would often pull older children out of school to watch the younger ones at home. We knew these kids needed to be in school; so we began a little day-care center and served lunch to the kids, some of whom were suffering from malnutrition. Soon we were asked to become the center for Headstart for Simpson County.

Working with the children opened the door to us and allowed

us to see how sin worked itself out in the community, to see how economic self-interest coupled with racism could institutionalize itself and create a cycle of poverty and despair that trapped the lives of black people. There was spiritual poverty in our black community to be sure, but that spiritual poverty was heightened by the "niggerizing" dependence of the system; crises in housing, health care, nutrition, education, skills and economics were crippling the hearts and minds of black people. To proclaim God's glory in the community was to ask ourselves as Christians, How can we break this cycle of poverty? How can the love of God reach into the whole of a person's life and heal them?

I wish I could take you there. One lady, who became our friend, was Mrs. Hester Evans. Everyone calls her Miss Hester.

From the outside, Miss Hester's place looks like an abandoned shack. Walls slant at different angles. Children come out as you drive up and stand on the broken steps. The roof is tattered and off center. The whole structure, much of it rotten, leans so much that when you walk close it seems like you're losing your balance.

Inside there are four rooms. Every one but the kitchen has beds in it. Gaps in the walls and around the fireplace are stuffed with pieces of tin and rags. There are mice and rats. In the kitchen is a broken refrigerator, a sack of meal and a jar of jelly. About three months ago, behind a torn plastic curtain, one of Miss Hester's daughters lay whimpering on a bed. Corrine had gotten sick and was now so malnourished that it looked like her skin had been sewn tightly over her bones. She looked like a living skeleton. At 36 she appeared older than her mother, although she was once a beautiful black woman. She had bedsores.

One thing that is striking about Miss Hester is her spirit. Even having to raise kids and now grandkids in that condition, she never seems broken. In her living room hangs a plaque that reads, "Believe on the Lord Jesus Christ and You Shall Be Saved."

But can I be happy with that? What does the Spirit of God in me say when I see such frighteningly limited salvation? What about Corrine? She is dead now. But what about the other children playing outside? And what about the children like them in shacks and housing projects all over this country? We desperately need to declare God's glory in the community.

After a few years Voice of Calvary (that is what we called our little mission) became involved in voter registration and integration, and started small business co-ops in the country. We marched, we prayed, we carried signs, we organized people to help themselves, we sang freedom songs. All of this was a result of asking the questions, How can God break the cycle of poverty through us? How can we declare his glory in our community?

As a result, some of us were thrown in jail. Some of us were beaten almost to death by Mississippi highway patrolmen and Rankin County sheriffs. And some of us have been called by God to go through that deep forgiveness process so that we wouldn't be crippled by the hatred that began to infect us too. God had to show us that he wanted us to love instead, to be reconciled and to be a reconciling force in the community. Since then God has called us to tutor, to educate adults, to build a health center and thrift store—to be the body of Christ in Mendenhall.

The New Testament Meaning of the Church

I believe that through the last sixteen years' struggle, God is doing something unique. I see it happening at Voice of Calvary, but also in a much larger movement in the church at large. I see God giving back to us an understanding of the local church as a means to declare his glory in the community.

I believe that God is doing something in our lifetime and especially in the last ten years: He is giving us the New Testament meaning of the church. It seems like the Holy Spirit is restoring to us an understanding of our local church as the replacement of Christ's body in a specific neighborhood, drawing people that they might be "nourished and knit together through its joints and ligaments," growing with a "growth that is from God" (Col. 2:19).

I believe two things are happening as the worldwide church rediscovers the importance of the local body, and as we commit ourselves to being that replacement of Christ's physical body in our neighborhood and to carrying on the ministry he began 2,000 years ago.

First, I believe that God is showing us, again and afresh, the meaning of the gospel. This is something that has been lost in the evangelical church. The real meaning of the gospel has been clouded up with doctrine.

You see, if you were to ask almost any evangelical in this country, "What is the gospel?" chances are he would say to you, "The gospel is the death, burial and resurrection of Jesus Christ." And if he is really fundamental, he will add the Second Coming. Now I believe in all these things. These are the propositional facts of the gospel. But the gospel is more than that. *The gospel is the manifestation of God's love in history*, the making visible, the incarnation of God's love in time. The death of Jesus Christ on the cross was God's way of showing to the world in one act, at one point in history, that he loved us.

That act of love happened once and will never be repeated (Heb. 7:27). Yet God desires his love to be made manifest over time, throughout history. And this is precisely where the body of Christ comes in. As we rediscover the local body, we also rediscover that God wants to duplicate throughout all history that once-in-history manifestation of his love. He wants to put the same life and love of Jesus Christ in a church so that people can again see Christ.

This is what Jesus meant when he said that we are to let our light so shine before men that they may see our good works and glorify the Father. This is what he meant when he said, "I am the light of the world" (Jn. 8:12), and then turned to his disciples, and said, "You are the light of the world" (Mt. 5:14). He gives us the same high calling that he himself fulfilled when he lived and taught here on this planet. And God never gives us a call to be or do something without also providing the necessary resources.

This is the second thing that happens when we rediscover the importance of the local body of Christ: *God is restoring to the local body the gifts of the Spirit.* People in local bodies are dealing with each other in ways that hold them accountable to the high calling of replacing Jesus Christ's body on earth and we are beginning to recognize the gifts of the Spirit within them. This can happen only as we rediscover the local body. Because the gifts of the Spirit are not mentioned in terms of glorifying individuals—but usually in the context of the body (Rom. 12; 1 Cor. 12). These gifts are not given to glorify persons individually, but to help build the body, to cause it to function as a powerful whole (Eph. 4:11-12).

The exciting aspect of this is that as people become the body in a local community, we can see Jesus walking the earth again, able to carry on the same ministries he carried on when he was here before as one person. Just as he said, "The Father who dwells in me does his works" (Jn. 14:10), so now the Son who dwells in us, Christ's new body, does his works.

This is one aspect of the promise: "Greater works than these will [you] do because I go to the Father" (Jn. 14:12). Jesus meant that his body would be embodied in local fellowships, scattered throughout the world and that the multiplied effect of these bodies would produce a greater quantity of healing works. The body is God's strategy for declaring and multiplying his glory in communities throughout the earth.

I know it is relevant to the poor community because I have seen and lived among the damaged in our communities. I have seen the poverty and the racism and the ignorance of the gospel. And I know that it is only when God's glory is declared in local communities of need that real healing takes place. Scripture says that we are made "God's own people" in the community so that we can "declare the wonderful deeds of him who called [us] out of darkness into his marvelous light" (1 Pet. 2:9). The promise is that God has chosen the church to make known his "manifold wisdom" not only to people but even "to the principalities and powers in the heavenly places" (Eph. 3:10). God wants to make known all the facets of his wisdom—his justice, his compassion, his economics, his holiness, his authority and power. All of these will be made known as we become his body in the local community. This is what he has done in Mendenhall. And this vision has special relevance in any community where the needs are out of control.

This then is my hope. I see it in the growing number of sharing

Christian communities, the small group movement, the church renewal movement and the heightened evangelical concern for social action. There is a *good basis for hope that God's glory may be declared in the community in new and exciting ways* through his body.

But there is also for me an element of despair. It is the despair I feel when I see the victims in our communities—victims of hunger and disease and oppression, victims of injustice and poor housing and welfare. It is the despair I feel when I see that the dynamic life of the body of Christ has not been brought to bear on the needs of poor people in this country. It is the despair I feel when I see that many times the church is a part of a system that afflicts the afflicted and comforts the comfortable rather than the other way around.

When I am told about the growing hunger problem in the world, I am not startled because I have seen the hungry grow retarded and the retarded live a life of misery and poverty right here in Mississippi.

When I am told that the world with its growing number of victims can at any time explode into a state where possibly all of us will be victims, I am not startled because I have seen too many people already victimized by a cycle of poverty which has manufactured brokenness since as long as I can remember.

When I am told that the fabric of life and culture as we know it is threatening to unravel, I am not startled because I have seen the tattered remnants of many lives already destroyed by the faceless power of oppression.

But what does startle me is the church and the lack of response by the people whom God has called to be the salt and the light in a decaying world of deepening darkness.

It startles me when I look out and see that the only people equipped with the faith, the love and the values necessary to redirect life in our society and heal some of its many victims are without a comprehensive strategy. It startles me to see Christians more intent on getting their piece of the action than on saving people from being destroyed by poor health, poverty and an ignorance of the plan of salvation.

We need to make visible God's glory in the community!

The Three "Rs" of the Quiet Revolution

There is, I believe, one key issue which, if addressed by the church today, would give power to the body movements. This issue is this: How do we as Christians relate our lives and our resources to the real needs of the human victims around us? This issue could take the form of some specific questions too. Like, How do we as Christians get rid of and replace the welfare system in America? Or, How do we as Christians preach the gospel in the Mississippi Delta? Or, How do we as Christians begin to minister in the hill district of Pittsburgh?

How can we be part of declaring the glory of God in a local community?

To me, our legitimacy and our identity as the church of Jesus Christ is wrapped up in our response to the victims in our world. As Howard Snyder puts it in *The Problem of Wineskins*, IVP, p. 51, "The gospel to the poor and the concept of the church are inseparably linked. Failure to minister to the poor testifies to more than unfulfilled responsibility; it witnesses to a distorted view of the church."

But how can we minister to the poor? Evangelism could be part of the answer. Social action could be part of the answer. But we lack a comprehensive strategy for community development because we have cheapened our evangelism to a smile and "Jesus saves." We have cheapened our social action to charity and welfare. We have for the most part lost the sense of power that comes from being the body of Christ, a quiet revolution in the local community. The longer we worked in the community of Mendenhall, the more God unfolded to us the real power of the body of Christ, that it is not just a group; it is Christians coming together, cemented by their central unifying commitment to Christ. We began to see how we could be transformed into corporate power confronting corporate sin, corporately giving our lives in the direction of evangelism or justice, or economic development or relieving human need, and make a difference.

We must relearn what it means to be a body and what it means to continue Christ's ministry of preaching the gospel to the whole person. And I believe there is a strategy to do this. We have seen three principles work that seem to be at the heart of how a local body of Christians can affect their neighborhood. We call them the three "Rs" of the quiet revolution: *relocation, reconciliation* and *redistribution.*

First, we must relocate the body of Christ among the poor and in the area of need. I am not talking about a group of people renting a store-front through which to provide services to the community. I am talking about some of us people voluntarily and decisively relocating ourselves and our families for worship and for living within the poor community itself.

A living involvement with people turns poor people from statistics into friends. I am not willing to lay down my life for a statistic. But I am more willing to lay down my life for my friends. Again, Jesus is our model.

Relocating myself makes me accountable to the real needs of the people because they become my needs. A person ministering from within the neighborhood or community will know and be able to start with the real needs of those around them, instead of forcing on the people what he or she has assumed their needs are. After meeting some real needs, you can begin to communicate through these "felt needs" to the deeper spiritual needs of a person. When this happens, we are beginning to transport God's glory into the community.

Second, we must reconcile ourselves across racial and cultural barriers. I hear people today talking about the black church and the white church. I do it too; it's reality. But it's not in Scripture. We should not settle for the reality our culture presents us with.

You see, the whole idea of the love of God was to draw people together in one body—all reconciled to God. That is supposed to be the glory of the church! And we are not manifesting the love of God today that can really move across racial and cultural barriers. What we do is to go on preaching the gospel within the limits of our own culture and tradition.

The test of the gospel in the early days of the church was how it was going to affect Samaria. I believe the gospel is being tested again today. To reconcile people across racial lines—black people, white people, all people—is to stage a showdown between the power of God and the depth of the damage in us as human beings. It has been my experience that the power of God wins, and the result is a dynamic witness for Jesus Christ that brings others to confront him in their lives.

When reconciliation is taking place across cultural lines—between blacks and whites, between rich and poor, between indigenous and those who are new in the community—we are beginning to make visible God's glory in the community.

The final result is redistribution. *We must as Christians seek justice by coming up with means of redistributing our goods and wealth to those in need.* How well a ministry can begin the process of creating a stable economic base in the community determines the motivation of that ministry. Is it simple "charity"? Or is it really trying to develop people and to allow them to begin to determine their own destinies? It also determines the long-range effectiveness of a body's commitment to a neighborhood. For without an economic base there will never be a launching pad for ministry. A ministry in the poor community which has no plans to create economic support systems in the community is no better than the federal government's programs which last only as long as outside funds are budgeted. The long-term goal must be to develop a sense of self-determination and responsibility within the neighborhood itself.

We need a change created by Jesus Christ in our institutional behavior equal to the change that can occur in the life of an individual. And as we commit ourselves to just redistribution in terms of creating a new economics in broken communities, we can see how Jesus, through us, offers himself. The body of Christ becomes the corporate model through which we can live out creative alternatives that can break the cycles of wealth and poverty which oppress people.

When this happens, we are spreading God's glory in the community.

God's Spiritual Saboteurs

What if the churches began to relocate, reconcile and redistribute? What real effect could it have in the battle to make the gospel known in America?

I believe the welfare system in this country is one of the most wasteful and destructive institutions created in recent history. The dependence and exploitation it encourages, its inability to deal with the real, deep-seated needs of people is pitiful. In a speech he gave in the fall of 1973, however, Senator Mark Hatfield reveals some startling statistics that reveal the depth of the impact the church could have on our country and in meeting needs:

If each church and synagogue [in the U.S.] were to take over the responsibility of caring for 10 people over the age of 65 who are presently living below the poverty level, there would not be any need for the present welfare programs focused on the aged.

If each church and synagogue took over the responsibility of 18 families—a total of 72 adults and children—who are eligible for welfare today, there would not be any need for the existing Federal or State welfare programs to families.

If each church or synagogue cared for less than one child each, the present day care programs supported by Federal and State funds would be totally unnecessary.

Our religious institutions would be a natural focus of community activity directed toward meeting the human needs of one's fellow citizens. (The Congressional Record, Vol. 119, No. 145, Monday, October 1, 1973, Senate)

As churches become those centers for community activity, what a witness, what a testament, what an opportunity they would have among not only the needy (and primarily un-churched) people, but also to the world at large! It could be the most effective environment for evangelism ever seen on the face of the earth since the time the Master himself walked among the people healing, teaching and calling them to himself.

The civil rights movement died right on the brink of some real human development. We must have some people who will keep moving after the movement dies, after it is no longer popular to do what is right.

If we as Christians can see the issues of our day, the poverty, the racism, war and injustice, if we can use the skills and resources that we get from our training at school or on the job, and if we can really be open to being equipped by the Spirit of God, then we will be used. We must lie on our beds at night and wrestle with how we can individually and collectively bring our faith from talk to power, how we can bring our faith and works to bear on the real issues of human need.

I believe that right now we are facing a most difficult time in history.

Do we see the battleline? Can black Christians and other oppressed Christians get beyond survival and blame? Can white Christians get beyond charity and the American dream? Can conviction be stronger than culture? Can we, like Zacchaeus, take responsibility for our past because of the presence of Jesus Christ in our lives now? Can we pay our dues and move creatively ahead to claim the joy of overcoming past injustice? Can we move beyond racism? Can we seek partnerships with brothers and sisters of another race? Can we seek the confrontations that will come from these partnerships and let Christ provide each other with the culture shock necessary to deeply question our values, to seriously investigate our lifestyles, our motives, to become skeptical about any good which we find in our deepest selves? Can we be called to a brotherhood like the one described in Proverbs where "Iron sharpens iron and one man sharpens another"?

My hope is in Jesus Christ and the new life he can bring to a community. The people I work with and I have put our resources behind an alternative. But we cannot do it alone. We must create models that will break the cycle of poverty wherever it is. We must create models of health that will show the Kingdom to the world. Not only do we need cooperative development and local leadership, but we also need supply lines, transports, shock troops and guerrillas working as bodies in the system organizing resources and skills around areas of need. We need God's people to declare a salvation that saves people from their personal sins and goes on to make them whole and healthy.

The world is tiring, but we are to endure. The world will become frustrated, but we can have hope. The world will withdraw, but we must strike. We are God's guerrilla fighters, his spiritual saboteurs. We must now go in bodies to battle in our communities armed with the evangelism, social action, economic development and the burning desire for justice through which Jesus can continue to declare his glory in our communities.

fourteen
Qualifications for Declaring His Glory

Isabelo Magalit

I speak this morning as a representative of the third world—the traditional recipients of missionaries. Much of what I have to say I address also to myself, and to all who are concerned for the spread of the gospel throughout the world. For the principles involved in making the good news known, particularly across boundaries of land and culture are the same for Christians everywhere. Nevertheless, the outworking and application of these principles can be made sharper and do greater good if particularly addressed to you as North American Christians by a Filipino believer.

The Philippines was a U.S. colony for nearly 50 years (1898-1946) and was ruled by Spain before that for more than 350 years (1521-1898). Both the Roman Catholic and Protestant versions of the Christian religion reached our people as part of our colonial experience.

What kind of people are required to declare God's glory

among the nations? What qualifications are needed for missionary service in the world today?

It is possible to put together a long and thorough list of missionary qualifications. Within the time we have this morning,
however, I would like to suggest three essentials.

Knowledge of the Holy God

The first qualification for declaring God's glory among the nations is *a growing personal knowledge of the holy God*

We need to know our God. Unless we know him, how can we
declare his glory? Such knowledge must be profoundly theological, requiring our clearest thinking as we respond to God's revealed truth. We must beware of all forms of subjective short
cuts. One of the most helpful books in recent years has been
James Packer's *Knowing God*. But such knowledge is more than
rational for it is personal knowledge of another person. You and
I worship a personal God.

How can we grow in our personal knowledge of God? The
answer is very basic but it is something that we never outgrow.
We must spend time alone with God, regularly, in prayer and in
Bible study. There is no substitute for the daily quiet time. Daily
we need to go to the Word of God because our knowledge of him
is only by revelation and that revelation has been given in his
Word. Daily we need to draw aside and worship and praise God
from our hearts in disciplined prayer, confessing our sins to
him and bringing to him our needs as well as the needs of others.

The practitioner of Transcendental Meditation spends time
daily in reciting his meaningless mantra. Why should you and I
spend less time in communion with our holy Creator-Redeemer
God? We must make time for what the late A. W. Tozer called
"the pursuit of God"—though we discover that it is he who pur-
sues us, who longs to reveal more of himself to us, showing us
something of his awesome majesty!

Like David we need to hunger after God: "Oh God, thou art
my God, I seek thee, my soul thirsts for thee; my flesh faints for
thee, as in a dry and weary land where no water is" (Ps. 63:1;
cf. Ps. 42:1-2).

The supreme example of one who deliberately set aside time

to be alone with God is the Lord Jesus. You remember the incident in Mark 6, after the twelve returned from a mission: "And he said to them, 'Come away by yourselves to a lonely place, and rest a while.' For many were coming and going, and they had no leisure even to eat" (Mk. 6:31). So they went away on a boat, but the people followed them on foot so that a large crowd was waiting for them when they landed. Jesus taught the people again, and towards the end of the day fed five thousand men as well. His disciples who assisted him must have been really weary, for he put them on a boat and sent them away while he dismissed the crowd. What does Jesus himself do, after such a long arduous day? He went into the hills to pray (v. 46). He must have prayed all night, for it is not until at least 3 a.m. that he links up with his disciples again. Even the Lord Jesus found it essential to spend time alone with his Father.

What is the evidence that we are growing in our personal knowledge of the holy God? A holy life among men. We are to be holy for he is holy. He is our Father and we are his children. Our likeness to him should become more and more evident in our daily lives. What is a holy life? Certainly there is a negative element: We are to be separated from all that is sinful and displeasing to God (2 Cor. 6:17). But holiness is positive too: To be holy is to be separated for God's special possession and his service (2 Cor. 6:16; 1 Pet. 2:9-10). This is the calling of every Christian, for all Christians are called to be saints (Rom. 1:7). God has called us to be conformed to the image of his Son (Rom. 8:20; Gal. 4:19; 1 Jn. 3:2). Holiness is to be like Jesus. That is why it is important to read the Gospels constantly, so we can keep fresh in our hearts and minds what Jesus was really like when he lived among us, as a man among men.

This personal knowledge of God in Christ is surely the secret of endurance. Why was the apostle Paul willing to undergo the hardships he describes in 2 Corinthians 11:24-27? Because his one great ambition was to know Christ and the power of his resurrection and the fellowship of his sufferings (Phil. 3:10). After many years of fruitful missionary labor, Paul's ambition was still to know Christ. He knew him and knew him well, but he also knew how much more there is to know in experience. To

know God in Christ must be our ambition in this life for it will be
our preoccupation in eternity. Or, to revise slightly the words of
a well-known hymn: "When we've been there ten thousand
years, bright shining as the sun; we've no less days to know God
and sing his praise, than when we've first begun."

When the going gets rough and the missionary star dust is
gone, only he who knows his God will persevere. When one has
to move from the bursting congregations of Phnom Penh to the
unfriendly flats of Hong Kong, only she who knows her God will
stay on. When language learning is tough and loneliness even
tougher, only those who know their God will endure.

Nearly twenty years ago I went to my first IVCF camp. It was a
tough month-long training camp, the first for the Philippine
movement. What was the main thing I learned? How to spend
time alone with God in Bible study and prayer. In spite of all
the years, I feel I know so little of the God I serve. Do you feel the
same way I do? We need to say to God, "Oh God, how little I
know of you, but give me a longing, a hunger to know you better,
and to become more and more like you. Then I can declare your
glory among the nations."

Identification with People

The second essential qualification for declaring God's glory is a
deepening identification with needy men and women.

More than 4 billion people inhabit this planet today. At least
2.7 billion of them do not know God in Jesus Christ. That's about
seven persons out of every ten. The vast majority of these are in
the third world: China, India and the world of Islam together
already account for 2 billion people.

We live in a world of great needs. Most people in the world
are poor, many go hungry every day, and have no decent place to
live in. Many cannot read or write, are unable to find adequate
employment and die without seeing the shadow of a doctor. Yet
their greatest need is to be reconciled to the holy God from whom
they are separated by their sin.

We have the message of reconciliation, God making his appeal
through us. But people are not reconciled to God simply by our
words, however clearly we may say them. We need to incarnate

our words, clothing them with our own flesh and blood, in deep identification with people in their need. We evangelicals tend to be weak here, perhaps because we are so conscious that *we* have *the* message. If we declare that message with verbal precision, we think our task is done. We fail to realize that the message and the messenger cannot be separated, that our word must be shown in deed. Further, we have not understood the example of the Lord Jesus, who came to give his life a ransom for many but did so as the culmination of a life of service to others (Mk. 10:45). He ministered to the total person as he preached and taught, fed the hungry, healed the sick and cast out demons. His mission is our mission (Jn. 20:21).

What does it mean for us to identify with men and women in their need, as we seek to share the glorious gospel with them?

First, it means a serious effort to understand them. We must learn to listen and to put ourselves in their shoes. "To the Jews I became as a Jew, in order to win Jews; . . . to the weak I became weak, that I might win the weak. I have become all things to all men, that I might by all means save some" (1 Cor. 9:20-22). Most of us come from the comfortable middle class; do we really understand what it means to be poor? Americans take pride in being patriots, but they find it difficult to understand a Filipino nationalist. Many Christians are passionately anti-Communist, but they never bother to find out why Marxism is such a live option for many in the Third World. They need to understand its moral attractiveness, its appeal to the downtrodden's sense of justice in this world; they must understand its tantalizing promise to achieve in one generation what took the West a hundred years to accomplish.

Part of your difficulty in understanding comes from a tendency to equate American culture with the gospel. To distinguish these two is not always easy, but it is a necessary exercise. We thank God for a greater willingness to recognize the problem and do something about it, especially since Lausanne 74.

We need more than understanding. We must actively pursue ways of rendering loving service to people in need. "Though I am free from all men, I have made myself a *slave* to all, that I might win the more" (1 Cor. 9:19). If we accept ministry to the whole man as our total mission, this is not the old social gospel. It is putting our ministry of proclamation in its proper context— that of a life of service to others. What can we do to help the poor, feed the hungry, teach the illiterate, create jobs for the unemployed, heal the sick and give hope to the oppressed? Plenty, if we were ready, in the words of the Lausanne Covenant, "to develop a simple life-style . . . and to empty ourselves of all but [our] personal authenticity in order to become the servant of others" (paragraphs 9 and 10).

Many doors are closed to the traditional missionary today. Many more will close in the years ahead. But these same doors remain open to people who come and render loving service to meet obvious human need. Why can't the missionaries of tomorrow come as professionals with expertise in these areas of need and declare God's glory in the context of their work?

Kenneth Scott Latourette, describing the first three-hundred years of church history, tells us, "The chief agents in the expansion of Christianity appear not to have been those who made it a profession or a major part of their occupation, but men and women who earned their livelihood in some purely secular manner and spoke of their faith to those whom they met in this natural fashion" (*A History of the Expansion of Christianity: The First Five Centuries*, p. 116).

Such identification will be costly but will bring glory to God. I remember an American missionary couple who lived among the poor people of Manila for a while. When they sent their young son to the local public elementary school, they were criticized for throwing away his future. God has honored their faith: This son recently came back to the Philippines with a Ph.D. in anthropology.

Mother Teresa received a call to serve the poorest of the poor. She has lived and worked in the slums of Calcutta since 1948. Malcolm Muggeridge has written of putting her on a train in Calcutta: "When the train began to move, and I walked away, I felt as though I were leaving behind me all the beauty and all the joy in the universe. Something of God's love has rubbed off on Mother Teresa." Isn't that what it means to declare God's glory?

A Healthy Relationship to the Body

A third essential qualification for declaring God's glory is *an increasingly healthy relationship to the body, God's church.*

Ten years ago, a seminary professor did a survey of the religious organizations at work in the Philippines. He counted nearly 400 of these groups, and he did not even claim to be exhaustive! Perhaps I do not have to tell you where most of these groups come from: the United States of America.

Two months ago, 127 people from all over Asia gathered in Hong Kong for a seminar on Christian communication. During a session, we were discussing the whole question of cooperative effort and the kind of structure required to make it possible. A perceptive participant raised the question: Brothers, can we really work together out here without the consent of our parent organizations in the United States and elsewhere?

My North American brothers and sisters in Christ, your strength is your weakness. The same pioneering spirit, rugged individualism and competitive drive that made you mighty and wealthy in the world are responsible for the setting up of your spiritual empires. I do not deny that many such ventures have been used greatly by God in building and extending his kingdom on earth. I am suggesting that God's kingdom does not have its headquarters in the United States or Canada or England.

How many times have missionaries from the West come to us and said in effect: "Here I am. I've got a powerful new program (with the dollars to fuel it). Help me to accomplish my dream." May I suggest that it is better for you to say: "I have come in response to a need. How can I help you in building up God's people here and reaching out to the lost?"

Some have said that we in the Third World are making these suggestions because we are hungry for power and authority ourselves. We want to be recognized for our spiritual maturity and want to make the decisions. Are we merely proving the truth of Lord Acton's dictum: power corrupts? This is a temptation we must conquer, but it is not an adequate objection to the principle at stake.

What is the principle? The hand is not greater than the foot—because they both belong to the one **body** (1 Cor. 12). Or, as

Jonathan Chao of Hong Kong argued in a seminar in Lausanne, there is parity among churches. Before God, churches are equal in status—the rich and the poor, the young and the old, the large and the small. If so, in desiring to begin a work in a locality, I cannot bypass the local body of believers without sinning against the body. It is true, there are some hard questions to be answered: How does one define "the local body of believers"? What if the local body is absolutely sleepy and does not care about its mission? Once more, these hard questions are no excuse for evading the force of the biblical principle involved.

Ideally, when you send a worker to us, he must be one who has healthy relations with a local body of believers—a local church. This local congregation has helped to confirm his call to work across boundaries of land and culture, as well as helped him to recognize and exercise the spiritual gifts that God has entrusted to him. Such a worker will then be received by an equivalent body of believers "in the field"—a local congregation—which will provide him the fellowship he needs, as well as supervision over his work. Whether we need intermediate structures between these two local congregations, or what form these should take, can be left open-ended. The principle I want to argue is this: The missionary must have a healthy relationship to the body at home and must be properly integrated into the body in the field.

The amount of duplication and wastage of people and money arising from each man doing his own thing is incredible. Not only do we sin against the body when we do this; we will also be called to account for sinful pride in seeking to build our own empires, as well as for bad stewardship of God's resources.

This is another argument for the multiplication of thousands of missionaries who do not carry the "missionary" label. Because they come as professionals, in the course of their work, they do not have to represent some powerful organization that seeks to establish "branches" all over the world. I think of a wonderful Canadian couple who have lived and worked in the International Rice Research Institute in the Philippines for some years. He is an entomologist—a highly competent one!—and also a zealous Christian who has closely identified with the local congregation and done a lot of good in winning people to Christ and encouraging them to reach out. May their tribe increase!

Provided the ones you send are those who know their God, are willing to identify with people in need and are properly related to the body, we welcome from you a whole variety of people—young and old, men and women, singles and families, the extremely gifted and the patient plodders, the traditional, full-time missionaries and the professionals. All kinds are needed, for there is much land to be possessed: the mature experienced man who can give counsel to a growing congregation in Tokyo that is interested not only in neighborhood outreach but also mission abroad, as well as the physically strong young men and women who will brave the forests of Kalimantan in Borneo to reach the tribes. We must work—together—while it is day. The Lord Jesus is coming soon. Amen.

fifteen
The Cost of Declaring His Glory

Helen Roseveare

During the hymn sung just prior to her address, Dr. Roseveare stepped to one side of the podium and there dismantled a large (about six-foot), stylized, artificial forsythia branch. She first removed all the blossoms and leaves and then, from within the branch itself, removed a bright, florescent shaft. Dr. Roseveare then fixed a large arrowhead to one end of the shaft. This transformation completed, she held the arrow up for display to the audience.

What is *cost?*—an entirely relative term that can only be understood in reference to the value set upon the object obtained.

If I say that I have just been out and spent a thousand dollars, you would consider it an enormous "cost" if you thought I were buying a pair of fur gloves: but it would be an extremely low cost if in fact I were buying a sports car!

As you have watched me "destroying" this lovely imitation

branch of forsythia—ruthlessly pulling off the brilliant blossoms (destroying its ability to breathe and feed); snapping off all side branches, cutting off knots and smoothing rough places (destroying its shape and form); and even stripping its very bark (its protection against rain and sun, destroying even that which gives it personality and the power to live)—what a pointless waste, you think, and at what a "cost," especially in midwinter!

But wait a moment! As the stripping and whittling and sandpapering processes are complete, what results from the rough (though beautiful) branch? An *arrow*—a polished shaft, fit to carry the arrowhead direct to its target. A perfect balanced tool in the hand of an expert archer to achieve a destined goal.

Does the "cost" now seem quite so high? Was it really a pointless waste? God says that he will make of his Branch (Is. 11:1) a polished shaft (Is. 49:2). And he longs to make you and me more "like unto Jesus," conformable to the image of his Son. Am I willing for the stripping and whittling and sandpapering, through circumstances, companions or committees, to make me into that perfect arrow to achieve his wonderful purposes in and through my life? "For we are his workmanship, created in Christ Jesus for good works which God prepared beforehand that we should walk in them" (Eph. 2:10).

During my thirty years as a Christian, twenty of them spent in central Africa, I have known something of the pressure of the Hand of the Master Archer, whittling away on my life—at my character, my habits, my attitudes—and there have certainly been times when I've felt like crying out to him, "Stop! Hold off! I just can't stand any more!" And yet, he graciously whittles on. Perhaps you think I'm being facetious? Strangely enough, not really.

Seven months after I was converted, July 1945, I stood at the great missionary gathering at Keswick Convention in North England to declare publicly that I would go anywhere he sent me "whatever the cost." Afterwards, I went up into the mountains and had it out with God. "O.K. God, today I mean it. Go ahead and make me more like Jesus, whatever the cost. But please (knowing myself fairly well), when I feel I can't stand any more and cry out, 'Stop!' will you ignore my 'stop' and remember that today I said 'Go ahead!'?'' And thank God, through the years, he has kept me to it.

The first and great commandment says that I should love the Lord my God with all my heart (which will involve a spiritual cost), with all my soul (involving an intellectual, emotional and volitional cost) and with all my might (involving a physical cost).

With All My Heart

We were well taught in missionary training college to "count the cost," involving such things as leaving home and loved ones, the possibility of remaining single, leaving my job and therefore the security of a settled salary or future pension, accepting that God is responsible, not only for myself, but also, should one marry, for the husband/wife and the children, and their education and safety. One would also leave the comparative safety and security of our home system of justice. There would be problems of communication—not merely language, but of cultural expression, which could well lead to loneliness. There might well be long hours of thankless toil at a job for which one doesn't feel really trained (such as a doctor building a hospital!) leading to over-tiredness and sore hands. Often there could be a load of responsibility dumped on one that almost crushes and leaves little time for the essential "waiting on God" alone to receive the needed daily strengthening.

After building a 100-bed hospital and maternity complex, developing a training school for national para-medical workers, caring for a growing number of regional clinics and health centers, the day came, when on a medical ward round in the hospital, I got mad with a patient and let rip with a fluency in Swahili rarely surpassed! As we left the ward to cross the courtyard, my African assistant quietly put his hand on my arm and rebuked me. "Doctor," he said, "I don't think Jesus would have spoken like that." I'm sure he wouldn't, but it was humbling to be told it by a student from the forest land. We returned to the ward, I apologized, and John, my assistant, preached the gospel.

This was merely a symptom of my state of heart. Shortly afterwards my African colleagues made it possible for me to go away for a ten-day break from the hospital, to our local pastor's home —basically that I might sort myself out with God. Eventually, after three miserable days, Pastor Ndugu came to my help. "Helen," he said quietly and patiently, "why can't you forget for one minute that you are white?" It was the first of many appalling shocks as he opened up to me something of my heart condition, including this race prejudice. Subconsciously, I didn't really believe that an African could be as good a Christian as I was or could know Jesus just as I did. Slowly Pastor Ndugu led me back to the cross to a new level of identification, for a new cleansing from this racial pride and many other subtle forms of pride that he made me recognize and face up to, and then for a new filling with Calvary love.

When I returned to our hospital-village, I was met by a group of my African team, and before I could begin to explain, one burst out, "Hallelujah!" I looked at him astounded. "Oh," he said, "you don't need to say anything, your face tells us. We've been praying for you for four years!" And I had gone out to them as their missionary! The first major "cost" was to my pride, but from then on, I entered into a new heart identity, not only with the Lord Jesus but also with my African friends and co-workers.

With All My Soul

Second, God had to teach me that his service would cost me all my soul (mind, emotions and will).

During my first five years in Africa, I had a growing desire to be married, to have a husband and home and children. I urgently wanted someone to carry the load of responsibility, someone to share with, someone to whom to "pass the buck" when things went wrong. There's another side to womens lib! I came home on my first furlough determined to get what I wanted, a Christian surgeon called to missionary service with Worldwide Evangelization Crusade in Congo/Zaire, willing to be my husband!

But such things don't grow on trees. God kept on saying, "Pass the buck to me; I can carry it. Lean on me; I can support you. Love me and let me be a husband to you." But I hit out and argued back. That wasn't the sort of "spiritualized" husband I wanted: I wanted a husband with two arms! I told God that he just didn't understand.

After two bitter years of struggle, I gave in, at least outwardly and went back to Africa single, to do the job God gave me, to obey him—but with a chip on my shoulder. I was almost bitter against him. I was not satisfied emotionally. I felt God had offered me "second-best."

For four years God wooed me to accept him in a new sense of emotional unity, but I kicked against his way. I did what I should do; I said what I should say. I taught in church and in schools. I was a "good missionary" so far as all others could tell. But on this level of emotional involvement I held myself aloof from God.

But he wouldn't let me go! So the rebellion came and I was taken captive by rebel soldiers. They stole my possessions, they stole my privacy and eventually they stole even my purity. And through the brutal heartbreaking experience of rape, God met with me—with outstretched arms of love. It was an unbelievable experience. He was so utterly there, so totally understanding, his comfort was so complete—and suddenly I knew—I really *knew* that his love *was* unutterably sufficient. He *did* love me! He *did* understand! He understood not only my desperate misery but also my awakened desires and mixed up horror of emotional trauma. I knew that Philippians 4.19, "My God will supply every need of yours according to his riches in glory in Christ Jesus," was true on all levels, not just on a hyper-spiritual shelf where I had tried to relegate it.

But I found that this new exquisite joy was going to cost me my prerogative to choose my own way, to exercise my own will. He demanded, as it were in exchange, a total acknowledgement of "no rights to myself." It would indeed cost me my soul. When I returned to Zaire after the destruction of the rebellion, six missions were led to unite their efforts to create a medical center with a training college for national medical auxiliary workers. I was invited to develop the latter. In other words, to be architect and builder, medical director and lecturer of the college.

A few years later, as more staff joined us, national and foreign, I found myself becoming more and more a glorified office-boy, keeping the accounts and doing all the behind-scene administration. I didn't like it. Wasn't I a surgeon? The college principal? A senior missionary? "Surely, God," I grumbled, "any old bod could do all this." He appeared to say, "Yes, that's why I've put you there!"

An African staff member reminded me, when I expressed my frustrated dissatisfaction, "We can't all be the last link in the chain." And I had to learn teamwork! As a result of accurate office work and government liaison, the college was ultimately recognized. Today one hundred graduates with official diplomas are reaching over eight thousand patients daily with a good medical service and also with the clear preaching of the gospel.

All rights to self—what I want to do, whom I want to love, where I wish to serve—have to go: This is cost number two, if I am to be fully identified with him, and to love him with all my soul.

With All My Strength
Third, God had to teach me the living sacrifice of the body (Rom. 12:1-2), being physically identified with our Lord—loving him with all my strength.

I well remember the night I was converted. Dr. Graham Scroggie was at the house party giving the Bible studies. He wrote in the flyleaf of my Bible Philippians 3:10: "That I may know him, and the power of his resurrection, and the fellowship of his sufferings, being made conformable unto his death" (KJV). "Tonight," he said, "you have entered into part I of that verse, 'that I may know him.' My prayer for you is that you will come to know more and more the power of his resurrection as you go out to serve him." Then very quietly, looking straight at me, he added, "Maybe one day he will give you the privilege to know something of the fellowship of his sufferings."

That night as I went up to bed, I tried to thank God for the amazing joy that flooded my whole being, the sense of newness and of belonging. Then I added, somewhat incoherently perhaps, "And please God, if you can possibly agree to it, would you give me the privilege of serving you as a missionary?" and almost under my breath, "at any cost." At that time I probably viewed the cost as giving up those things that I most enjoyed— lovely clothes, a good home with decent furniture, the use of flush toilets rather than the "pit down the garden path" that was common in areas of missionary service. Maybe I knew little of what that so-called cost might involve, but this made my prayer no less real.

When I eventually reached Africa, I was completely happy in a mud-and-thatch home, and I hardly even noticed that the "pit down the garden path" was less convenient than the old-fash-ioned flush toilet of my youth! But other trials came, most noticeably periods of ill health. In 1954 I had malaria and jaun-dice pretty badly. In 1957 I had meningitis complicating a bout of flu. In 1961 a severe attack of cerebral malaria nearly ended my time of service in Africa. In 1971 an attack of tick-typhus fever made me extremely miserable and low.

Each illness brought with it the normal post-infectional de-pression, during which questions and doubts crowded into my mind. When one is ill in missionary service, so many others become involved. Someone has to care for you, on top of their own workload. Someone else has to carry your workload on top of theirs. Why did I keep getting ill? Was I just becoming a bur-den to the team? Would it be better if I went home?

Each time I guess God offered to explain to me the "Why?" but I was not listening—only complaining and asking questions! At last he did get through to me. Each of us in the natural likes to be needed; it feeds the ego to know we are needed. For years I was the only doctor in the area, and so I was always needed. Thus I was always on the giving end, and the Africans always had to say "thank you" on the receiving end. This can soon become demoralizing: But I had not seen that the roles had to be reversed if the Africans were to know fulfillment and the joy of being needed.

Only when I was ill did I obviously, unequivocally need them. They nursed me, they cared for me, they fed me, they washed me. And I said, "thank you." And they had the tremen-dous joy of knowing for once that they were needed and had a role to fulfill. But their joy cost me my physical health.

Then during the rebellion, on the night of October 28, 1964, cruel men broke into my home around midnight. It was a wicked, savage night. I had tried to escape from them. What a hope! Six soldiers, armed and with powerful flash lights, surrounded the house and moved in on me as on a trapped animal. Numbed and terrified, I lay in the mud beneath a meager hedge. Pulled roughly to my feet, I was struck across the face. My glasses went, and my nose was gashed and bleeding. A second blow felled me to the ground where the leader's boot crashed cruelly into my face and then my ribs. My back teeth were broken, my whole body bruised. I was driven back to the verandah of my home, jeered at, cursed and insulted. My benumbed brain was only able to keep me one step ahead of them, one inch out of reach of each succeeding lunge. I wasn't praying. I was beyond praying. Someone back home was earnestly praying for me. If I had prayed any prayer, it would have been, "My God, my God, why hast thou forsaken me?"

Suddenly, there was God. I didn't see a vision or hear a voice, but I just knew with every ounce of my being that God was actually, vitally there—God, in all his majesty and power. And he stretched his arms out to me, surrounding me with love, and seemed to whisper, "Twenty years ago you asked me for the privilege of being a missionary. This is it. Don't you want it?"

Fantastic. The privilege of being identified with our Savior. As I was driven down the short corridor of my home, it was as though he clearly said to me, "These are not your sufferings. They are not beating you. These are my sufferings. All I ask of you is the loan of your body." And an enormous relief swept through me: One word became unbelievably clear. That word was privilege. He did not take away pain or cruelty or humiliation. No, it was all there, but now it was altogether different. It was with him, for him, in him. He was actually offering me the inestimable privilege of sharing in some little way in the fellowship of his sufferings.

In the weeks of imprisonment that followed and in the subsequent years of continued service, I have looked back and tried "to count the cost," but I find it all swallowed up in privilege.

The cost suddenly seems very small and transient in the great-ness and permanence of the privilege.

Can you, will you, believe it and enter into it?

As the branch to become the arrow had to lose its leaves and flowers, so I perhaps the pleasant home, fixed salary and married joys. (Nothing wrong in leaves and flowers—essential to the life of the branch—but a hindrance, a weight, to the balanced arrow). So also the side branches, roughnesses and knots—my temperament, my sensitivities, my habits—the sin that does so easily beset us, of bad temper, of being hurt, of throwing my weight about. And even to the bark, the final in-dividuality of the branch—my personality, my right to be my-self—that I may be crucified that Christ may live wholly in me: so will we be able to run the race that is set before us, looking unto Jesus, who has paid the cost and offers us only the privi-lege.

sixteen
The Joy of Declaring His Glory

Eric Frykenberg

There is great joy in serving Jesus. I was in a young people's camp, and they sang "Happiness is to know the Lord." And I said, "Amen to that." The primary text which we are discussing at Urbana 76 is Psalm 6:3: "Declare his glory among the nations." But I want to direct your attention to three other portions of Scripture. All three texts have at their heart, the center, the Lord himself.

The first is Exodus 15:11. Put that verse, which is in the very heart of Moses' song, in your pressure cooker and let it simmer and see what the Holy Spirit will say to you. "Who is like unto thee, O LORD, among the gods? Who is like thee, glorious in holiness, fearful in praises, doing wonders." This verse has to do with the holiness, the majesty, the greatness, the righteousness of our God.

There is no greater emotion that could stir our hearts, no greater thought that could fill our minds, no greater word that

could ever be on our lips than the word *God*. That is the way
the Bible begins. I love all the psalms that begin with that like,
for example, "God is our refuge and strength" (Ps. 46:1). The
book of Hebrews begins with God. Some years ago a boat was
leaving Boston, and before they tied up the hatches someone
said, "There is a man down among the packing boxes. Is he
mad? He's crying something." The man was crying one word:
"God, God, God." His name was Dr. A. J. Gordon, the founder
of a Christian school. So this Scripture has to do with the greatness of God.

Holiness is linked to the inner sanctuary of the tabernacle;
it was called the Holy of Holies. There was the Shekinah glory.

The second Scripture is in Isaiah. There is a crisis in Israel.
For five chapters Isaiah, a faithful man of God, had cried, "Woe,
woe, woe unto the people." Though he lived in a time of almost
unparalleled prosperity in Israel, second only to the days of
Solomon, violence was abroad in the earth. There was immorality. Standards were thrown to the wind. There was corruption in the government. And Israel was headed for judgement.

Then King Uzziah died, and the last human restraining influence for good was gone. Do you remember the tragedy of his
death? He was smitten with leprosy. He had to live in a hut and
give the quarantine cry for himself, stamped with death while
he was still living.

Isaiah was burdened and didn't know what to do. So he went
into the sanctuary and we read: "In the year that king Uzziah
died, I saw the Lord" (Is. 6:1). One of the greatest prayers is that
of Moses, "Show me thy glory." And the Lord said, "You can't
see my glory and live. I'll show you my goodness as you stand
in a cleft of a rock." But here God revealed himself to this burdened servant. Isaiah saw the glory of the Lord.

Then the flaming servants of the Lord, his ministers, the
seraphim, cried out, "Holy, holy, holy." That's a doxology if
ever there was one. They declared the whole earth to be full of
his glory.

It didn't look like that at the time. Were they speaking in
prophecy? God is the eternal One—yesterday, today and forever
—a present-tense God. So I think those seraphim saw things

from heaven's point of view and judged from the dimension of eternity. Nothing in history has ever thwarted the purpose of our God. When one of the seraphim touched his lips with a burning coal from the altar (a beautiful symbol pointing to the cross of Christ), Isaiah had a living, burning experience. It saturated his whole being, and the tympanum in his ear got on heaven's wavelength.

"Who shall we send, and who will go for us?" said the voice of the Lord.

And he said, "Lord, here am I." Would you have like to be in his place?

"Be assured," said the Lord, "people are not going to listen to you. I'm going to make their hearts fat and their ears heavy so they can't even listen to you." When Isaiah came back to the annual conference meeting in chapter 53, he didn't have much to report: "Who hath believed our report, and to whom is the arm of the LORD revealed?"

Maybe some of the executives said, "Strike him off the list. He's not a producer." But he was a faithful servant of the Lord. What made him faithful in the remaining sixty chapters of his wonderful prophecy (a record of a man who magnified the glory of his God)? A living, personal experience from the altar. We too need a vision of the Lord Jesus Christ. That's what puts the go into life.

Fifty-four years ago I gave my first testimony to the Lord Jesus Christ as a new Christian. I was a mason. Billy Graham said he has a sense of fear every time he speaks. For fifty-four years I get a new crop of goose pimples all over before I stand and speak. I get over it after I get up and open my Bible. Then what makes us go?

Years ago Dr. Rimmer, a scientist friend who was a Christian, returned from an expedition in Alaska. He brought with him one of his guides, an Alaskan Indian that he had the joy to introduce to the Lord. When he got to San Francisco he saw a streetcar and he was baffled. They didn't pull it; they didn't push it. "What makes it go?" he asked.

Dr. Rimmer said, "You see that wire? That brings power, electricity, from the power station, and that scraping thing brings it into a motor, and the power is relayed through gears to the wheels and that propels it." And the Indian said to Dr. Rimmer, "What makes it go?"

He didn't understand. And Dr. Rimmer thought to himself, "What's the use of explaining. Who can explain electricity?"

Rather than stumbling and grumbling in the dark we let our faith be functional, and we turn on the switch. It is really by faith, practical like that.

When they got back to the hotel, Dr. Rimmer said, "Come over here." He got up on a chair, unscrewed the bulb and said, "Wet your thumb and hold it in this a moment." Then he turned on the switch, and the Indian blurted out, "There's fire in that thing." Dr. Rimmer said, "That's what made it go."

Isaiah had an experience with the living God. That's what put the go in him.

Just before I left for the mission field with my wife in 1929, I asked an older Christian, "Have you got any little word, as an older brother in Christ, for a man who is going to the mission field? God willing, I'm going to serve him in the jungles of India."

"Only one thing, my young man," he said. "Remember fire has a tendency to go out."

I profited from that little word for over half a century. Sometimes I have been ill. I had malaria five times, twice almost dying from it. I had plenty of persecution, opposition, naturally. If you serve the Lord faithfully, you get your share of that. But there has been nothing so serious as when my own heart has grown cold toward Jesus Christ. Then it's time to close shop, get alone, turn to Matthew 27, read it slowly, prayerfully, and let the Holy Spirit show you what God has done to redeem your soul. God broke his heart to save me from my sin. Read it again until your heart melts. After a while the fire is rekindled, and you are ready to go again. As Paul said, "Stir up the gift that is within you" (2 Tim. 1:6). Fan the fire, give it fuel, give it oxygen, and you will be ready to go.

The theme for our convention starts with an exhortation: "Sing unto the Lord" (Ps. 96:1). Song has always had a great place in God's economy. We read in the Bible that the morning stars sang together when the Lord laid the foundations of the earth. You and I were wired for sound. We should look to the Lord, and then we should praise him.

You say, "I'm not much of a singer." Neither am I. But I try to sing sometimes. On the road my wife bears with me when I sing. I try in my humble way to imitate George Beverly Shea, "Little lamb can go astray; Little lambs can lose their way. Shepherd, shepherd teach me where to go." We love to sing the praises of our God.

You say, "The environment is not conducive to praising God." It's not a matter of convenience. It's an imperative to praise our God. It's a sacred duty. We are redeemed. We are twice his.

I remember as a new Christian I worked for Morgan Construction Co. in Worcester, Massachusetts. There was another Christian lad there, and we prayed together and witnessed to other workers. They used all sorts of bad language and they chewed black tobacco and they spit. They were hard men. But I kept on and when it got so I could hardly breathe, I would sing.

My friend and I made a covenant. I said, "I need more prayer, brother. You pray." Then I tried in my humble way to sing. I didn't know how much got through. That was almost fifty years ago.

A little while ago I was asked to speak in a prayer meeting in Pleasant Creek Baptist Church in Worcester, Massachusetts. A man, Mr. White, whom I didn't even recognize said, "I come on behalf of three old men living in Shrewsbury. We're too old to drive. We saw your picture in the paper, and so my friends said, 'Go over there and tell Mr. Frykenberg that we are still hearing your hymns in our ears. We still hear about Jesus meeting us just inside the eastern gate.'"

So we should sing the praises of our God! Jeremiah said that praising the Lord is a great power; it is our strength. Today we are learning a little bit about that. They crack petroleum with music now; they mix paint with music; they homogenize the milk with music nowadays. Why shouldn't the Christian sing? So the psalmist said, "Praise the Lord"; this is the center of everything. We sang together that wonderful hymn, "Take my life and let it be" by Frances R. Havergal. "Take my moments and my days," she wrote. "Let them flow in ceaseless praise." A few years ago among the ten outstanding women in British history she was voted second to Queen Victoria.

Years ago a man from India spoke at Princeton, I believe, at the close of the college year. He addressed himself to the seniors: "I don't know your aim and ambition in life. Maybe some of you want to accumulate wealth, and very likely you will become men of means before life is over. Others may desire power, and maybe you will come to wield influence. Maybe some want fame. But somewhere along life's way you will meet some little fellow who doesn't care for any of the three. Then you will feel very poor." If we put the Lord at the center of our hearts, let him fill our whole horizon and sing his praises, no matter what the situation, we can't go wrong. During my senior year in a little college in Boston we had a young freshman from the state of Maine. He was a new Christian, flaxy hair, effervescent, happy in the Lord. He sat toward the front during chapel. We had chapel speeches, some good, some not so good. But his heart was hungry and he said with gusto, "Hallelujah! Praise the Lord." But, you know, Boston is rather conservative. We could tell by the faces of our beloved dean and president and faculty that they were not altogether delighted with the effervescent spirit of this brother. They said he needs a little help. So we seniors took him up in the dormitory and had a lovely, Christian, brotherly talk with him. They said, "You know the Bible says the spirit of the prophets is subject to the prophets. And we think you could magnify God and glorify him better if you sit back further in the chapel service and subdue your spirit a little bit. You can still be happy in your heart."

He said, "Thank you, brethren, for being so helpful and kind. Thank you, thank you for helping me. I was just so happy I didn't think."

So to be sure there were no ragged edges, some of the men asked him, "Are you doing all right in the studies?"

"I'm not getting As but I'm doing pretty well. I got several Bs."

"How do you make out financially?"

"Fine," he said. "I'm working here at the gas station next door. Yesterday morning I had the privilege of praying with a man while I serviced his car. And he broke down and told about his home breaking up. I saw that he wanted to know Jesus Christ. I think the man got saved. Then I work on the street here in the restaurant. The other day I talked to one of the waitresses, and she asked me to come inside and talk to the cook and her. We prayed together; I read the Scripture. I think the Holy Spirit honored his Word. I think both women were born again and became the children of God."

One of the seniors, without saying anything, got off his chair and down on his knees. We all got on our knees and started to pray. The first one said, "Lord, don't let me graduate and get out before you give to me what this young brother has."

After many years, I sat over a cup of coffee in Chicago with a leading Christian man, editor of a paper. I said, "What's the greatest experience you can remember from those college years?"

He referred to that very experience and said, "It has done more to challenge me and to remind me of the need of being on the beam for our wonderful Lord Jesus Christ in declaring his glory than anything I can think of from college."

God bless you. Thank you for letting an old missionary from the jungles of India that didn't die, that's just fading away, come along here. When Billy Graham said that he's scared, how do you think I felt? I think the coming of the Lord must be very close at hand. I don't know if we will be privileged to meet again. But if we don't meet here, we can always make a date to meet together just inside the eastern gate. And I'll see you on the updraft. God bless you.

seventeen
The Unfinished Task of Declaring His Glory

Luis Palau

Missionaries sometimes look very solemn, very quiet. But they can be funny if you give them a chance. I once met a Wycliffe missionary in Peninsula Bible Church in California. He had been serving in Mexico. He said that one day he was seated outside his cabin in the jungle translating the Bible, and he saw a cow going by in front of him very slowly. As he was looking at this cow and thinking about what it was doing, he said to himself, "Missionaries are just like that. Missionaries are like manure. If you pile them up together, they stink. But if you spread them around, they can do a lot of good." I want to talk about spreading missionaries around, not stacking them up together.

I love missionaries. My dad would be in hell today if it were not for a British missionary that came to Argentina. He died singing a Christian chorus when he was only thirty-five years old, having known the Lord Jesus for only nine years. My mom too belongs to Christ, my Grandma is with the Lord Jesus, and my five sisters and my brother were won to Christ, all thanks to missionaries.

I came to know the Lord Jesus when I was twelve years old, thanks to a Jewish British missionary, Charles Cohen. He came to Argentina and taught in the British boarding school that I attended. He insisted on giving me the gospel, paid for my expenses for a week at camp, and at that camp I received the Lord Jesus as Savior.

You can understand, then, why I get very impatient when people start criticizing missionaries. It is appropriate to criticize missionary methods, but it is intolerable to malign the missionaries themselves. When the critics are through, sometimes you feel that missionaries have got to be the biggest fools there ever were. They have made big mistakes, so bring them home, get rid of them.

Yes, they made mistakes. Don't you ever make mistakes? I make a lot of mistakes. But I hope that when I die people will not be pointing and say, "Louie Palouie, look at all the mistakes he made" and write a book about it. Actually missionaries are among the greatest men and women of God. Think of the sacrifices that they and their families have made in order to declare the gospel. We ought to be saying, Lord Jesus, glory to your name that these men and women went out to finish the task. Matthew 9:35—10:1 says,

Jesus went about all the cities and villages, teaching in their synagogues and preaching the gospel of the kingdom, and healing every disease and every infirmity. When he saw the crowds, he had compassion for them, because they were harrassed and helpless, like sheep without a shepherd. Then he said to his disciples, "The harvest is plentiful, but the laborers are few; pray therefore the Lord of the harvest to send out laborers into his harvest." And he called to him his twelve disciples and gave them authority.

The church is planted in every continent. Every nation has a church. And who do you think was the human instrument? Missionaries. They have done a fantastic job to the glory of God. But the task is unfinished. There is still a lot to do. There are 2.7 billion people who have never even heard the gospel truly explained.

I want to discuss seven principles and illustrate them from the lives of missionaries in my life.

Vision

First, notice that the Lord Jesus had a big vision: He "went about all the cities and villages, ... [and] when he saw the crowds, he had compassion for them." The vision has geographic dimensions. He went about from city to city, from village to village. The Bible says the Lord Jesus saw them all—the multitudes. There is nothing spiritual about being puny and small.

I didn't have that vision. Though I was brought up in a marvelous church, we were self-centered. Then this missionary showed up. His name was Keith. One day, to my pleasant surprise, he said, "Luis, every Wednesday after work"—I worked in a bank—"why don't you come and let's pray."

The first Wednesday we got on our knees and he started to pray for me. And he prayed up a storm. He prayed for my mom, for my sisters, for our local church, and he seemed to know all the elders by name, though he had never been to our church.

The next Wednesday when we got together, he began to pray for the whole city of Córdoba, the second city of Argentina. He began to pray first for our church, then for all the churches in our group, then all the Baptists, the Methodists, and the Assembly of God. He began to pray for all the denominations—35 of them in that city—one by one. I didn't know there were 35 until Keith began to pray.

The following Wednesday, he showed up with a map of the province of Córdoba. He said, "Luis, how many towns and cities are there in Córdoba?" I never thought of such a thing. Who cares how many towns and cities there are in Córdoba? He said, "There are just slightly over 900. Now we are going to pray for them." I couldn't believe it. Then he said, "Do you know how many of them have evangelical churches? Only 90 of the 900." He had studied it. We got on our knees and he started praying up and down this province. He began to pray for every town that had a church. If he knew the minister or the missionary in town, he began to pray for him.

The next Wednesday he brought a map of Argentina. We began to pray from south to north, province by province—and he knew all the statistics. My heart began to expand. It was like taking a jet and flying all over the country and praying for it.

Next Wednesday he came with a map of all the Americas. He knew missionaries all over. And he began to pray—Argentina, Uruguay, Paraguay. But it wasn't a quickie, flimsy little prayer. He took his time. And my heart began to open up. The next time he showed up with a map of Europe. And finally, after several weeks, he brought a map of the world.

He taught me about vision. Right then and there I said, "Lord, I want to be an evangelist. I want to be a missionary. I want to get out there." When you begin to pray, you realize that you can't just pray, you must go. A dream began to form in my heart, the desire that someday the Lord Jesus would give us a team and that we would have campaigns, and not just pray for all these millions, but get out and do something about it.

So a vision is the first thing.

This vision also has to be anthropological. Verse 36 says that the Lord Jesus felt "compassion for them, because they were harrassed and helpless, like sheep without a shepherd." He felt for them. He was moved with compassion when he looked at people. We need that.

Sometimes I like to sit in a restaurant or an airport and just look at people. When I was with my sons in London, our flight was delayed and we were put up in a hotel near Heathrow airport. I said, "Boys, we've got three hours. Let's look at people and try to guess what's going on in their minds." As one walked out, very cocky, I said, "Look at that guy. He thinks he's rich, and see how he looks at everybody." Then we'd look at the bellboy. What is he thinking? Counting the pennies that they gave him? As I looked at people, I wanted to share the gospel with them. Just so, when the Lord Jesus looked at people, he had compassion for them.

If we are going to finish the task, we have to have a faith vision. The Lord said, "Go into all the world and preach the gospel to every creature. Declare his glory among the nations." If this means that it can be done, then we must say, "Lord Jesus, in this generation, by your power, it shall be done."

For the past two months I have been burdened for the Arabic countries. And I have discovered that there are scores and hundreds of students with the same burden. I have faith that in our generation the Arabic world will be open to the gospel and Islam will hear the gospel in a powerful way. Those of you who have a burden for Islam, don't rest.

But the vision also has practical dimensions. So you might do this: Get on your knees, take a loose-leaf notebook and until the Lord sends you out write down some of the plans and objectives you have concerning how to proclaim his glory among the nations in our generation. It can be done because the Lord said so.

Priorities

The second principle is priorities. Notice Jesus' priorities in verse 35: "Jesus went about . . . [first] teaching in their synagogues . . . [secondly] preaching the gospel of the kingdom, and [third] healing every disease and every infirmity." We must keep these things in proper perspective: first, teaching the body of Christ; second, preaching the gospel to the lost; third, social action—healing every disease.

We are very concerned about people's physical hunger, and we should be. But it is unpopular to talk about people going to hell. We must have as our number one conviction that spiritual starvation is the most horrid and devastating starvation. We run the risk of being so overwhelmed by the physical that we almost sneer at the spiritual. Yes, we need the balance of emphasis on loving and caring for people, but we can be overwhelmed by publicity and forget the priorities.

Another missionary—George Mereshian, an Armenian—taught me about priorities. When I was nineteen years old, Mr. Mereshian invited me to his home three days a week; this went on for three years. When I would arrive in his home, he was usually on his knees by a couch with an open Bible. I would come into his home (I worked in a bank, and I had half a day free), we would get on our knees and he would teach me the

Bible for three or four hours. I learned most of what I know today
on my knees with Mr. Mereshian. On weekends we would go
door to door helping the poor, older people especially, and
preaching the gospel. But I learned it on my knees. He seemed
to be always on his knees. What a lesson it was to me. He taught
me to love and to help, but first of all to be with the Lord.

Compassion

The third principle I had to learn through missionaries was the
principle of compassion. When the Lord saw the multitudes, he
had compassion for them. We need to get the tender compassion
from our Lord's heart into ours.

One of the greatest dangers of the intellectual is cynicism
and a cool detachment. We do not want to get too emotional
about people getting lost. And the more statistics you have in
your head and the more knowledge you cram in it, the greater is
the danger that you will say, "Oh yeah, 2.7 billion. Well, at
least 1.3 billion people are in the kingdom." And you forget that
2.7 billion people is lots of people who suffer, and you lose
compassion.

Do you know how I get compassion? I remember that in Latin
America every two months an average of 500,000 people die.
Every two months! And my heart breaks when I think of it. I have
a book with pictures of Latin America—the Indians and city
people, rich people and poor people. When I begin to feel that
my heart is getting hard, I go through this book and look at the
old people and poor people and the blind, and I begin to cry almost every time. We must not be embarrassed to cry a little bit
for those who are lost. Compassion in my mind has got something to do with crying. When people are suffering and dying
and lost, and there are so many millions of them that we cannot
even imagine what 2.7 billion is, how can we not cry?

Urgency

The fourth principle is urgency: "Pray therefore the Lord of the
harvest to send out laborers into his harvest" (v. 38). We must
sense the urgency of the time in which we live. How long must
people wait before they hear the gospel? How many more gen-

erations must pass before some parts of the world hear for the first time the message of the Lord Jesus? The task is urgent.

It is exciting to see that in most of the so-called Third World today there is a harvest like there has never been before. In Latin America people are ready to come to Christ. Children, older people, people with religion and some without religion are hungry and open. They tell me that it is the same in much of Africa, and in many parts of the Orient also.

Right now the doors are open as perhaps never before in history. Much of the world, despite some closed doors, is open to the gospel of Jesus Christ. And, humanly speaking, we have the money and the communications media to do the job. All this is in our hands in this generation. But it could pass in such a short time. Certainly you want to prepare for service. And you must not rush madly ahead. But there is an urgency. The unfinished task says, "Do it, and do it now before it is too late."

Servanthood

The fifth principle is servanthood. Missionaries must be servants. Yesterday I was talking to a man with a Ph.D. He asked me, "What can an American missionary do overseas? Honestly, just between you and me, do you really think there's room for us any more?" I believe there is.

One way to serve is to go to the lonely spots, to the remote areas, to the jungles, where people still do not want to go—and where many of us nationals would not go for anything. We still need missionaries like that.

But even in the big cities we need American missionaries. The best approach in my opinion is for an American missionary to become a member of an international team. Do not come thinking of yourself as a Christopher Columbus discovering America. Most Americans would be much more comfortable and fruitful as a missionary if they were part of an international team.

Our evangelism team works this way. I'm Argentinian, and we have Guatemalans, Ecuadorians, Dominicans, Chileans— and some Yankees—all kinds of people. We don't feel that the Yankees on our team are superior or inferior. We just love to have them. They know more theology than we do because they have been to seminary and most of us have not been. So we go to them when we need help with theology.

There are at least three areas North Americans are well suited to help in. The first is "platform building." In other words, help the nationals, but put the national out front.

Mr. Dick Hillis, the founder of Overseas Crusades, is a great example of a servant missionary. He is a great writer, a great evangelist and a man of God, and yet he always stays in the background. He says: "Build a platform under the national and you missionaries stay behind." That is what he has done. You can be the supporting platform for gifted nationals.

Second, you can have a life-building ministry behind the scenes. Many nationals are not as spiritual as they sometimes appear to be. We may be more emotional than North Americans, but not necessarily more mature or more spiritual. You can teach us how to live in the power of the indwelling Christ. If you can teach people how to walk controlled by Jesus Christ, then there is great need of you behind the scenes.

The third area where help is needed behind the scenes is intellect building. This is necessary if the task is to be accomplished. Most of you are in the university, many of you will go to seminary. But most of the nationals with whom you may work will not have finished high school. Some will have had a year or two of Bible school. A missionary with knowledge and an ability to organize can provide a tremendous service.

Mr. Mereshian used to give me books and American and British magazines. He always said, "I've got an extra magazine, do you want it? I can loan you a book, do you want it?" And other missionaries were always giving me books. I used to wonder why. But now I understand that they were building me up intellectually. These missionaries gave me an appetite to read, and now I devour books. If you have this attitude as a missionary, there is no limit to how the Lord can use you.

My first and most memorable lesson in servanthood came when I was thirteen years old. I was in a Bible class called Crusaders; it was in English and was run by some Britishers. In the English style, we had a little tea after class. Two little ladies, who were very old, and a Chinese woman that was blind were there. We paid no attention to them. They were the kind of old ladies you used to joke about and say, "What can they do, the little things."

But soon these two women began to speak to us. Their names were Mildred Cable and Francisca French. They had been missionaries in the Gobi Desert in the interior of China for fifty years. They had been spat upon; they had been dragged by their hair; they had been kicked and otherwise mistreated in the interior of China. Though they had been raised in upper-middle-class British homes, the two of them, with their Chinese friend, had gone into the middle of China by themselves, and stayed fifty years. They called themselves "ambassadors for Christ."

A few years later we were singing that old hymn that says, "Am I a soldier of the cross, a follower of the Lamb? And shall I fear to own his cause or blush to speak his name?" We were singing it loud and with real martial spirit, when suddenly the Holy Spirit seemed to say, "Luis, what soldier of the cross are you? Remember those three little ladies you saw that used to be dragged by their hair and kicked and spat upon? You call yourself a soldier of the cross? What have you done for the Lord Jesus?" And I said, "Lord, I want to be a missionary."

Three little ladies went all the way from England in the last century to the middle of the Gobi Desert in the nineteenth century in order to finish the task of proclaiming his glory, even to people who didn't want them. That is the spirit of servanthood.

Laborers
In verse 38, the Lord Jesus says, "Pray therefore the Lord of the harvest to send out laborers into his harvest." Notice he says "laborers." There is room for laborers anywhere in the world. Everyone likes to have a servant. If you come as a laborer, a servant, you will always be welcome on anyone's team.

The Lord Jesus said to pray for laborers. He did not say send executives into his harvest. Now executives are needed, but even this role must be carried out with a servant attitude. Do not wonder if there is room. If you come as a servant, there is room all over the world to finish the task.

Holiness

The last principle is the authority of holiness. Matthew 10:1 says that the Lord called his disciples to himself and gave them authority. In order to finish the task we must have authority. And authority comes from holiness. There is power in a holy life. In a biography of Billy Graham, a newsman said not long ago that the thing that frightened him about Mr. Graham is his "arrogant humility." This seems like a contradiction. I think he was trying to say that Billy Graham is humble, but that there is an aggressiveness about the humility. I think this is a result of holiness.

One day two single, women missionaries showed up in our city in Argentina. Theda Krieger and Margaret Tyson were with Child Evangelism Fellowship. They wore their hair in a bun, wore long skirts and used no make-up. They were very quiet and not aggressive. But there was something attractive about them. My sisters and I were teenagers, and they invited us to take some Child Evangelism classes.

But there was an authority about them. I remember talking to my sisters and saying, "What have they got? They have something!" It was holiness. There is spiritual power and authority with the man or woman who has a pure heart and a pure mind. Men and women who have the authority of holiness are needed in order to finish the task.

That famous contemporary missionary, Mrs. Lillian Dickson, once told a visiting minister in Taiwan, "Remember, young man, your life is like a coin. You can spend it any way you want, but you can only spend it once." The unfinished task is enormous. Three billion people mostly in cultures other than our own. Will you spend your life to reach them? Are you available to God? Are you willing to be wasted for the sake of declaring his glory worldwide? Will you end your life on a victorious note, whether you're young or old, when he calls you home, or on a I-wish-I-had-done-it note?

The victory and the joy will come when we get to heaven. May God help us to say with Corrie ten Boom, who is a great evangelist: "When I enter that beautiful city, and the saints all around me appear, I hope that someone will tell me, 'Hey, it was you who invited me here.' " Let's finish the task.

eighteen
His Glory
in My Life:
Six testimonies

During the Urbana 76 convention, six persons told briefly how God had declared his glory in their lives. Bernie Smith ministered to high school students for seven years (1958-1965) with IVCF Canada, has been on the staff of the Baptist Leadership Training School in Calgary, Alberta and is now doing freelance youth work with Bridging the Gap Ministries. Anne McCarthy is a campus staff member with IVCF in Chicago. Thomas Cook is a student at the University of Washington, Seattle, in Classical studies. He was president of the IVCF chapter there in 1974-75. Dr. Andrew Foster is director of Christian Missions for Deaf Africans. Ruth Lichtenberger, a former staff member with Nurses Christian Fellowship, U.S.A., is director of N.C.F. International and lives in London. Cindy Hoffman is a campus intern with IVCF in Ann Arbor, Michigan. The testimonies are arranged here in the order they were given at the convention.

Encounters with Christ (Bernie Smith)

In June 1954, at the end of my first year at Kent State University, I went to a Christian training camp in northern Ontario and there I gave my heart and life to Jesus Christ. Within eight months the Lord dealt with me in three specific ways with three specific encounters which were destined to change and reshape the rest of my life.

The first thing God dealt with was that I was playing for dances. God said to me—there was no voice to hear, but the thought was pressed on my mind continuously—"Bernie, your bass is standing between you and God." I haven't time to go into the detail of the encounter, but it went on for quite awhile, and eventually I was convinced God was trying to speak to me. And so I said, "Okay, Lord, I won't play for any more dances."

Then I had another encounter. Shortly thereafter God seemed to be calling me to the ministry. I was in the field of education and had no desire to be a preacher at all. So I told the Lord this. And I reasoned with him that I would be much more effective as a teacher. But God has a one-track mind. He didn't change his mind. So I said yes to God because I had heard preachers say how they had rebelled and their lives were miserable as a result.

The third encounter was very difficult. During the winter of the year that I became a Christian, in the midst of my quiet time it seemed as though God said, "Bern, I don't want you out for track this year." Now this upset me because track was the only sport in which I could compete on a university level. After awhile I was convinced it was God. I spoke to one of my buddies and asked what he thought. He said, "Maybe God doesn't want you out for track." I thought, "Profound revelation!"

You can imagine the difficulty I had when I went in to speak to my track coach, because in my freshman year another fellow and I had done—not all that outstanding—a 10.2 in the 100, which was better than the Varsity guys were doing. So I went in to let him know I wouldn't be out for track in the spring. I had no sophisticated language. I simply said I was having my quiet time and the Lord seemed to say . . . . That was pretty hard. We got into a theological discussion. I was a new Christian. I had no strong rebuttals. I just knew I wanted to get out of the office as quickly as I could because I felt very foolish and very small.

That was twenty years ago. Any person looking at my life at that time from the outside would think God was a kill-joy because what I enjoyed most he took from me. But now I look back over the twenty years and see what God was doing. For one thing, I was anxious to go into show biz, and dance work was one way in. God took the show biz and the dance work—because I played jazz—and he took the jazz and sanctified it. Since that time, in the past three or four years, I have written a musical drama, somewhat in the jazz idiom, and a choir from the Leadership Training School in Calgary has performed it from Winnipeg to the coasts, in some cases to a standing ovation. So God didn't take it; he just removed it until I grew up strong enough to handle it properly. He sanctified it and gave it back.

As far as track is concerned, it's almost as if God was saying to me, "Bern, would you rather be a little track star for the next three years or would you rather enjoy track for the next twenty?" Now if I had to take a choice like that, I'd say the latter. And, if I may say this to God's glory, he's given me health, and every year I try to get clocked in the 100-yard dash just to see how close I am to my best. Last spring I was clocked in running shoes and sweat shirt and did 11.1. That's not one full second from my best and I'm forty-four years old.

Lastly, as far as preaching is concerned, I taught elementary school five years, and I taught at the Baptist Leadership Training School three years. I looked back recently and discovered that most weekends when I was free I was out preaching weekend conferences or out filling some minister's pulpit. I say to myself, "Wait a minute, God said I want you to be a preacher and you said no." And I find my greatest joy, my greatest fulfillment, is not in music which I enjoy immensely, but in preaching the gospel and getting a response.

I want to say one more thing with regard to the work of Jesus Christ in my life. After working for seven years for Inter-Varsity Fellowship, through a process of a number of circumstances I felt led of God to function independently, that is to say, to preach wherever the calls came with no guaranteed income whatsoever. And for three years I did this. And you know, I was never short.

In 1972 my wife and I bought a 1972 Dodge Coronet and paid *cash* for it. And I had no guaranteed income. There were about eight couples who would contribute to me regularly, the smallest amount was $10.00 and the largest amount $50.00. I'm a married man with a wife and three children. God provided my needs for three solid years.

Do you want to hear the latest? I'm free-lancing again, and I get a kick out of God's sense of humor. He has sent many whites to black Africa, but he sent black Bernie to white Canada. And recently I was contacted by a church in Calgary, Brentview Baptist Church of the North American Baptist Conference, which is German background—and there aren't black Germans, you know. This is a church of 350 members, 500 in attendance on Sunday mornings. They invited black Bernie—the only black spot in the church—to be their interim minister from December to June. So I say this to God's praise that I have found life in him exciting. I find him unique. And I can say with David finally, "I delight to do thy will, O my God." Amen.

Meeting Christ in a Foreign Land (Anne McCarthy)

I met Jesus Christ a little over seven years ago in a country about 10,000 miles away. I was seventeen at the time, just beginning my senior year at an American high school in Karachi, West Pakistan.

I had been at Karachi American School for three years and was proud of all I had done and who I had become. Among other things I had been president of the student council and had dated one of the most popular and talented guys around. And now I was looking forward to college. I had no spiritual hunger in my life at this point, though I was quite sure that God existed. My parents, both strong Catholics, had done a good job of building an awareness of God in our hearts. But what I was to do with that awareness, I didn't know. And how God could ever affect my life in a personal way, I knew even less.

I probably would never have bothered to seek answers to those questions had not two significant things happened. The first was that my boyfriend left for college. Because we had spent a great deal of time together, his absence put a big hole in my life.

Then on top of that, my best friend's father was found to have a malignant tumor, so the whole family had to return to the states. Another substantial hole.

There were a number of kids at KAS who were children of missionaries. I hadn't paid them much serious attention before because they didn't seem to enjoy the same things we did. But now I felt drawn to them. I began to spend time with some of them, talking with them and asking questions. One of the things that struck me about them was the impression they gave me that they knew God. My knowledge of his existence was not making a whole lot of difference in my life. In fact, I really didn't know what to do with God on any day other than Sunday. But somehow it was making a difference in these kids' lives—a big difference. I wanted to know why.

Then one day my sisters and I were asked by a missionary if we would like to sing in a youth choir that was preparing for a rally to be held in the city. We loved to sing so we immediately said yes. Through the songs that we rehearsed, the Holy Spirit finally brought me to my place of emptiness and need. After singing "Great Is Thy Faithfulness" and "He's Everything to Me," songs I had never heard before, I knew that I wanted to know God personally.

At the rally, a musical group from the states shared Christ through song and testimony. I was overwhelmed the first night of the rally before the program was even half over. I had never before heard Jesus Christ talked about as a personal Lord. Nor had I ever really understood that Jesus had died for me, to set me free from sin. I finally understood that I needed to make a personal response and commitment to God. So I did so that night, along with several Pakistanis and at least one other American, who happened to be my sister.

I'm eternally grateful to these missionary friends, some of whom are right here tonight, for wanting to share the reality and love of God with me.

Through personal counseling and a Bible-study group, I was encouraged to begin a daily walk with God. What a discovery it was for me to begin reading the Bible. I had never done it on my own and I couldn't believe it. It was like a treasure book!

I always used to wonder why God went to so much trouble to draw me to himself—coming all the way to Karachi and working in my life through missionaries. Then I realized, of course, that it wasn't any trouble for God, nor was it out of his way, because all the world is his and he was at work in all the world to bring his own back to himself.

In Karachi it was obvious who was a missionary and who wasn't. I wonder how obvious it is here, to people we work and live with. Do they know that we have answers about eternity? I hope they do, for their sake and for Jesus' sake.

My Role in Overseas Mission (Thomas Cook)

"Where do I belong now?" Do you remember your first week on your campus? "Do I fit in?" You had been admitted, but getting into student life was another story.

One year ago, I found myself in this position concerning my role in overseas missions. I had been here at Urbana in 1973, but as graduation approached, I found it hard to connect the overall mission of the church with my own future. I found a basic difference between understanding the mission of the church, and discovering whether I am called to serve overseas. I applied to Overseas Training Camp, asking God to give me some sense of his direction concerning missions. I went to Guatemala with questions about my own fitness, my gifts and training, my stamina, my maturity and the pace of the work. I wanted to know what no training manual could tell me—do I, Tom Cook, have a place declaring the glory of the Most High God in another land?

One reason that OTC was a rewarding experience for me is that it was the kind of training Jesus gave his disciples. We studied, then we were prepared to go out, and then we took part in the life and ministry that we had studied. And as Jesus provided his own example as a round-the-clock text for the disciples, so the examples of the missionaries I lived and worked with convinced me that God could make me part of that work.

I found that the daily struggles of these men and women are mostly the things I struggle with: quiet time, obedience, guidance, temptation, living only under grace. I found that the rules don't change when you go through customs. I found that missionaries don't walk on water, but that they are not losers, either. They are people like you and me, who live as faithfully as they can, who have some victorious times, and some days when it's hard to get the right shoe on the right foot. None of them were starry-eyed idealists; they weren't there primarily to right all the wrongs or to save all the souls. They dealt with these things constantly, but they were there because they sensed Jesus Christ calling them there, and they obeyed that call. I knew that I could do that much; I could hear the Lord's call, and follow him.

I was able to get my feet wet, too: living with Montezuma's Revenge, trying to communicate the gospel through an interpreter, carrying a bag of cement up a mountain trail. Some things went better than others, but I found that the work was not beyond me and that these experienced missionaries had started from the same point I am at now.

The day before we left for New Orleans, my journal entry reads, "I look forward to going home, but I have also come to a settled sense that I will probably be back overseas someday." Over the month of OTC, God showed me that I can live in a different culture, that I can serve him overseas and that he will meet me there as he has met the other men and women who have followed him obediently. If OTC might be on God's agenda for your life, pray about it and see what develops. I can guarantee that God is as faithful overseas as he is here today.

Declaring God's Glory to the Deaf (Andrew Foster)
It's good to be here again. Thank God for the theme, "Declaring His Glory among the Nations." For over nineteen years we have been doing just that among the deaf in Africa!

My special interest in witnessing Jesus Christ to the deaf in Africa stems from the fact that I am totally deaf myself. Meningitis destroyed my hearing at the age of eleven. At seventeen, through the sign language used by the deaf, I came to know Jesus as my Lord and Savior. Then followed a burden for reaching Africans afflicted like myself.

This vision began to materialize in 1957, with the launching of our first ministry in Ghana. To date we have opened a total of eleven schools for the deaf in both English and French-speaking West Africa. Besides education work, our ministry includes new gospel ministries, Bible teaching, a Bible institute, Bible correspondence courses and camp work.

Most deaf Africans were in darkness—illiterate, without any means of communication, without Christ, without hope, without God in the world. But, praise the Lord, many now have the light of education and the blessing of communication! A good number have confessed Jesus Christ as their Lord and Savior and followed him in baptism. A few, praise God again, are actively witnessing for him.

Of course we give God the glory for these accomplishments. We only try to follow as he leads. Furthermore, we use the means of communication which he has taught us, though this system continues to be enlarged.

Finally, I would like to demonstrate our primary means of communication, which are signing and finger-spelling. Here is how to say, "Jesus loves me." "Jesus" is expressed by using the middle finger to show the scars in his hands. "Love" by pressing the heart—where love is supposed to be. And "me"—pointing at self. How about following me as I repeat this phrase?

In finger-spelling, words are spelled out with the fingers. For example, L-O-V-E. See how the finger-letters resembles the written letters? The same goes for most other letters, too.

Communicating with the deaf is fun and easy to learn. Why not try it? You might discover a new dimension for prayer and service.

Declaring God's Glory to Nurses (Ruth Lichtenberger)

I was prompted to enter nursing school by an interest in missions. Nurses Christian Fellowship and Inter-Varsity missionary conferences kept that interest in missions alive. Seminary created a stronger desire to communicate God's love to people overseas. However, after many discussions with the Lord, I accepted that his will for me was to be a campus staff member with NCF— USA, for at least three years. Urbana missionary conventions continue to move me towards involvement with internationals and work overseas.

In 1970 God provided the opportunity to go around the world

to visit missionaries and international friends. My diary reveals the emotional struggle I went through when confronted with all kinds of poverty—people without shelter, food, clothing or spiritual light.

I visited NCF staff and student groups in some countries. As I talked with the missionaries, nurses and faculty, I realized that nursing was different in other countries because of their cultural and religious backgrounds. From the Judeo-Christian view, man is worth something, a life has value because we have been created by God. He holds us dear as stated in Isaiah 43.

In many cultures, life is cheap, people die all the time. What does it matter if they receive care that acknowledges their personal worth, whether they get medication as ordered, whether their temperature is taken and recorded accurately? They will die anyway.

The trip around the world climaxed in Scotland at the 7th NCF International conference where I was challenged with the needs of nurses and nursing from many countries. An outstanding need was for evangelicals in Spain to allow their daughters to go into nursing school—not an acceptable profession to Christians in that country.

Months later I wrote, "I still have no freedom to go overseas but am certain God has something in mind for me. Until he discloses that plan clearly, I'll beg him to care of their physical and spiritual needs." And still later I wrote, "Help me think through logically how we can reach nurses for you who will share their faith with the sick, the poor, the disturbed around the world."

I was invited to teach at the NCFI conference at Schloss Mittersill in 1974. The first morning, while reading the chapter, "Prayer That Makes Dreams Come True," from *Beyond Ourselves*, I committed myself with God's help, to review my work and extracurricular activities in light of my dream in order to say that these things were contributing towards my dream being accomplished. That evening the NCFI executive committee asked me to consider the possibility of becoming general director.

My concern is to encourage nurses around the world to see nursing as a vocation, a call from God, to think through their view of man, how their culture views man and life, and how they can become involved in the profession, in their country in order to develop or maintain nursing as a caring profession, which recognizes that the person is of value to God. My goal is that people not only be reached for God but be cared for the same way as Jesus cared for people when he walked on earth. That kind of caring can only be given as we know Jesus Christ personally.

Is this a possibility? Last October I met with eight out of the twenty some nurses meeting regularly at the Evangelical Hospital in Barcelona. Now they need to scatter as the early Christians did and reach other nurses in Spain. In January 1977, Christian faculty in Denmark will discuss how a Christian philosophy of nursing can be implemented in their schools. Three NCF staff in South America will meet in March to discuss the development of a Christian philosophy of nursing applicable to Latin-American culture.

God is at work giving nurses a concern to teach students and nurses to care as Jesus cared for those who are in need.

My Student Training in Missions (Cindy Hoffman)

A year and a half ago in the summer of 1975, the Lord took me into a new realm of understanding him and his work and myself. I was in Johannesburg, South Africa with Inter-Varsity's Student Training in Missions program. STIM tries to place you according to your interests, and mine was student work. So I spent three months on the campus of a major university in Johannesburg working with the staff member of the Evangelical Student Union. Most of the time I worked with the women students in trying to get Bible studies going in their residence halls. Since that time, I'm happy to say, God has accomplished that.

I learned a great deal in that three-month period, and it is hard to distill the most important things. But in retrospect, the most significant and lasting lesson has been in my concept of God and what he is doing in people's lives.

There is, of course, real excitement in seeing God's presence and power with you on foreign ground, and at the same time in knowing that he is working in the lives of your friends back home. I learned to trust God as I experienced fear and loneliness and disorientation. God is faithful.

But the most astounding thing for me was that as young and inexperienced and insecure as I felt, God could be glorified in me and he could use me. By living and working in another culture, I began to develop a deep love and concern for other people, and that concern has expanded into a conscious awareness of the many people beyond my little "world" who daily try to live a godly life and are daily making decisions about their relationship to God. He cares immensely about them. And I feel that I've only just begun to be aware of their living, breathing humanity.

Going to Africa showed me an additional small bit of the work of God in the world. But it was enough to help me understand that as a Christian I am part of something very big. The kingdom of God is huge and alive and growing. And while the world-wide work of God may be beyond my understanding, I am able to grasp that somewhere in it he has a part for me, and that's amazing. Of course, he is concerned about my "backyard." But he is concerned about so much more. How great to realize that wherever you go God is still God, and he is at work!

nineteen
God's Work in the World of Students Today
Chua Wee Hian

The International Fellowship of Evangelical Students is primarily a missionary movement operating in the world of students. All 62 member movements of the IFES are committed to present and uplift the Lord Jesus Christ in campuses where he is not known or named. Today we are pooling our resources and manpower to pioneer evangelical student witness in about 30 different countries, including Eastern Europe and some very difficult lands in the Islamic bloc. I would like to share with you some of the highlights of our missionary thrust.

Six months ago Leni Sison, a young Filipino worker, went to Mexico City. She had received a clear call from the Lord through participating at the Asian Student Missionary Convention in the Philippines to go and help the Mexican movement pioneer high school work in Mexico City. When she got there, her Mexican brothers and sisters in Christ welcomed her most warmly. Within a matter of weeks she was able to establish eight high-school groups in Mexico City.

In Mexico City there are half a million high-school students who do not know Jesus Christ personally. There is no Christian work done among this large group of students. Leni is there working with her Mexican colleagues and also with an IFES staff worker, Douglas Stewart, in establishing high-school groups in that particular city.

There is another interesting sidelight to Leni's ministry. She is backed up by prayers and by giving from students in Trinidad, Malaysia, Japan and Canada.

Missionary involvement has been expressed by students in different parts of the world. At the beginning of this year, Brazilian students began to work out new models of missionary service. A group of young medical doctors went into the interior of Goias State to start a hospital, to be engaged in a ministry of loving service and healing; at the same time, they endeavor to share the eternal gospel of Jesus Christ to the neglected community in that area. So in the IFES, we seek to minister and preach the whole gospel to the whole man.

Literature plays a very vital role in student evangelism. It helps to break down prejudices and to introduce men and women to Jesus Christ. Students in the Philippines have distributed several thousand copies of The Jesus Book, a selection from the Gospels portraying the life of a dynamic, living Jesus Christ. The same approach has been adopted by many of our movements in Latin America. They have published a book called Jesus: the Model for the New Man and students are being invited to study the Gospels together and to rediscover the living Jesus Christ, not one trapped in the institutional garb of ecclesiastical traditions.

I suppose the greatest experiment of evangelism in the field of literature is that done by graduates in Hong Kong. They produce a monthly magazine in Chinese called Breakthrough. It is the vision of Josephone So, a young lady who graduated from Wheaton College about ten years ago. When she was about to return to Hong Kong, she was told that she had cancer in her throat. Her prayer was that God would spare her life. She shared her vision with other Chinese graduates especially in Taiwan and Hong Kong. Four years ago they produced a magazine which could compete with the glossy magazines of Hong Kong.

This magazine is meeting the need of young people in the colony. Some 25,000 copies have been sold, mainly in secular newsstands and bookstores. Thus many unchurched young people learn about Jesus Christ through the evangelistic periodical. Some write or phone in to talk to counselors who try to explain to them who Jesus is. There is a full-time worker who can meet with these inquirers. Because of the impact of this magazine, a radio station in Hong Kong has given the editors free time to answer the questions and problems of young people in that bustling city. So God has used *Breakthrough* as a tool to capture the minds and hearts of these students.

God has also used Inter-Varsity Press in Britain and the States, and also Ediciones Certeza, the publishing arm of IFES in Latin America, to produce books for thinking Christians and Bible study guides for tools for pastors and church leaders, so that the Word of God can be expounded, taught and applied in our changing situations.

IFES movements are also committed to thorough evangelism. In my home country of Singapore, Inter-Varsity Christian Fellowship has a membership of over 600. This fellowship is divided into 100 action groups that meet regularly for fellowship and also for evangelism. They sign a covenant committing themselves to the Lord and also to one another. The only time when they can be excused from attending a cell group or action group meeting is when they are fatally ill! Because of this commitment to Jesus Christ and to one another, the groups have grown and multiplied. More than half the university enrollment have heard the gospel and the claims of Jesus Christ clearly presented.

In Africa I could show you many Christian Unions with large student memberships. In fact, the largest Christian Union of black students in Africa is at the University of Makere in Uganda. In spite of the unstable political and social situation of that country, this group is thriving. Hardly a week passes without a student committing his or her life to Jesus Christ.

The IFES also believes in church commitment and involvement. In my travels around the world, it is wonderful to meet pastors who received a clear call from God while they were students in an Inter-Varsity chapter. I have met many missionaries serving in different fields telling me how God met with them at Urbana or at a Christian fellowship meeting. Involvement in the life and activities of the chapter had exposed them to needs around the world.

There is much for which to praise God in terms of growth and advance in all the continents. Doors are still open to preach the gospel to students in lands like Sri Lanka, Nepal and Bangladesh, but we do encounter certain problems and obstacles.

We had to withdraw a team of staff workers because of the civil war in Lebanon. A few students were killed in the strife. In spite of the war, the students were able to have Bible studies. At one time, all links to the outside world were cut off. The students, however, had access to telephones and they developed an ingenious method of "telephonic" Bible studies. They would phone one another and agree to study a set passage. Later, over the telephone, they would exchange insights gained. They would then pray for one another, thus sustaining one another in the midst of much bloodshed and struggle.

Early in 1976 Muslim leaders from various countries in the Middle East and North Africa met in Pakistan. They recommended to their own governments that all Christian missions and enterprises be asked peacefully to withdraw from Islamic lands. It seems that the door to open missionary witness to these countries could be closing; the curtains are about to fall. But God has not closed these doors.

Some of the papers in England and the United States are carrying advertisements put out by the governments of the Middle East and North Africa for engineers, doctors, university lecturers and for those who can teach English. The IFES would like to challenge some of you to buy up these opportunities, by going to these countries as teachers, as educators, as professional men and women. The salary is very high, yes, even higher than in the United States of America. Go, then, and work; earn these huge salaries and give half of your income to the Lord's work. At the same time, help us, give us a hand to build up Christian groups in these nations.

We would also urge you to assist us in our work in Europe. At Urbana 73 I mentioned Italy. Some of you might remember an incident that I related concerning my visit to the University of Rome in October 1973. As I walked through that ancient university with an enrollment of 100,000 students, I asked a colleague of mine, "How many Christians are there in this university who are witnessing to Jesus Christ?" She said to me, "As far as I know, Wee Hian, only one." One out of 100,000 students! Thank God there are several more students who are now witnessing to Christ. We need to pray that more people would go to study in Italian universities and also universities of Belgium and Greece so that we can establish vital Christian fellowships in these countries. We recommend that you not go out alone. Go in twos or threes as teams; go out in fellowship with IFES and be certain that you are faithfully backed up by prayer support and by the concern of other Christians.

Finally, you might ask, What can we do to be active partners in the ministry of IFES? First, pray. We can only advance when we are on our knees. How I thank God each day for some letters that I receive in my office in Harrow, England. Some are letters from retired missionaries who are in their 80s assuring me they pray for us every day. Thank God for those mighty prayer warriors. May it please God to increase their tribe, not only of the older friends but the younger ones as well!

Second, we need financial support. We thank God that 65% of our income comes from students. We pray that students will continue to give sacrificially and regularly to help us assist our staff and our member movements to advance and grow.

Third, I hope that some of you with cross-cultural gifts will consider going to places like Greece, Belgium, Italy, the Middle East, the Islamic world and parts of French-speaking Africa where vast spiritual needs still exist. In Eire (southern Ireland) where Americans are particularly welcomed, there are unique opportunities to befriend Irish students and to lead them to a personal commitment to Jesus Christ. As Christian Fellowships are started or strengthened in these countries, as movements are built up and as Christian students are brought into spiritual maturity and equipped to go out to win their contemporaries to Jesus Christ, we—all of us together—in the family of IFES can declare his glory and praise among the nations.

part IV

Communion Message

twenty
Following in the Footsteps of Footsteps of His Glory

A. Donald MacLeod

One of the truly miraculous things the Spirit of God has been doing this week is drawing our attention in many different ways to the prayer of Moses in Exodus 33: "Show me your glory." The passage in full reads:

And the Lord said to Moses, "This very thing that you have spoken I will do; for you have found favor in my sight, and I know you by name." Moses said, "I pray thee, show me thy glory." And he said, "I will make all my goodness pass before you, and will proclaim before you my name 'The LORD'; and I will be gracious to whom I will be gracious, and will show mercy on whom I will show mercy. But," he said, "you cannot see my face; for man shall not see me and live." And the LORD said, "Behold, there is a place by me where you shall stand upon the rock; and while my glory passes by I will put you in a cleft of the rock, and I will cover you with my hand until I have passed by; then I will take away my hand, and you

shall see my back; but my face shall not be seen." (vv. 17-23)
The Apostle Paul, commenting on these chapters and the inci-
dents related there, gives us insight into this as he describes the
story of the brilliance of God's glory revealed to Moses and the
even greater brilliance of the glory that we know in the new
covenant in Jesus Christ.

*Now if the ministry that brought death, which was engraved
in letters on stone, came with glory, so that the Israelites could
not look steadily at the face of Moses because of its glory, fading though it was, will not the ministry of the Spirit be even
more glorious? If the ministry that condemns men is glorious,
how much more glorious is the ministry that brings righteousness! For what was glorious has no glory now in com-
parison with the surpassing glory. And if what was fading
away came with glory, how much greater is the glory of that
which lasts!*

*Therefore, since we have such a hope, we are very bold.
. . . Now the Lord is the Spirit, and where the Spirit of the Lord
is, there is freedom. And we, who with unveiled faces all reflect the Lord's glory, are being transformed into his likeness
with ever-increasing glory, which comes from the Lord, who is
the Spirit.* (2 Cor. 3:7-12, 17-18, NIV)

"Show me your glory." What an extraordinary prayer this
was! Can you picture the scene? Mt. Sinai towers above with the
shekinah glory of the holy law-giving God. In the valley below,
the people of Israel, stretched out before the sham deity they
had erected, worship the golden calf, aided by the very priest
of God himself, Aaron, the brother of Moses. Then there is
Moses, coming down from the vision of God to the apostasy of
the people of God. And all he can pray is, "Show me your glory."

I would have prayed anything but that, if I had been in Moses'
position. I would perhaps have said in desperation, "Lord,
you've got to clean up this mess. It's beyond my control. How
could these people do this? After all the concern and prayer and
the intensity of my vision for them, how could they do this?
Lord, I can't take any more. It's too much. Do something, and do
it quickly." But I would hardly have prayed as Moses prayed:
"Lord, show me your glory."

How will you apply the lessons you have learned at Urbana 76 in the new year 1977? What has God told you and me about declaring his glory among the nations? What have you discovered about the glory of God that will make a difference in your life? Is your prayer "Lord, I want you to show me your glory"?

Henry Scougall, a 17th-century Scottish minister, in a classic that every Christian should read and re-read, *The Life of God in the Soul of Man*, says that you and I are called to walk in the footsteps of God's glory, that day by day, hour by hour, minute by minute we are called to follow in the footsteps of the glory of our God: "We cannot open our eyes but we must behold some footsteps of his glory; and we cannot turn them toward Him but we shall be sure to find His intent upon us; waiting, as it were, to catch a look, ready to entertain the most intimate fellowship and communion with us. Let us endeavor to raise our minds to the clearest conception of the divine nature." The clearest conception of the divine nature—that is the way God answers the prayer: "Show me your glory."

The Glory of God: Greatness
God showed Moses three aspects of his glory. First, to see the glory of God is to know his greatness. "Show me your glory:" Do you think that was a legitimate request to ask of God? Many commentators have said that Moses was being presumptuous. Moooo, thoy oay, had no buoinooo aoking tho almighty God to show him his glory. He knew enough of God from the shekinah glory to know that his prayer was inadmissible.

But there is no prayer that our heavenly Father enjoys answering more than the heart cry of the child who comes to his heavenly Father and says, "Lord, I want to know more about you. Lord, tell me about yourself." Our hearts, so often mired in the horizontal, need that vertical dimension. "Oh God," the psalmist says, "thou art my God, I seek thee, my soul thirsts for thee; my flesh faints for thee, as in a dry and weary land where no water is. . . . beholding thy power and glory" (Ps. 63: 1-2).

God deals gently with Moses in this story. You cannot see my face, he says, for no man can see me and live. But "behold, there is a place by me where you shall stand upon the rock; and while my glory passes by I will put you in a cleft of the rock, and I will cover you with my hand." He hides my soul in the cleft of the rock, and as with Moses, lest I be consumed by his greatness, he covers me there with his hand. The Apostle Paul said the rock of Horeb was a figure of Jesus Christ. So we sing the familiar hymn, "Rock of Ages, cleft for me, let me hide myself in thee. Let the water and the blood from the riven side which flowed be of sin the double cure, cleanse me from its guilt and power."

The greatness of God in the person of Jesus Christ was prefigured to Moses. Jesus stooped to our weakness, mighty as he was, and hid us from the wrath and judgment and justice of the holy God. The blood that flowed on Calvary's cross which we celebrate in the wine of communion reminds us of the glory of God, who covers us with the hand of Jesus Christ so that we may know that God is great and yet not be consumed or judged by that knowledge. What a Savior we celebrate in the eucharist!

What kind of God do you know? Is he just the projection of your imagination? Is he merely a product of wish fulfillment? Or is he the Jehovah God who showed his glory to Moses and who has revealed his glory in the person of Jesus Christ? If that is the God whom you know, then he will be with you throughout your life because you and I need to follow in the footsteps of the glory of this great God. Our weakness is more than balanced by his greatness; our failure, by his greatness; our fear of others, by our confidence in his greatness; our uncertainties about the future, by our confidence in his greatness.

The Glory of God: Goodness

"Show me your glory." To be shown the glory of God is to know not only his greatness, but his goodness. In Exodus 33:19 God says, "I will make all my goodness pass before you, and will proclaim before you my name, 'The Lord.' " Moses needed to know not only that God is great, but also that God is good because Moses must have asked, as many who have been called to lead God's people subsequently have asked, "Lord, why did you bring me into this place? Why have you put me in this kind of predicament? I have been frustrated over and over again in my desires for this people. They have rewarded me only with ingratitude and unfaithfulness."

In Exodus 33 and 34 God says repeatedly to Moses that he is a good God. And he is good not only to Moses, but also to the people of God. This is important because often in the community of God's people, Christians become embittered, not because of the world but because of the hypocrisy and superficiality of other Christians. But Moses continued to be sweet and loving in the presence of the apostasy of God's people. When God, in response to this apostasy, said, "Let me alone, that my wrath may burn hot against them and I may consume them," Moses pleads with the Lord: "Turn from thy fierce wrath, and . . . remember Abraham, Isaac, and Israel, thy servants" (Ex. 32:10, 12-13). Moses could argue this way with God only because he had been convinced of the goodness of God. "Oh, that men would praise the Lord for his goodness and for his wonderful works to the children of men," the psalmist says. The Lord God is merciful and gracious, long-suffering and abundant in goodness and truth. But Moses had to be continually reminded of God's goodness to his children.

But what about the future? What if I am called upon to suffer in the way that we have heard? What if I go out in God's service and find that things happen to me that I have not wished for myself? We need to know that the glory of the God that we are called to declare among the nations is the glory of a good God. "Surely goodness and mercy shall follow me all the days of my life; and I shall dwell in the house of the LORD for ever" (Ps. 23:6).

Other potential problems come to mind: What about the ridicule of those I live with? How can I share my faith with someone I work or study with? What about my family? What about my boyfriend who is a non-Christian? We can trust God in all these things and follow in the footsteps of God's glory because God is good. With Charles Wesley we sing, "Before my face's enlightened eyes make all thy gracious goodness pass. Thy goodness is the sight I prize; thy nature in my soul proclaim; reveal thy name, thy glorious name."

The Glory of God: Graciousness

Finally, to be shown the glory of God is to know his graciousness. God is not only a great and good God, he is a gracious God. Earlier he had said to Moses, "I know you by name, and you have also found grace in my sight." Now he says, "I will be gracious to whom I will be gracious, and will show mercy on whom I will show mercy" (Ex. 33:19). God who calls himself the Lord Jehovah is merciful and gracious.

Grace is the greatest word in my experience, as it is in yours and as it is in any Christian's experience. It is the greatest word in our vocabulary. " 'Tis grace that led me safe thus far and grace will lead me home." Grace is amazing and free. The sacrament of holy communion is a demonstration that God's unmerited grace comes to us by his invitation—we are guests at his table. The invitation is his. The gift of life is his alone to give, for he alone died for us. And lest I stumble as I walk along in the footsteps of his glory, I will need to receive the bread and the wine over and over again as a reminder that God is gracious.

When difficulties come, when circumstances arise in my life that I cannot cope with, God is a God of grace. The glory of God might dazzle me were I not to remember that Jesus Christ reflects the glory of God. We have beheld his glory. The Word made flesh has dwelt among us, full of grace and truth. "For you know the grace of our Lord Jesus Christ, that though he was rich, yet for your sake he became poor, so that by his poverty you might become rich" (2 Cor. 8:9).

You may have come to Urbana with the thought that your uncertainties about the future would be solved, that you would have a new shot of spiritual adrenalin that would carry you out into an effortless and failure-free future. Moses discovered that there are no money-back guarantees in the Lord's service. He learned that God who shows his glory is a God of grace and that that grace is daily, continuous and unchanging.

A communion service is a festival of grace. It is a place for you and me to begin to follow in the footsteps of the glory of a gracious God. "Show me your glory." Open my eyes, Lord, that I might have the clearest conception of your nature. A great God? Yes. A good God? Yes. But, hallelujah, a gracious God as well—

sovereign and gracious. "All of us who are Christians . . . reflect like mirrors the glory of the Lord. . . . We now can enlighten men only because we can give them knowledge of the glory of God, as we see it in the face of Jesus Christ" (2 Cor. 3:18; 4:6, Phillips). Declare that glory among the nations.

Convention Speakers

John W. Alexander is president of Inter-Varsity Christian Fellowship—USA, Madison, Wisconsin. Previously he served as Chairman of the Department of Geography at the University of Wisconsin. His publications include *Scripture Memory 101, Managing Our Work* and *Economic Geography*.

Edgar S. Beach is a staff member of Wycliffe Bible Translators, assigned to Guatemala. He was president of the Inter-Varsity Christian Fellowship chapter at the University of Illinois at Urbana during his senior year.

Chua Wee Hian is General Secretary of the International Fellowship of Evangelical Students. Born and raised in Singapore, he has studied in London and the USA. He served as Associate Secretary of IFES for East Asia before assuming his present position and also has been Editor of *The Way*, a quarterly magazine for Asian students.

Edmund P. Clowney is President of Westminster Theological
Seminary, Philadelphia, and Professor of Practical Theology. He
has been a pastor and former moderator of the General Assembly
of the Orthodox Presbyterian Church. He is the author of *Called
to the Ministry* and *The Doctrine of the Church*.

Eric Frykenberg is a retired, though not inactive, missionary.
Born in Sweden and trained there as a civil engineer, he became
a Christian while in the United States on a study leave in 1923.
From 1929 to 1953 he was a missionary in India. Since 1954 he
has served in the United States, speaking about missions and
ministering to weary missionaries.

Billy Graham is perhaps the most well-known evangelist in the
world. He has held crusades in almost every state in the United
States and in more than 50 other countries. He leads the weekly
"Hour of Decision" radio program and is the author of a news-
paper column, "My Answer," as well as of several books including *Peace with God* and *World Aflame*.

Samuel T. Kamaleson is Vice-President-at-large for World
Vision International. He also pastors a church in Madras, India.
The author of several books and many magazine articles, he is
widely known also through his radio and preaching ministry.
He participated in the International Congress on World Evangel-
ization at Lausanne (1974).

Festo Kivengere is leader of a team of African evangelists
associated with African Enterprise, and has been called the
outstanding black evangelist in Africa today. He was chairman of the Pan-African Christian Leadership Conference
(Nairobi, 1976) and serves on the executive of the Continuation
Committee for the Lausanne Congress (1974).

Elisabeth Elliot Leitch served in Ecuador among Colorado,
Quichua and Auca Indians from 1952 to 1963. She is the widow
of Jim Elliot, martyred by Aucas in 1956, and was widowed
again in 1973 upon the death of her husband Dr. Addison

Leitch, professor at Gordon-Conwell Theological Seminary. She is the author of many books, including *Shadow of the Almighty, Through Gates of Splendor, Liberty of Obedience* and *A Slow and Certain Light.*

A. Donald MacLeod has been General Director of Inter-Varsity Christian Fellowship—Canada since 1975. In 1967, after serving as pastor to churches in British Columbia, Quebec, Ontario and Nova Scotia, he started the Bridlewood Presbyterian Church in Agincourt, Ontario. While ministering there for nearly eight years, he was also president of the Evangelical Fellowship of Canada.

Isabelo Magalit is Associate General Secretary of the International Fellowship of Evangelical Students in East Asia. A native of the Philippines, he received the M.D. degree from the University of the Philippines in 1964 and shortly thereafter became a full-time staff worker with Inter-Varsity Christian Fellowship—Philippines. In 1966 he was appointed General Secretary of IVCF in the Philippines, and in 1972 he was appointed to his present position with IFES.

John M. Perkins is founder and President of Voice of Calvary Ministries in Mendenhall and Jackson, Mississippi. He is an active organizer as well as the author of many magazine articles and two books: *A Quiet Revolution* and *Let Justice Roll Down.*

Helen Roseveare is on the staff of the Missionary Training College of the Worldwide Evangelization Crusade. She was trained as a medical doctor at Cambridge University and practiced in the Congo (now called Zaire) from 1953 to 1973. She has written a number of books, including *Give Me This Mountain* and *He Gave Us a Valley.*

John R. W. Stott is Rector Emeritus of All Souls Church in London. He is also honorary chaplain to the Queen of England and has a worldwide ministry as a Bible expositor and conference speaker. He has written many books, among them *Basic Chris-*

tianity, Christ the Controversialist and *Christian Mission in the Modern World.* He was also one of the framers of the Lausanne Covenant (1974).

Lemuel S. Tucker is a student at Westminster Theological Seminary, Philadelphia, Pennsylvania. He is a graduate of William and Mary College (1974), where he was president of the Inter-Varsity Christian Fellowship chapter and the Fellowship of Christian Athletes.